LIKE Diamonds FROM Dirt

ESSAYS *and* **INTERVIEWS** *about David Dabydeen's Creative Writing*

Edited by LYNNE MACEDO

First published in 2024 by Hansib Publications
76 High Street, Hertford, SG14 3TA, United Kingdom

info@hansibpublications.com
www.hansibpublications.com

Copyright © Lynne Macedo and contributors, 2024

Lynne Macedo and the contributors have asserted their right to be identified as the authors of this work in accordance with the Copyright, Designs and Patents Act 1988.

ISBN 978-1-0686993-4-4
ISBN 978-1-0686993-5-1 (Kindle)
ISBN 978-1-0686993-6-8 (ePub)

A CIP catalogue record for this book is available from the British Library

All rights reserved. No part of this publication may be reproduced, stored in a retrieval system, or transmitted, in any form or by any means, electronic, mechanical, photocopying, recording or otherwise, without the prior permission of the author.

Produced and printed in Great Britain

Founded in London in 1970, Hansib Publications has played a crucial role in documenting the Caribbean experience and bringing Caribbean perspectives to a wider audience. It is renowned for its extensive catalogue of Caribbean fiction and non-fiction, spanning a diverse range of genres, including historical novels, biographies, poetry anthologies, political commentaries and social narratives. It has also made significant contributions to Caribbean scholarship by publishing insightful works on history, culture, politics and social issues.

Today, Hansib Publications remains a significant force in the world of Caribbean publishing and continues to publish books that reflect the vibrant diversity of the Caribbean region and the global Caribbean diaspora. Its legacy of promoting Caribbean voices and perspectives has made it an invaluable resource for those seeking to understand and appreciate the rich cultural heritage of the Caribbean.

This book is dedicated to Rachel, Surya, Moses and Teddy Dabydeen; Robin and James Dabydeen; Chrishna Ely; Russ, Selma and Nazli Harland; John and Susan Mair; Ian Marshall; Michael Mitchell; Chris, Elly, Philip, Carmen, Paul and Matthew Niland; Indeera Payne; and Krishna and Veronica Prasad.

DAVID DABYDEEN
LYNNE MACEDO

CONTENTS

ACKNOWLEDGEMENTS 9
INTRODUCTION 11

PART I
Essays about David Dabydeen's Creative Writing

CHAPTER ONE 19
Beauty and the Beast: White women, Black men and the question of the animal in *Slave Song* by Renée Landall

CHAPTER TWO 30
Shoring Up the Nation: David Dabydeen's Oceanic Sublime by John Clement Ball

CHAPTER THREE 41
Identity negotiations in *Disappearance* (1993) by Marta Fratczak-Dabrowska

CHAPTER FOUR 52
Spatial Transgressions and the Search for a Non-Identitarian Ethics in David Dabydeen's *Disappearance* by Sten Pultz Moslund

CHAPTER FIVE 72
'Telling it how *I* want': Reading the liminality of David Dabydeen's *The Counting House* by Mark Tumbridge

CHAPTER SIX 93
Racial Capitalism and Racial Intimacies: Post-Emancipation British Guina in David Dabydeen's *The Counting House* by Najnin Islam

CHAPTER SEVEN 116
Slave Narratives and (Black) British History in David Dabydeen's *A Harlot's Progress* by Sofia Muñoz-Valdivieso

CHAPTER EIGHT 138
Infinite Worlds: Eighteenth-Century London, the Atlantic Ocean, and Post-Slavery by John Clement Ball

PART II
Interviews with David Dabydeen

CHAPTER NINE 165
Interview between Alison Ward and David Dabydeen conducted at Warwick University in August 2013

CHAPTER TEN 191
Interview between Diane Barlee and David Dabydeen conducted at Warwick University on 18 May 2016

CHAPTER ELEVEN 217
Interview between Ruzbeh Babaee and David Dabydeen conducted online in spring 2016

ABOUT THE CONTRIBUTORS 225

ACKNOWLEDGEMENTS

The following articles have all previously appeared in a modified form. We are grateful to each of the publishers for their permission to reprint.

Ball, John Clement: 'Shoring up Britain: David Dabydeen's Oceanic Sublime' in *The National across the World: Postcolonial Literary Representations*, ed. Harish Trivedi, Meenakshi Mukherjee, C. Vijayasree, and T. Vijay Kumar, Oxford University Press, New Delhi, 2007, pp. 115-124.

Ball, John Clement: 'Infinite Worlds: Eighteenth-Century London, the Atlantic Ocean, and Post-Slavery in S.I. Martin's *Incomparable World*, Lawrence Hill's *The Book of Negroes*, David Dabydeen's *A Harlot's Progress*, and Thomas Wharton's *Salamander'* was first published in *Transnational Literature* 5.1, May 2013.

Fratczak-Dabrowska, Marta: 'Identity negotiations in *Disappearance* (1993) by David Dabydeen' was part of a book published by Adam Mickiewicz University Press in 2016. It is updated and reprinted here with their kind permission.

Islam, Najnin: "Racial Capitalism and Racial Intimacies: Post-Emancipation British Guiana in David Dabydeen's *The Counting House*" has previously appeared in *Interventions: International Journal of Postcolonial Studies* (05 Apr 2021). https://doi.org/10.1080/1369801X.2021.1892516. It is reprinted here with the kind permission of Taylor & Francis.

Moslund, Sten Pultz: 'Spatial Transgressions and the Search for a Non-Identitarian Ethics in David Dabydeen's *Disappearance'* is a shortened and slightly edited version of chapter twelve, "Spatial Transgressions and Migrant Aesthetics in David

Dabydeen's *Disappearance*", in Sten Moslund's monograph *Literature's Sensuous Geographies. Postcolonial Matters of Place* (Palgrave Macmillan, 2015). It is reprinted here with their kind permission.

INTRODUCTION

It is now almost forty years since David Dabydeen published his first creative work – a collection of poetry entitled *Slave Song* (1984) – which won both the Commonwealth Poetry Prize and the Quiller-Couch Prize. Since then there have been two further collections of poetry – *Coolie Odyssey* (1988) and the long narrative poem *Turner*[1] (1994), as well as seven novels. His first novel, *The Intended*, was published in 1991, followed by *Disappearance* (1993), *The Counting House* (1996), *A Harlot's Progress* (1999), *Our Lady of Demerara* (2004), *Molly and the Muslim Stick* (2008) and *Johnson's Dictionary* (2013). Like his first collection of poetry, several of his novels have attracted critical acclaim and awards. *The Intended* won The Guyana Prize for Literature in 1992, *The Counting House* was shortlisted for the 1998 Dublin Literary Prize, *A Harlot's Progress* was shortlisted for the James Tait Black Memorial Prize and also a winner of the Guyana Prize for Literature, and *Our Lady of Demerara* won Dabydeen's third Guyana Prize for Literature in 2004.

Like Diamonds From Dirt begins with a newly commissioned article which takes us back to Dabydeen's first fictional publication, *Slave Song*. Landell's primary focus is on Dabydeen's 'representations of the non-human [animal] world and how they have informed race', an area that scholars previously paid little attention to in these early poems. Landell suggests that Dabydeen draws parallels between constructions of Black masculinity and animality, whilst also raising questions about gender politics and the role of the white woman as the 'feigned victim' of Black male desire. Highlighting the intertextual nature of Dabydeen's writing with its ambivalent linkages to Fanon's views on white womanhood, Landell argues that the poems' connections between man and animal really 'expose[s] the contradictions' in the stereotypical constructions of gender and race in representations of colonial sexuality.

Chapters Two to Four shift the focus from Dabydeen's poetry to one of his early and most widely analysed novels – *Disappearance*. In Ball's exploration of the novel's narrative, he reads Dabydeen's representation of the sea as emblematic of earlier cultural associations with 'nation and empire' as well as linking it to the sublime with its shift from a place of peril to one of 'pleasure and personal uplift'. The sublime is more frequently associated with Dabydeen's long narrative poem 'Turner'[2], but here Ball equates it to the nameless narrator's contradictory views of the sea as a space of energy and mystery, but one that is resistant to human intervention such as his own attempts to shore up the crumbling cliffs of Hastings. Ultimately, the shifting, dangerous, and fluid nature of the sea and its disintegrating shoreline is shown by Ball to be a complex metaphor for both constructs of identity that elude and evade the narrator, and the failing 'post-imperial [notions of] Englishness' that run throughout the novel.

The transgression of ethnic boundaries and the issue of identity is a key theme in Fratczak-Dabrowska's article on *Disappearance*. Her analysis of the novel grounds it firmly within its Guyanese context, and explores the notion that the narrator's own struggles with a sense of identity and a lack of belonging may be able to 'reveal…universal truths about identity formation in today's world'. Dabydeen's writing suggests that both fluidity and hybridity can co-exist with a sense of national identity, something which Fratczak-Dabrowska believes 'does not demand questioning **any** of one's cultural loyalties' (my emphasis). The narrator's ability to reconcile conflicting notions of identity into one 'hybridized body' are to be read as a blueprint for the contemporary world, where questions of identity continue to remain a key issue within an increasingly multicultural environment.

The final chapter on *Disappearance* is by Sten Pultz Moslund. His is a more theoretical examination of Dabydeen's writing, which explores two modes of spatial transgression – *discursive* and *sensuous* – that combine to form 'a phenomenological challenge to oppressive Western histories and narratives'. His essay demonstrates how the novel subverts and challenges preconceived ideas about nation and modernity whilst also creating 'a great deal of unrest about the spatial references and metaphors that circulate within its narrative'. By resisting assimilation into the cultural 'centre', Dabydeen's narrator deliberately draws attention to the self-contradictory nature of the construction of English identity, as well as insisting upon his own hybridity that was itself 'shaped by a multiplicity of narratives'.

Chapters Five and Six are concerned with Dabydeen's third novel – *The Counting House* – which is set in India and British Guiana during the time of Indentureship. Tumbridge's sustained reading of this novel pinpoints connections with the writing of V.S. Naipaul, alongside the intertextual connections[3] to Jenkins' 1877 work *Lutchmee and Dilloo*. Aside from the obvious naming of the main protagonist as 'Vidia, whose mother's name is Droopatie' (as was Naipaul's), Tumbridge highlights a series of allusion's to Naipaul's 1961 novel *A House for Mr Biswas*. The main thrust of his essay is, however, more directly concerned with exploring *The Counting House* as a work of 'cultural re-appropriation' from Jenkins. By inverting the power relationship of Rohini and Vidia compared to that of Lutchmee and Dilloo in the earlier work, Dabydeen is shown to have 'incorporate[d] a greater sympathy towards the interiority of the subjects while maintaining enough objective distance to allow them to flourish'. The ruthless and pessimistic outlook of Dabydeen's novel that is stripped of all forms of sentimentality is, Tumbridge asserts, an (in)direct riposte to Jenkin's romanticised notion of life in colonial India and British Guiana.

Islam's analysis of *The Counting House* has a somewhat different focus as it is concerned with reading the novel in terms of its exploration of racialization. Rather than reinforcing historical views of racial conflict between Indians and Africans within a colonial plantation context, Dabydeen's novel instead highlights 'moments of empathy and intimacy among these communities'. This, she argues, was largely rendered invisible by the colonial archive, and reinforced by cultural theory which 'has tended to study these diasporic groups as separate, insulated units'. Whilst the novel clearly does explore antagonisms between Afro-Creole characters such as Kampta and Miriam with the Indian characters Vidia and Rohini, these are skilfully juxtaposed with other scenes of solidarity and 'mutual empathy' between them. By imagining an alternative environment wherein interracial intimacy replaces resentment, *The Counting House* can therefore be perceived as a challenge to the 'foundational premise of racial capitalism'.

Part I of *Like Diamonds From Dirt* concludes with two essays on the 1999 novel *A Harlot's Progress*. This novel takes its inspiration from Hogarth's 1732 engravings of the same title which provide a compelling series of images of that period in time, despite being clearly staged and essentially fictitious in nature. Similarly, Dabydeen's fourth novel appears to present a detailed account of life in 18th century London, yet is riven with narrative ambiguities and uncertainty which undercut many of its most significant events.

Chapter Seven by Muñoz-Valdivieso situates *A Harlot's Progress* as a direct link to the slave narrative genre, and in particular to the memoirs of Mary Prince (1831) – who narrated her story to one Thomas Pringle – and Olaudah Equiano who wrote and published his own story in 1789. In Dabydeen's novel, his irrepressibly unreliable narrator Mungo finds himself in straitened circumstances in London, and reluctantly tells his story to a 'Thomas Pringle' of the Abolition Society in exchange for basic provisions. The character of Mungo is deliberately made into a stereotype, who shifts and alters his story to make it palatable for a British audience, paralleling the way that Equiano would also have adapted his narrative to further the cause of abolition. By placing a Black character like Mungo in 18th century London, she suggests that Dabydeen actively 'contributes to the recognition that Black history is part of British history' and that slavery was not something that just happened in far off shores. She also highlights the prescient nature of the novel which 'predates the explosion of historical studies on the Black British history in the new millennium'.

The second article by Ball picks up on the outpouring of novels by Black British writers that Muñoz-Valdivieso introduces in the preceding chapter. It explores *A Harlot's Progress* alongside three other similar works of historical fiction that are all 'associated with infinity and unboundness, and with relational identity and transnational worldliness'. By examining the ways in which Dabydeen's Mungo 'asserts control over his narrative' through his continual contradictions and 'unstable narrative', Ball suggests that 'what happened or could have happened to Mungo…becomes its own kind of infinite text'. Although the four novels contain highly disparate portrayals of the Black urban subject, he concludes that they all enjoy a 'shared effect…of teasing out the multiple infinities implied by the Black subject's move from slavery to freedom' and 'respond to the paradox at the heart of the concept of infinity'.

Part II of *Like Diamonds From Dirt* shifts focus away from critical analyses of Dabydeen's writing to a more intimate look behind the works through the transcripts of three interviews with the author himself. Their diverse range of topics which encompasses areas such as his academic career, inspiration for his fiction, politics, history, and identity, all serve to highlight the fact that his often provocative style of fictional writing will continue to challenge the reader and critic alike. Conducted between 2013 and 2016, these interviews show how Dabydeen refuses to be constrained by any racial or linguistic boundaries, whilst also highlighting a more mischievous side to his personality that undercuts many of his more controversial pronouncements.

Aside from the wealth of scholarship dedicated to Dabydeen's fictional output, his influence on the world of literature has been recognised in a number of important ways. In 2000 he was made a Fellow of the Royal Society of Literature – the only Guyanese writer to be thus recognised to date. In 2007 he was awarded the Hind Rattan Award for his outstanding contributions to literature and the intellectual life of the Indian diaspora, and in 2021 he was elected Honorary Fellow of Selwyn College, Cambridge. He is currently working on another novel, inspired by his time in Beijing (2010-215) as Guyana's Ambassador to China, whilst also serving as Director of the Ameena Gafoor Institute for the study of Indentureship and its Legacies. Whatever the themes and context of that new novel, it will doubtless inspire the academic world to search for further insights into Dabydeen's often subversive, but always fascinating, relationship to literary tradition.

Lynne Macedo
March 2024

NOTES

1. A separate collection of essays on 'Turner' – *The Hook of Desire* – has just been published by Hansib Publications, see note ii below.
2. See, for example, Mark Frost: '"The Guilty Ship": Ruskin, Turner, Dabydeen, and their Critics' in Macedo, L. (ed.) *The Hook of Desire – Slavery and David Dabydeen's 'Turner'*, Hansib Publications, 2023, pp. 28-51, or Aleid Fokkema: 'Caribbean Sublime: Transporting the Slave, Transporting the Spirit' in Macedo, L. & Karren, K. (eds.) *No Land, No Mother- Essays on David Dabydeen*, Peepal Tree Press, 2007., pp.17-31.
3. Intertextuality is most frequently associated with Dabydeen's first two novels – *The Intended* and *Disappearance*, although there is rarely a straightforward connection between his writing and the books or authors he obliquely 'writes back' to. See, for example, Russell West-Pavlov: 'Intertextuality and the 'Spatialization' of Reading' in Macedo, L. (ed.) *Talking Words – New Essays on the Work of David Dabydeen*, University of the West Indies Press, Jamaica, pp.58-72.

PART I

*Essays about David Dabydeen's
Creative Writing*

CHAPTER ONE

Beauty and the Beast: White women, Black men & the question of the animal in *Slave Song*
Renée Landell

ABSTRACT

A substantial body of critical literature provides a postcolonial analysis of David Dabydeen's *Slave Song*. However, comparatively little scholarly attention has been paid to his treatment of gender, his representations of the non-human world and how they have informed race. In this collection of poems, Dabydeen vividly presents the Black male body, Black male sexuality, and the violent sexual histories of enslaved Black men. Such depictions expose and contextualize the historical construction of the Mandingo stereotype on the grounds of race, gender, sexuality and animality. The colonial construction of Black masculinity as tantamount to animality has had detrimental effects on the Black male psyche, the Black male body, and in turn, the lives of historically villainized and racialized animals. Using Dabydeen's poems, I maintain that the human-nonhuman binary is central in the racialized formations of gender and sexuality. In *Slave Song*, Dabydeen's representations of the white woman and the Black man expose how the Mandingo is grounded in the weaponizing of victimhood by white women. Such victim-playing has masked white women's participation in the racial domination of Black men and animal subjugation. Additionally, the animalization of the Black male body justifies the violent 'taming' of both the Black man and the animal.

KEYWORDS

Black masculinity, white womanhood, animality, the Mandingo stereotype, gendered racism, victimhood.

* * * * *

From the pestering "cush-cush ants", "cackroach" and "masquita" to the "black crappau" and the "bush-haag", animal images figure glaringly in almost all the poems in David Dabydeen's *Slave Song* (1984). Dabydeen's use of animal imagery speaks to the diversity of Caribbean wildlife where the tropical rainforests, coastal plains and savannas are home to various animal species. The songs of frustration, revenge and pain sung by African slaves and indentured labourers in the collection tell the violent histories of enslavement in Guyana. However, while a substantial body of critical literature provides postcolonial analysis on poems from Dabydeen's collection, little to no scholarly attention has been paid to his representations of animal life. Across the Anglophone Caribbean, Guyana is the only country where a substantial Amerindian presence survives, and so, ancestral practices of interspecies bonding have remained of significant importance. It is no wonder, then, that Guyanese writers like Dabydeen use animal imagery in their work to a greater extent than writers in other parts of the region. [1] Despite the comparative insertion of animals on a literary level, the scholarly lack of attention on the animal representations in Dabydeen's collection may concern something deeper than simply a proclivity for the human to centre self.

As Lucile Desblache remarks, "enslaved black Caribbeans were treated like beasts and were considered as 'not quite' human, [and so] there emerged a desire to establish strong boundaries between human and non-human animals" (2012, 125). Many slavery scholars, particularly of the Caribbean, have been reluctant to embrace the animal turn because of the dehumanizing nature of enslavement, but also as a way of avoiding the "dreaded comparison". [2] Critics such as Zakiyyah Iman Jackson and Bénédicte Boisseron have criticized scholarship that has analogized human suffering as animal suffering instead of reading them together in ways that expound how one has also informed the other.[3] I argue that scholars risk repeating racist and speciesist practices which have pitied Black people against animals incipiently increases when resting on comparison alone. For instance, in literature and throughout history and western philosophy, Black people as beastly animals became a common trope, and this anti-Black discourse coincides with depictions of the animal as 'Other' to the human within these same discourses. Dabydeen's poetry is a helpful resource for reading the entanglements of race and animality in ways that unearth violent human practices and animal practices. One of the critical ways Dabydeen draws on these concerns is through his treatment of gender (white femininity and Black masculinity). However, much like the animal, Dabydeen's representations of gender in *Slave Song* have also received little scholarly attention.

In this chapter, I critically analyze several poems from Dabydeen's collection to initiate a dialogue on the Mandingo stereotype – the popular and pervasive caricature of Black men as hypersexual and violent animals commonly described as sexually victimizing white women. The Mandingo simultaneously calls into question the entanglement of race, animality and gender. Drawing on representations of the Mandingo in Dabydeen's poetry, I argue that speciesism and gendered racism work in tandem to manufacture the violent weaponizing of victimhood by white women. Ultimately, this is important for understanding the circuit from white women's tears to white men's rage – the Mandingo stereotype made it easier for white women to hide their desire through accusations of rape and violent abuse; this then resulted in several punishments such as lynching by the white male master. Understanding the racially gendered crossing from tears to rage is also helpful in understanding how the villainization of certain animals has led to mass-killing and extinction.

Indeed, the main corollary of the Mandingo is its accentuation of white women as beauties (innocent and virtuous) and Black men as beasts (violent and dishonourable). The white damsel's appearance of powerlessness provokes a constant need for protection from the Mandingo beast. In his eponymous poem 'Slave Song' and throughout the collection, Dabydeen signifies how the abject bodies of enslaved Black men are othered limb by limb ("haan", "eye", "teet", "neck", "foot", "lip" and "leg") and how they are reaffixed in the colonial imaginary so that the Black man becomes a "h'animal", an "African orang-utan / [...] cannibal / fit fo slata fit fo hang" (Dabydeen, 2005, 29). Dabydeen suggests that the mythologisation of the Black body has been instrumental in shaping a split identity, in this case, of an interspecial 'Other':

> I suppose that's all I wanted to say, that ultimately, the plantation experience has severe and traumatic changes in epistemologies and philosophies, but overwhelmingly had to do with what is the very ground of our being, which is our body. (Grant, 1997, 220).

Additionally, the simianisation or 'ape-ing' of the enslaved Black man in the poem 'Slave Song' is particularly pertinent to this conversation on the weaponization of victimhood by white women and the Mandingo stereotype. In popular films and novels, the unspoken fear about Black-white sexual relations and the anxieties about Black male hypersexuality is figured by the human and non-human, Black and white, masculine, and feminine nexus. For example, the 1933 film *King Kong* has been extensively criticized for its gendered, racist, and speciesist overtones by many historians and critics. The film is set on a fictional island inhabited by native Africans and tells the story of a giant, black ape who falls in love with a white woman who is terrified by his 'disgusting' existence. The white woman plays the role of damsel-in-distress, and ultimately Kong is killed. Kong, like the Black man who defiantly and satirically urges the white man to call him an "African orang-utan" in 'Slave Song', also draws on the origin of scientific racism, which helped to shape hierarchal epistemologies of both human and nonhuman species and subsequently resulted in the enslavement of African people.[4] Claiming victimhood, according to Cheryl E. Matias, continues to be a "strategic manoeuvre used in gendered whiteness to relinquish a white women's culpability" of manipulation through victim-playing, but also her psycho-sexual violations of Black men (Matias 2019, 161).

In reading *Slave Song*, I argue that white supremacy and a racialized anthropocentrism are central functions of the Mandingo, which in the case of white women is actuated through performances of powerlessness. The title of the poem 'Nightmare' implies anxiety, fear, and disturbance, shaped in the imaginary. Beyond the emotional responses to mental images, the title 'Nightmare' can also be read as a delineation of the Mandingo stereotype. The word 'nightmare' etymologically derives from the Old English' mare'. The word 'mare' can be traced back to the reconstructed proto-Indo-European root '*mer-', which means 'crushing', 'pressing' and 'oppressing.' In Germanic and Slavic folklore, legends and myths, the 'mare' is a demonic entity that sits on the chest of its sleeping victims, causing them to feel suffocated and paralyzed. In thinking about how the Mandingo is conceptualized through 'wildness' and animality, it is interesting to note that in mythology, mare demons commonly take on bestialized forms of animals, including dogs, horses, frogs and hares. The association between the animal and the demonic spiritual world signifies the human anxieties about nonhuman species, and this conflation works to distort our perception of the non-human in the natural world.

Whether it is Dabydeen's intention or not, reading the poem through the etymological context of its title provides an alternative way to examine the representation of Black masculinity and animality. Additionally, it is also worth considering the association of Black men and animals with darkness and evil and the psychologically conceived threat they pose to whiteness. From the Latin translation of the word "nightmare" (incubo: to lie upon), the mare demon is often used interchangeably with the incubus night-demon, a male beast that sexually violates sleeping women and assumes the form of animals. In Dabydeen's poem, the Black men are bestialized ("crawl dung hole, lay dem egg"), they are violently rendered ("Bruk dung de door! / [...] drag she aff she bed [...] crack she head") and they perform their violent acts in the darkness ("deep in de night") much like the mythical mare. Their figuration is reminiscent of the Black animalistic beast in the famous eighteenth-century painting *The Nightmare* (Fuseli,

1781). In the painting, the focal figure is the unconscious white woman lying across her bed, her arm and hair falling to the side, her back arched and legs slightly bent. Sitting on top of her chest is an ape-like demon, an incubus, who stares threateningly at the viewer and a seemingly terrified horse. Figuring these characters, Fuseli's use of chiaroscuro (meaning: "light-dark") emphasizes the binary of good and evil.

The stark contrast between the dark/black and light/white elements of the painting work to illuminate one figure (the white woman) and almost conceal the 'other' (the ape-like incubus). In so doing, natural darkness and spiritual darkness become assigned to Blackness and the animal. According to Peter Wagner, "the (black) incubus in Fuseli's *The Nightmare* (1781) embodies…dominant prejudice concerning blackness…in conjunction with the construction of (white European) femininity and virility" (Wagner, 2009, p. 35). The psychological codifying of race by colour association in the painting is reflected in Dabydeen's "Nightmare" through images of Blackness and darkness ("dark surging wata", "deep in de night", "de moon", "black bat"). Such images are further reinforced in the poem 'Love Song':

> Black man cover wid estate ash
> E ead haad an dry like calabash,
> Dut in e nose-hole, in e ear-hole,
> Dut in e soul,
> In e battie-hole
>
> (Dabydeen, 2005, 31)

In contrast, religious and colour coded symbols of purity and light are used to represent the white woman in the poem 'Canecutter's Song':

> White hooman walk tru de field fo watch we canecutta,
> Tall, straight, straang-limb,
> Hair sprinkle in de wind like gold-duss,
> Laang lace frock loose on she bady like bamboo-flag,

An flesh mo dan hibiscus early maan, white an saaf an wet
Flowering in she panty.

(Dabydeen, 2005, 26)

This codifying of white femininity on a natural and spiritual level further justifies the violent 'taming'/civilisation of both the Black man and the animal as they are conflated with natural and spiritual darkness.[5]

Furthermore, as animals continue to be exploited and subordinated, I argue that attempts to bring violent animal practices to an end must rely on postcolonial discourses which explore how darkness and blackness work to abject Black men and animals. Looking beyond the title and into the narrative, the narrator in the poem 'Nightmare' describes how "waan gang sweat-stink nigga" violently intruded the space of the white woman; an allusion to wolves follows this in the third stanza. The animal imagery provides an opportunity to read the historic villainization of wolves, the mythic rendering of the werewolf, and the Mandingo stereotype together. Robert Busch argues that "no other animal in history has suffered the amount of misplaced animosity as has the wolf" (Busch, 2018, p. 109). Trevor Hulz hypothesizes this 'misplaced animosity', claiming that "the greatest threat to wolves is prejudice, fear and misunderstanding about the species" (Hulz, 2019).

The wolf has long been demonised in myths, legends, novels, music, art, and film. In examples such as *The Boy Who Cried Wolf* to *Little Red Riding Hood* and *The Three Little Pigs*, the wolf is not only imagined as a natural predator in literature but as an evil and barbaric intruder, much like the "waan gang sweat-stink nigga" in Dabydeen's 'Nightmare' (2005, 34). Indeed, the irrational fear of wolves speaks to the power of literary and historical myths and misrepresentation, which has provided cause for hunters to kill the canines to near extinction in fear of them trespassing and endangering their livestock. In thinking about the Mandingo stereotype, which mischaracterises Black men as sexual intruders/rapists, the Black man becomes allegorically associated with the infamous 'Big bad wolf.' As such, we cannot think about animal-life liberation without examining how animal abjection is entangled in gendered racism and mythologisation. One of the main symbols which have maligned wolves in Western literature is the moon; as a spiritual symbol, the moon represents the dark side of nature. As such, the poem conjures the mythical werewolf with which Blackness, humanity and spiritual darkness can be redrawn into question. In the third stanza of Dabydeen's poem, the narrator describes the perceived 'wolfish' nature of the Mandingo men after having devoured the white woman's body: "When dem dun suck dem raise dem red mout to de moon / An mek saang" (34). Lurking between wilderness and civilisation, the werewolf who transforms at night is situated at "the border between the beast and the 'human' qualities of man" (Jesse, 2000, p. 34).

Likewise, the white woman's forbidden desire of the Black man must be kept in the dark, always violently rendered and never desired in the public domain, so that the purity of her whiteness is maintained. Dabydeen leaves it until the final line of the poem to reveal that this 'nightmare' is, in fact, the white woman's rape fantasy: "wet she awake, cuss de daybreak!" (34). According to Dabydeen, "the final line glances comically and perversely at the 'aubade' convention in which Medieval lovers lament the coming of the sun which disturbs their secret nocturnal joy" (61). There is something about the light ("de daybreak"), its revelatory faculty, that exposes the contradictions in the construction of the Mandingo and the performative victimhood of the white woman. The darkness/Blackness and animality are not only feared but desired as an appealing and yet temporary egress for the white woman from societal constraint.

Reading Dabydeen's representation of the white woman in this way can unveil "the continuities between Dabydeen and Fanon", as Carl Plasa argues (Plasa, 2011, p. 118). In his controversial yet arguably most notable book *Black Skin, White Masks*, psychoanalyst, and postcolonial scholar Franz Fanon notes, "If we go farther into the labyrinth, we discover that when a woman lives the fantasy of rape by a Negro, it is in some way the fulfilment of a private dream, an inner wish" (Fanon, 1986, p. 179). Fanon further suggests that this concealed desire is a longing for the white woman to rape herself with the Black man's penis ("I wish the negro would rip me open as I would have ripped a woman open") (ibid). I contend that this masochistic desire exposes the anxieties of Self and emphasising Fanon's argument this desire to "rip" womanhood open is a desire to escape from an oppressed category. However, I argue that the social constraints of white womanhood do not make the white woman an actual victim but rather a perpetrator at odds with her split identity. An identity, where the oppressed part of her 'Self' (gender) is used for violence to uphold the oppressive parts of her 'Self' (whiteness). Her desire for pleasure is coupled with a desire for power for herself, substantiated by her feigned victim-identity, both of which come at the expense of the Black man, and in turn, the animal.

What I have argued in this chapter is that the Mandingo stereotype (where Black masculinity is tantamount to animality) has had detrimental effects on the Black male psyche, the Black male body and in turn, the lives of historically villainised and racialised animals. Dabydeen's poetry, like many other Caribbean, authored literary pieces, provides an opportunity to read the bestialisation of the Black man and the racialisation of animals together. However, an analysis of how such an entanglement has given power to colonially constructed white identities must also be explored to a greater extent.

NOTES

1. In an essay on Human-animal contact in Caribbean literature, published in A. James Arnold's *Monsters, Tricksters, and Sacred Cows*, Jeremy Poynting states that "if one surveys a wide range of Caribbean poetry in English, the truth is that there are really very few poems (certainly in comparison with English verse) that focus on animal life" (1996, 211).
2. Chattel slavery and factory farming were orchestrated to enforce a hierarchy of power where a distinction can be made between the 'human' (the white man) and the 'nonhuman' (animals, plants, and dehumanised humans, etc.) Comparisons helped to justify violence and tie one oppressed group to another. An example of this can be drawn from certain types of labour: the

exhibiting of Black bodies like meat on display at slave auctions, slave breeding 'farms', lynching, and the caging of Black bodies of which racialisation and animalisation become entangled.
3. Zakiyyah Iman Jackson in *Becoming Human* (2020) and Bénédicte Boisseron in *Afro-dog* (2018) both extensively highlight how drawing comparisons between animals and Black people are problematic and harmful in ways which trivialise suffering and reinforce hierarchies.
4. Darwin, along with many other scientists and philosophers, suggested that there were lower and barbarous races who are closely connected to animals such as 'anthropoid' apes (see, *Simianization: Apes, Gender, Class, and Race* by Hund, Mills and Sebastiani, 2015).
5. The bestialisation of the animal and the Black man upheld by the Mandingo stereotype, enables the weaponisation of victimhood by white women, which in turn emphasises the ineligibility of the Black male victim.

REFERENCES

Boisseron, B. 2018. *Afro-dog: Blackness and the Animal Question*. New York, Columbia University Press.

Busch, R. 2018. *Wolf Almanac: A Celebration of Wolves and Their World*. Lanham, Rowman & Littlefield.

Dabydeen, D. 2005. *Slave Song*. Leeds, Peepal Tree Press.

Desblache, L. 2012. Writing Relations: The Crab, The Lobster, The Orchid, The Primrose, You, Me, Chaos and Literature. In C. Blake, C. Molloy and S. Shakespeare (Eds.) *Beyond human: From Animality to transhumanism* (pp. 122-142). London, Continuum.

Fanon, F. 1986. *Black Skin, White Masks*. London, Pluto Press.

Fuseli, H. 1781. *The Nightmare*. [Oil on canvas] Michigan, Detroit Institute of Arts.

Grant, D. 1997. Ed. *The Art of David Dabydeen*. London, Peepal Tree.

Hulz, T. 2019. *THREATS TO WOLVES*. [online] New Wolves. Available at: <https://newwolves.com/blogs/news/threats-to-wolves> [Accessed 05 June 2021].

Hund, W., Mills, C. and Sebastiani, S., 2015. *Simianization: Apes, Gender, Class, and Race*. Münster, LIT Verlag.

Jackson, Z. 2020. *Becoming Human: Matter and Meaning in an Antiblack World*. New York, New York University Press.

Jesse, L. 2000. *Wolves in Western Literature*. [online] Trace.tennessee.edu. Available at: <https://trace.tennessee.edu/cgi/viewcontent.cgi?article=1391&context=utk_chanhonoproj> [Accessed 15 May 2021].

Matias, C. 2019. *Surviving Becky(s): Pedagogies for Deconstructing Whiteness and Gender*. Lanham, Lexington Books.

Plasa, C. 2012. *Slaves to Sweetness: British and Caribbean Literatures of Sugar*. Cambridge, Cambridge University Press.

Poynting, J. 1996. From Ancestral to Creole: Humans and Animals in a West Indian Scale of Values. In: A. Arnold, ed., *Monsters, Tricksters, and Sacred Cows: Animal Tales and American Identities*. Charlottesville, University Press of Virginia.

Spiegel, M. 1996. *The Dreaded Comparison: Human and Animal Slavery*. London, Mirror Books.

Wagner, P. 2009. Hogarth and the Other. In *Word & Image in Colonial and Postcolonial Literatures and Cultures*, Leiden, The Netherlands, Brill. Available From: Brill https://doi.org/10.1163/9789042027442_003 [Accessed 02 June 2021]

CHAPTER TWO

Shoring Up the Nation: David Dabydeen's Oceanic Sublime
John Clement Ball

ABSTRACT

The meditative narrative of Dabydeen's *Disappearance* (1993) depicts the efforts of an engineer from Guyana to protect some English cliffs against the "rogue and monster sea" that is eroding them and threatening a coastal village. Transcending the miniaturized waterscapes of his earlier novel *The Intended* in favour of an oceanic sublime that draws on ancient myths and fears of the sea's boundlessness and power, Dabydeen uses the ravaged English coast as a complex symbol for a crumbling post-imperial Englishness. The Black narrator's uncertain belonging is captured in his ambivalent identification with both the disorderly sea that preceded and still threatens 'civilization' and with the shored-up English landscape and community where he places himself as a new, if temporary, resident and protector. Moreover, his representations of the sea draw on eighteenth- and nineteenth-century cultural associations of nation and empire with the sea, and on the sublime – a way of framing the sea (and cliffs) that combined the eighteenth century's new sense of the sea's pleasure and personal uplift with older views of its primal mystery and danger. For Dabydeen and his unnamed narrator, the imperfectly protected shoreline represents the fluidity, liminality, and instability of national identity in post-imperial Britain.

KEYWORDS
England, Englishness, nation, empire, identity, ocean, shoreline, sublime

* * * * *

The sea is a multivalent sign in West Indian literature and culture. In the work of Jean Rhys, Derek Walcott, George Lamming, V.S. Naipaul, and Caryl Phillips, among others, ocean-space may signify the salt-sweat of slavery and indenture, the blank surface of ancestral memory and buried history, the circumscribed possibilities of "shipwrecked" lives, the restless fluidity of diasporic identity, a homesickness that can be as enervating as seasickness, and the complex relationality of what Paul Gilroy calls the "Black Atlantic" (1993). The cultural theorist Edouard Glissant, who defines "the Caribbean" as "a multiple series of relationships," also calls it a "sea [that] exists within us." This internalized space of outreach, this "estuary of the Americas," as he calls it, makes the Caribbean islands not isolated and "insular," as some would have it; on the contrary, Glissant writes, "each island embodies openness. The dialectic between inside and outside is reflected in the relationship between land and sea" (1989, p. 139). The many oceans and seas that separate lands and peoples around the globe are paradoxically also a single space of continuity and connection; a naval historian observed this at the height of Britain's imperial dominance of the world's oceans. "Though it has different names in different parts," Spencer Wilkinson wrote, the sea "is one single uninterrupted surface," a fact that "implies some kind of community between all mankind" (quoted in Behrman, 1977, p. 27). Glissant would doubtless want to qualify that universalizing sentiment, but his syncretistic view of Caribbean society and culture endeavours to transcend the obvious oppositions engendered by a brutal, violent history. His translator, J. Michael Dash, looks to the oceanic shoreline as a place to ground the migrant individual when he articulates one imperative at the heart of Glissant's relational poetics. "The 'unhoused' wanderer across cultures," Dash poetically writes, "must be 'rehoused' in the fissured history, the exposed sands, before the surging sea" (1989, p. xx).

One such transcultural wanderer is at the centre of David Dabydeen's second novel, *Disappearance* (1993). Its meditative narrative loosely depicts the efforts of an engineer from Guyana to protect some English cliffs against what he calls the "rogue and monster sea" that is eroding them and threatening a seaside village (1999, p. 20). Set near Hastings – the same bit of coast where canonical English history began in 1066 and where the protagonists of Salman Rushdie's *The Satanic Verses* would land over 900 years later – *Disappearance* turns the ravaged English shoreline into an ambiguous symbol. Reviewers typically describe the book as a "condition of England" novel (e.g., Jaggi); the disintegrating cliffs and the bucolic village on top thereby represent a nation whose empire has collapsed, shrinking its territory and its oceanic reach back to its original island shores. Dabydeen, who wears his metaphors on his sleeve in this novel, encourages such identifications. His unnamed narrator – a "self-consciously post-colonial" voice, in one critic's view (McWatt, 1997, p. 121) – writes that "the cliffs around Hastings were collapsing as the Empire had crumbled" (Dabydeen, 1999, p. 121); "the Empire had ended and what was left was a palsied decay, like the state of the cliff" (1999, p. 133).

Postwar decolonization coincided with the arrival in England of hundreds of thousands of West Indians – migrants who could be discursively rendered as either building a newly constituted nation or as eroding its foundations, depending on whether one took an open or an insular view of national identity. Given that context, what kind of England or Britain is implied by this novel's central image and event: a West Indian of African ancestry building a wall to protect the coast? If Dabydeen's protagonist is identified with the imperial and post-imperial sea – the slaves transported across the ocean as well as the waves of migrants washing up on England's shores and reshaping the nation's boundaries – can he without self-contradiction also be the one to, in his words, "conquer" that sea: protecting the houses and gardens of elderly white Britons from disappearance? Is there a coherent vision of the nation – the land – swimming around in this overdetermined imagery of assault and defence? In a text driven more by association than narration – by ideas rather than incident – Dabydeen invites us to wring his symbolic spaces dry for every ounce of significance, however slippery his meaning may seem to be.

The narrator has it both ways. In one important paragraph he identifies himself with both the sea and the seawall. The sea appeals to him as a something "more restless than myself, belonging everywhere and nowhere"; its ability to "dissolve" or erase the very history that was staged upon it liberates him, he says, from "all disquieting thoughts about how I could belong or not belong" (1999, p. 132). Indeed, "I was seduced by its endless transformations, which promised me freedom from being fixed as an African, a West-Indian, a member of a particular nationality of a particular epoch" (1999, p. 132). But he immediately goes on to say that he longs for definition, "to be a somebody, not any thing, and [I] resisted the sea's indiscriminateness" (1999, p. 132). He therefore thinks of the wall as "my identity, the obstacle I sought to put between shore and sea to assert my substantialness, my indissoluble presence, without reference to colour, culture, or age" (1999, pp. 132-33). This oscillation between the countervailing attractions of fluidity and fixity, the ephemeral and the permanent, connection and division, evokes something of the ambivalence towards the sea that has marked English and European cultural history.

In Guyana, where reclaiming and protecting land from the sea has a long history, the narrator learned to admire the sea's eternal, patient, mindless power; he felt dwarfed by it even as he worked professionally to "enslave it to my will" (1999, p. 18). "What destruction could Europeans wreak on Africans or Africans on Asians compared to the sea's frenzy?" he wondered: "How feeble were our strategies to colonise the land compared to the sea's ambition!" (1999, pp. 17, 18). The English did colonize many lands and celebrated that taming of purportedly wild overseas places and peoples – the unruly in need of rule – as a domestication of the wild, restless ocean. Britannia, as the song went, "rule[d] the waves"; as in Tennyson's characterization of Britain as "the mightiest Ocean-power on earth, / ... the lord of every sea" (qtd. in Behrman, 1977, p. 28), the workings of metonymy extend those "waves" to embrace the lands that Britannia crossed the waves to reach. It was a commonplace at the peak of Empire and of British naval supremacy to call the sea the "natural home of the Englishman," as James Anthony Froude did (qtd. in Berhman, 1977, p. 28). As Cynthia Behrman writes in *Victorian Myths of the Sea*, the English complacently claimed a sense of belonging to the sea, and a possession of it, greater than other nations' – a result of superior virtue and God's favour (1977, p. 22). This national feeling was part of the sense of entitlement to other lands that this substitution of sea for land and land for sea suggests. But as with all metonymic and metaphoric substitutions, the identification is imperfect, marked by difference as well as similarity. Foreign lands and peoples take enormous effort and power to rule, however incompletely; but no amount of effort or power can really enslave or control the sea, which will always be its own master.

This fact prompts Dabydeen to engage in some verbal punning with the word "rule" that helps contextualize the narrator's own efforts to tame the sea. In Guyana, the acerbic labourer Swami mocks the engineers he works for, including the narrator, as "straight-line folk" based on the way their "bulldozer blade does slice a line in the land." He says, "all-you does live along ruler's edge. The white man who used to rule you left you with a plastic ruler to rule you. If you take the ruler away, what you will do? Without the edge, you'll wander off in the bush and get lost" (1999, p. 36). The cluster of intersecting binaries this passage implies recurs throughout the novel: the straight and narrow "rule" of science – like that of imperialism – tames wild nature through the powers of civilization, culture, and technology. That which eludes or escapes such rule – that which is not straight or "straightforward" – is "the sinuous, the curved, the circular, the zigzagged, the unpredictable," and the "crooked" (1999, p. 75). The narrator's unconventional and anti-imperialist English landlady, Mrs Rutherford, recites that list as she encourages the narrator to transcend his engineer's habits of mind. But his work is premised on this very kind of hierarchical opposition: using science and technology to put a straight wall between the unruly sea and the crooked cliff, thus preventing the gardens and houses of civilization from being swallowed up and disappearing.

What they are threatened by is a sea that, as an implacable force in European history and global geography, comes saturated with symbolic and mythic associations that favour crookedness and anarchy over straightness and order. As Alain Corbin shows in his masterful cultural history *The Lure of the Sea*, prior to the eighteenth century the Biblical creation and flood stories underpinned a dominant attitude of horror and repulsion toward the ocean. It was seen as a primordial remnant of chaos, the disorder that preceded civilization and still threatened it, so difficult was it to contain the sea's power or predict its behaviour. The Garden of Eden has no sea and, as W.H. Auden observes in *The Enchafèd Flood*, "the first thing ... the author of the Book of Revelation notices in his vision of the new heaven and earth is that '*there was no more sea*'" (1967, pp. 6-7). Corbin writes, "the ocean spoke to pious souls. Its roaring, its moaning, its sudden bursts of anger were perceived as so many reminders of the sins of the first humans, doomed to be engulfed by the waves; its sound alone was a permanent appeal to repent and an incitement to follow the straight and narrow path" (1994, pp. 2-3). Add to that associations with sea-monsters, the cruelty of the underwater food chain, the many natural and human dangers involved in sea travel, and the amorphous openness of a space that has no visible pathways, and the ocean accumulates a host of negative and threatening associations. It becomes a space of purgatory and exile, of drift and madness, and life itself becomes figured as a perilous journey through a world as unstable as the sea. In such a world, the straight and narrow was not an easy course to follow; it might even require divine support of the sort Moses received in finding a straight and narrow path across the Red Sea.

Over the eighteenth century, however – a period of special interest to Dabydeen – ocean-space, along with the coastlines where it was imperfectly contained and accessed, was redeemed. The seaside became a place of renewal, refreshment, and pleasure;

a place of meditative seclusion away from the madding crowd but not entirely solitary; one could engage there in the pleasures of conversation with a select few individuals while being soothed by the rhythms of the waves. The narrator of *Disappearance*, with his solitary, meditative ways and his long conversations with just a few villagers, comes to the seaside with something of this agenda. The discursive taming of the sea in the eighteenth century led to a domestication and commodification of its benefits that continues in our own time: one went to the sea to be symbolically reborn or baptized by immersion in cold salt water that was now seen as physically and spiritually beneficial. Dabydeen's narrator doesn't bathe in the sea, but his perspective on it does draw on the sublime, a contemporaneous way of framing the sea (and other large phenomena such as cliffs) which combined that new sense of pleasure and personal uplift with the older view of the sea's primal mystery and danger. The sublime view emphasized the boundless vastness of the sea's surface and the profound mysteries of its depth, as well as its endless energy, mobility, and indifference to human activities or values. The very qualities that caused civilizing orders to construct the sea as a space of otherness now present what Edmund Burke would see as an "agreeable amazement" that overwhelms the senses and emotions, even as observers of this spectacle are reassured by their safe, if dizzying, position apart from it. Contemplation of primitive natural phenomena such as the sea, Corbin writes, "invite[s] the observer to delight in any setting that demonstrates that Nature has sufficient force to resist the pressures of civilization. From this desire for a compensatory tempo the sublimeness of the ocean is born. Remember that human activities leave no trace upon the sea. As a barren landscape that mankind can neither arrange nor endow with moral significance, the immensity of the waters is the antithesis of the garden" (1994, p. 125).

The garden, like the city, is a time-honoured emblem of human civilization. In my book *Imagining London* I discuss Dabydeen's rendering of the city in *The Intended* (see Ball, 2004, pp. 166-73), which also has some significant, if smaller and more contained, waterscapes. *Disappearance* makes fleeting references to London but picks the private garden as its chief representation of a settled world – a nature tamed by culture. Mrs Rutherford's obsessively tended garden runs "down the edge of Dunsmere cliff and a sheer drop of ninety feet" (1999, p. 3). It and the house are therefore directly opposed to – but also next to – the sea. The garden strikes the narrator as "the very picture of order"; "Everything she planted," he says, "was *engineered* to present a gentle spectacle of shapes and colours" (1999, p. 67; emphasis added). Moreover, that garden is essential to the narrator's acculturation since, in Mrs Rutherford's view, "You only know a place when you can identify the flowers"; he duly learns their names and comes to see her plants as "rooted in English history" (1999, p. 68). But as a fellow "engineer" of a sort, Mrs Rutherford is no more clearly identified with the traditional order of history, Englishness, and civilization's rule (in both senses of that word) than the straight-and-narrow-wall-building narrator. It is she who urges him both to resist Englishness and to favour the unruly and crooked over the straight. She insists that her garden is actually a "wilderness" (1999, p. 75) and is remarkably unconcerned about its possible collapse into the wild sea. As she blurs conceptual boundaries between her green and pleasant land and its supposed antithesis, she provides a model of Englishness that can help us better understand the narrator (whom she nurtures as avidly as her flowers) and his own contradictory affiliations with land and sea.

The sea-space in question here is, of course, the English Channel, the so-called "streak of silver sea" that provided Britain with what the Victorians celebrated as their "happy confinement" and "splendid isolation" from continental Europe (Behrman, 1977, pp. 38, 43). With its rough weather the Channel was seen as a protective "moat" or "barrier" against foreigners (1977, p. 46). As a Victorian anthologist smugly observed, "Thanks to the 'silver streak' which is worth an entire European army, the English race, instead of exhausting its force ... in defending frontiers, has been enabled to give all its energies to strengthening its limbs at home and finding fresh fields in which to exercise them abroad" (qtd. in Behrman, 1977, p. 47). The Channel, in other words, facilitated imperialism and a national identity premised on it. Among the many ironic reversals invoked by Dabydeen's novel is the Channel's changing image: the waters that used to protect have become waters from which England must be protected. Now that Britannia no longer rules the waves, a former colonial from across the waves (and identified with them) is charged with providing protection from them.

Once he has done so and finished the wall, the narrator feels ambivalent about his achievement. He thinks it looks out of place, too visible and obviously man-made. "Everything else was made by sea and wind," he says, but the wall interrupts the rhythms of nature and tide, settling, in his words, "monumentally and unnaturally in the sand, refusing to budge" so that it looks "monstrous and cruel, stubborn and brutishly arrogant, an awesome deformity. I regretted that I had made it and half wished that the sea would breach it, break it down to mere pebbles" (1999, p. 177). As another famous writer once opined, "Something there is that doesn't love a wall" (Frost, 1960, p. 94), and Dabydeen's ambivalent narrator seems to agree with that sentiment; however, as Robert Frost's poem makes clear, the walls that separate can also gather and connect, even if they have to be regularly broken down and built back up to do so.

Some important books on Englishness and empire show how the prevailing sensibilities of the imperial nation have historically vacillated between an inclusive, borderless, global version of English identity and territory and a more racially and territorially exclusive one. Ian Baucom's study of "spaces of instability in the geography of Englishness" argues that nineteenth-century uprisings such as the Morant Bay Rebellion in Jamaica "served to collapse any conception of England as a discrete, ocean-bounded space" (1999, p. 41). At its extreme, this global embrace leads to the "vision" John Stuart Mill and his contemporaries articulated of what Baucom calls an "empire without interruptions, ... without boundaries, or breaks, or, quite frankly, oceans" (1999, p. 167). Simon Gikandi, in "calling attention to the unstable zones and contested boundaries that conjoin and divide metropolitan cultures and colonial spaces," pursues some of the geographical and political implications of the fact that "it has never been clear where the identity between the colonizer and the colonized ends and the difference between them begins" (1996, p. 2). As Homi Bhabha, Stuart Hall, and Paul Gilroy have also shown, the tensions between inclusive and exclusive versions of Britishness or Englishness remain divisive, and in post-imperial, multicultural Britain the redefinition of the nation's territory, culture, society, and identity remains an urgent, ongoing project.

In this context, it is fitting that Dabydeen chooses the seaside for the investigation of post-imperial Englishness. The writer who once referred to England as "the third largest West Indian island" (quoted in Birbalsingh, 1996, p. 174) makes the restless sea and shoreline the keys to a migrant, Black British thematic. In doing so he chooses spaces that defy fixity, embodying fluidity and instability and transformation. While the sea is obviously a space, even the shoreline is most appropriately thought of as a space rather than a line. With its tides and shifting contours, its inclusion of land and sea – culture's houses and gardens and people as well as the forces of brute nature that threaten them – the shoreline is an in-between area, a liminal zone where differences collide but also overlap and vie for dominance. The nation, Dabydeen implies, is still a site of contestation, and locating "the 'unhoused' wanderer across cultures" at the seaside enables him and the novel to enact that contestation in a highly symbolic space: to shore up the nation so there will continue to be one and to break down any straight and narrow symbols of what its boundaries should be.

REFERENCES

Auden, W.H. (1967) [1950]. *The Enchafèd Flood: or The Romantic Iconography of the Sea*. New York, Vintage.
Ball, John Clement. (2004). *Imagining London: Postcolonial Fiction and the Transnational Metropolis*. Toronto, University of Toronto Press.
Baucom, Ian. (1999). *Out of Place: Englishness, Empire, and the Locations of Identity*. Princeton, Princeton University Press.
Behrman, Cynthia Fausler. (1977). *Victorian Myths of the Sea*. Athens, Ohio University Press.
Birbalsingh, Frank. (1996). 'David Dabydeen: Coolie Odyssey'. *Frontiers of Caribbean Literature in English*. Ed. Frank Birbalsingh. New York, St. Martin's. pp. 167-82.
Corbin, Alain. (1994). *The Lure of the Sea: The Discovery of the Seaside 1760-1840*. Trans. Jocelyn Phelps. Harmondsworth, Penguin.
Dabydeen, David. (1999) [1993]. *Disappearance*. London, Vintage.
Dash, J. Michael. (1989). Introduction. *Caribbean Discourse: Selected Essays*. By Edouard Glissant. Trans. J. Michael Dash. Charlottesville, University Press of Virginia. pp. xi-xlv.
Frost, Robert. (1960). *Robert Frost's Poems*. Ed. Louis Untermeyer. New York, Washington Square.
Gikandi, Simon. (1996). *Maps of Englishness: Writing Identity in the Culture of Colonialism*. New York, Columbia University Press.
Gilroy, Paul. (1993). *The Black Atlantic: Modernity and Double Consciousness*. Cambridge, Harvard University Press.
Glissant, Edouard. (1989). *Caribbean Discourse: Selected Essays*. Trans. J. Michael Dash. Charlottesville, University Press of Virginia.
Jaggi, Maya. (1993). Rev. of *Disappearance*, by David Dabydeen. *Times Literary Supplement* 3 December: p. 20.
McWatt, Mark. (1997). ' "Self-Consciously Post-Colonial": The Fiction of David Dabydeen'. *The Art of David Dabydeen*. Ed. Kevin Grant. Leeds, Peepal Tree. pp. 111-22.

CHAPTER THREE

Identity negotiations in *Disappearance* (1993)
Marta Fratczak-Dabrowska

ABSTRACT

This article focuses on one of David Dabydeen's most popular novels entitled *Disappearance*, and centres on the novel's main protagonist and his struggles with identity and belonging. It portrays the main character as a contemporary Everyman – a migrant from a peripheral space to the former metropolis – who tries to find his place in the globalized world. Trapped by fixed categories of belonging, which other people impose upon him, he negotiates his identity in-between concepts such as African, West-Indian, English and Guyanese. In the course of the novel, he learns how to reconcile his national and transnational identity, and finds his way back to his home(land). In such a way, Dabydeen shows that embracing one's national identity does not entail compromising on other, more fluid patterns of belonging available to us today.

KEY WORDS

Disappearance, national identity, transnational identity, hybridity, Guyana, migrations

* * * * *

Disappearance is one of Dabydeen's most popular and widely analysed novels. It is often compared with V.S. Naipaul's *The enigma of arrival* in terms of its landscape imagery as well as the Caribbean migrant experience of travelling (back) to the metropolis (Stein 2007).[1] Its countless interpretative dimensions make *Disappearance* an endless source of academic inspiration. Some, however, hold this multidimensionality against the novel. Mark McWatt, for example, accuses it of being a cliché of postcolonial theories. "Perhaps it is preferable for the reader to apply the theory to the text", he writes, "rather than have the text apply it to itself. Perhaps, too, this could be Dabydeen's point: that there is little substance at the centre of the self-consciously post-colonial text" (McWatt 1997)[2]. The present analysis, however, does not wish to prove that *Disappearance* is an exemplary postcolonial novel, but at the same time it does not forcibly separate it from its postcolonial background. Rather it places the text within the purely Guyanese context and investigates if Dabybeen's reflections on (non)belonging may reveal any universal truths about identity formation in today's world.

Disappearance may be read as a voice of Dabydeen's generation. As the already quoted critic and a friend of David Dabydeen – Mark McWatt – writes, when the country gained independence he was nineteen years old, seven years older than Dabydeen himself, and three older than the main protagonist of *Disappearance*. McWatt remembers his and his friends' enthusiasm for the country's liberation (McWatt 2005).[3] At that time they were all young, intelligent, ambitious and went to good Georgetown schools, which made them the elite of the nation. In 2005, McWatt gathered his old colleagues from Guyana, most of whom were now important people working in Western institutions, and asked them to finish their teenage project of each writing one short story on the occasion of Guyana's independence. Regardless of the stories' literary value, and the collection is indeed very interesting, McWatt bitterly concluded that their writing was a homage to the country that all had "abandoned" and which nowadays "seems in worse shape than it was at independence" (McWatt 2005).[4] Dabydeen, though not part of McWatt's group of writers, is nevertheless one of those Guyanese intellectuals of the post-1950s generation who left the country, but ultimately decided to engage himself more actively in the Guyanese political and social life. He was, for example, the Guyanese ambassador to UNESCO (1997-2010) and the Guyanese ambassador to China (2010-2015).

The Guyanese experience, hence, corresponds to that of many people who leave their homelands and seek their places in the globalized and theoretically border-less world. Such a universalist perspective is not ungrounded, as the main protagonist of *Disappearance* is left unnamed, which makes him a contemporary Everyman. However, if one looks closely at the novel, one may find many allusions to Dabbydeen's own life. He and his protagonist were both born sometime before political independence, they were both raised by single mothers and their formative years were overshadowed by ethno-national(ist) tensions. Though Dabydeen left Guyana as a boy, a few years earlier than his protagonist, they both emigrated to England where they tried to find their professional identity, Dabydeen as a professor and his protagonist as an engineer. Also, they both maintained an emotional relationship with their home country:

> David Dabydeen: (…) I think of Guyana constantly. I've just come back from Guyana. (…) I spent thirteen years there. Those are the experiences that form your character. Some people say writing is just about explorations and re-explorations of childhood experiences. So in a sense: yes, I feel Guyanese…. (…). But then one can't have these easy dichotomies either; but you know what I mean, there are grey areas as well (Stein 2004).[5]

Therefore the novel may be read as an intimate account of personal and universal identity struggles and an intriguing portrayal of a contemporary Guyanese man trying to reconcile many of his conflicting loyalties into one hybridized body.

Initially, the protagonist's critical investigations into his identity are triggered by a sense of alienation from his own community. From the very first page of the text, the unnamed protagonist is well aware that he is a cultural hybrid; even though he is part of the Afro-Guyanese community, he never calls himself an African or displays any ethnic loyalties. He is sent to an ethnically mixed public school, and then to the newly established state college, where he is brought up in the appreciation of English culture. From the beginning he calls Guyana "our country", but he is also convinced of its inferiority towards England. The desire of going abroad is shared by many of his compatriots, including a local drunkard, Alfred, who is a father-figure for the boy. "You does feel as if you got more than one life when you go abroad" (Dabydeen 1994)[6], Alfred preaches. As such, Guyana appears a country torn by negative differences where one learns the power of stereotypes and the unfairness of classification. The boy perfectly remembers a moment when his teacher called him a *nigger*, as well as when he himself used a word *coolie* "a reminder of [East-Indian] lowliness" against his school friend (Bahadur 2013).[7]

It is in escaping Guyana, then, that he sees a chance of escaping sectarian divisions. When he commits himself to emigration, he sees England as a solid alternative to his homeland, a land without the legacy of violence and hatred, where he could become everything he wanted: "... if there was a god he had long abandoned our land and gone abroad or back to England. I suddenly knew that I too must voyage abroad as soon as I grew up and could fashion a boat, even though I was not wholly convinced that such a place existed" (Dabydeen 1994)[8]. As Julia Kristeva argues: "[t]hose who repress their roots (...) fuel the same hatred of self [as those who are nationalist] but they think that they can settle matters by fleeing" (Kristeva 1993)[9] and Dabydeen's protagonist does exactly that, namely he tries to resolve his identity problem by running away from the country. When he finally arrives in his dream (Eng)land, despite his black skin and exotic national affiliation, he does not see himself as a foreigner but as a transcultural being who can claim place anywhere in the world and across any categories (Berg and Ní Éigeartaigh 2013).[10] This illusion of belonging is quickly shattered when England makes him acutely aware of his internal as well as external otherness.

The first one to make him feel a stranger is Mrs Rutherford, his landlady, who utterly ignores Julia Kristeva's rule of the privileged status of a foreigner, who "is from nowhere, from everywhere" and should never be sent back to his origins (Kristeva 1994).[11] Instead, Mrs Rutherford immediately inscribes him into a solid category of belonging, showing that identity is by no means our independent choice, but rather a constant struggle against the representations. "Cultural identities (…) have histories", being the "names we give to the different ways we are positioned by, and position ourselves within, the narratives of the past", as Stuart Hall once said (1990).[12] Here Mrs Rutherford offers the cultural identity to her guest. Her house is filled with African masks she collected during her travels and she naturally imposes an African(ized) identity on the engineer. She even expects him to manifest a passionate attachment to Africa, which he does not feel:

> 'I know nothing about art,' I said, when I meant to say was that I knew nothing about Africa. She looked at me as I returned the carving, seeing a Negro, his large black hands carefully holding up a sacred bowl (…) I was no African though, and my fetishes and talisman were spirit-levels, bulldozers, rivets. I was Black West-Indian of African ancestry but I am an engineer, trained in the science and technology of Great Britain (Dabydeen 1994).[13]

Mrs Rutherford assumes that her guest would be happy to claim his African heritage. Such a seemingly inclusive category of belonging, however, is by no means liberating. The 'true' Africa, embodied by the masks bears no affinity to the guest's cultural identity and triggers no emotional response. The guest is more than positive that he is "no African", the closest acceptable denomination being a "Black West-Indian of African ancestry"

(Dabydeen 1994)[14], though this term comes with its own history too. The adjective 'West-Indian' was first used as a geographic denominator by the Spanish to describe the location of the Caribbean and its native inhabitants; the term, hence, is not indigenous to the region. As George Lamming writes, they never placed themselves in this category; he learned its meaning when he arrived in England, where it was used to describe the new wave of newcomers to Britain, being tantamount to the word *immigrant* (Lamming 2012).[15] As such, Dabydeen's protagonist is trying to use the purely colonial and homogenizing term to describe a completely new, truly fluid, identity construct he feels entitled to. For him, West-Indian is a signifier of freedom from the burdens of the old world: "I was a West-Indian, someone *born in a new age for a new world*. (…) I was always present. I was always new" (Dabydeen 1994)[16].

It soon occurs that his vision of his West-Indian identity is dangerously close to a simple imitation of Englishness. This truth dawns on him when Mrs Rutherford starts alluding to his excessive admiration of English tradition brought, after all, from a country forcibly subdued to the domination of the English culture. She acts as a catalyst dismantling her guest's illusions as to his role within the system; in a Conrad-like manner, she reverses for him the categories of master/savage and gives him various evidence of English 'savagery', that could be realized only outside the tight grip of English civilization. The English, for fear of their own 'hearts of darkness', tried to "domesticate" *the Others* (Bhabha 2004)[17]. "I must admit that when you first came here I looked upon you suspiciously and a robot – something we had created (…) a Black man with an English soul" (Dabydeen 1994)[18], she says. Finally, her guest starts recognizing analogies between his desire of coming to England and his formative years spent in Guyana overshadowed by his beloved college professor, Fenwick, who appeared to him a paragon of Englishness. "When I grew up", he says, "I wanted to believe that professor Fenwick was the true Englishman (…) [his] influence on me was total" (Dabydeen 1994)[19]. For years, he has been fuelled by an unexpressed desire to be like Fenwick – an Englishman raised and shaped in a country unburdened with colonial violence and racial prejudice. The ultimate and irreversible collapse of Fenwick's authority comes when Mrs Rutherford turns out to have known the man as a simple crook, who ran to Guyana to escape from justice.

Resultantly, there collapses the façade of English ideals and a hybrid West-Indian identity conceived of by the protagonists. They invariably situate a postcolonial Caribbean man in relation to the metropolis and metropolitan culture, offering no space to coin an independent identity (Puri 2004).[20] From now on, the protagonist decides to think of himself simply as an engineer: "I'm me, not a mask or a movement of history. I'm not Black, *I'm an engineer*" (Dabydeen 1994)[21]. This brief statement is predicated on the belief that one may exchange one's cultural belonging for an unburdened, but utterly rootless, professional identity that would not necessitate a confrontation with the past:

> I was seduced by (…) endless transformations, which promised me freedom from being fixed as an African, a West-Indian, a member of a particular nationality of a particular epoch. (…) When Mrs Rutherford asked me why I became an engineer I couldn't answer, but deep down I knew a dam was my identity, and obstacle I sought to put between shore and sea and to assert my substantialness, my indissoluble presence, without reference to colour, culture or age (Dabydeen 1994).[22]

Such words may be read as a somewhat desperate attempt at becoming *himself* – a man free from any constraining ideals. After all, he is and always will be an engineer, and thus he will belong to the broad and undefined category of the engineers, even if he refuses to be African or West-Indian.

Dabydeen's protagonist's self-determination as an engineer, hence, is fuelled by both his yet unexpressed regret of breaking his ties with Guyana, and his silently harboured wish not to be marked out as a foreigner in England. However, even in a seemingly tolerant metropolis, the idea of being a nation-less and race-less engineer is an impossible construct. One of the characters who makes him fully understand this paradox is Christie, the manager of the building site. After long years spent in England, Christie introduces himself in the following words: "I'm a foreigner from Ireland" (Dabydeen 1994).[23] Christie's *otherness* comes to light literally the moment he opens his mouth: "He replied in a tongue I couldn't follow, an English so mangled and accented that I knew immediately that it was Irish" (Dabydeen 1994)[24]; Christie "mentioned the traumas of being Irish" so poignant to those of being a Guyanese. He also described Ireland as full of superstitions and a deep spiritual connection to the land: "from what Christie says Dunsmere might as well be a village in the Congo" (Dabydeen 1994)[25]. Moreover, Christie still harbours a deep sense of economic injustice done by the English to his people: "[t]he only ones who work are the Irish. They've been at it for centuries, they're the leprechauns of England, the ones who get things done by miracles" (Dabydeen 1994)[26]. As such, a Guyanese engineer and an Irish manager, both foreigners, are linked in their otherness. Even in their strangeness, however, they are not equal. Though the dam builders accept Christie's leadership, they have some reservations as to being governed by a 'Black man'. Even some of the narrator's new neighbours display an unhealthy interest in their 'Black engineer'. One day an unknown man tells him in no uncertain terms that "[i]n America they'd string you up for peeping under a white woman's skirt. We do things differently here, but *you're still black so don't forget it*" (Dabydeen 1994)[27].

The man denies the engineer his very right to the English part of his cultural heritage, implying that his stay in England is temporary and conditional. The immigrant is thought of as a foreigner whose right to stay is legitimate only if s/he contributes to the wellbeing of the receiving society. Indisputably, Dabydeen's protagonist fulfils the latter criteria as he is a legally employed professional, but it also means that his legitimacy is sanctioned only by the work he is capable of doing and not by his rightful claim to the English nation-state. For this reason, the chances of being harmoniously accepted into the receiving society without the stigma of foreignness are slim. His meeting with Christie, and the sense of being a stranger in England, force the man to critically rethink his national belonging. As Kristeva once said, "[l]iving with the other, with the foreigner, confronts us with the possibility or not of being *an other* and makes oneself other for oneself" (1994).[28] The foreigner, hence, leaves his land "only to return to oneself and one's home" (Kristeva 1994).[29] As if to echo her words, when the engineer completes the sea-wall he arrived in England to build, he decides to go back to Guyana.

Ironically enough, as Mrs Rutherford observes, the sea-wall makes him forever part of England: "You've shaped something in stone which will be here for a long time, if not for ever. And you've done it in England, so you've carved your name in our history" (Dabydeen 1994)[30]. The very fact of being part of English history, however, does not make him part of the English present. Now, for the first time in years, he starts thinking of Guyana as home:

> I would leave both of them [Mrs Rutherford and England] and return home. Guyana had its own legacies of deceit, and cruelty, but there was space to forget. The land was vast and empty enough to encourage new beginnings in obscure corners. I had to believe this, otherwise there would be nowhere to go and nothing to do but act out ritual public disputes (Dabydeen 1994)[31].

Even though Guyana has "no burial grounds holding the bones of slaves, no old sugar mills where they worked, no letters, no books that they left behind, no carvings" (Dabydeen 1994)[32], it is built on a truly non-codified, and thus flexible, memory, which opens endless possibilities of self-invention that could restore one's rootedness in time and space, while not forcing one to choose from the limited array of available and pre-defined patters of identification.

The vision of national consciousness re-discovered here by the protagonist is that of a cultural hybrid. It is inherently fluid, yet rooted, and it does not demand questioning any of one's cultural loyalties. *Disappearance*, then, shows that hybridity and fluidity – two defining features of the Caribbean world – need not preclude the sense of national belonging. Guyana is an inseparable part of the engineer's identity, though at the beginning it seemed a burden from which he wanted to run away. The right to claim national identity may be redemptive for a Caribbean man trapped in the paradoxes of the global(ized) world and having nothing in common with declaring nationalist sentiments. As Samuel Selvon observed, his native Trinidad is a "shadow" that follows him anywhere he goes and proves that his "roots are the same as a mango tree or an immortelle" (Selvon 1987).[33] Selvon stresses the need of national heritage being part of the broader Caribbean identity, as only reconciled with one*self* would one be able to face the challenges of the global(ized) world. The reader does not know if Guyana is the last stop in the protagonist's journey, but one may hope that his physical and metaphorical homecoming will help him emerge anew, hybrid-ized and stronger.

NOTES

1. Mark Stein, "Writing place: The perception of language and architecture in V.S. Naipaul's *The enigma of arrival* and David Dabydeen's *Disappearance*". In Kampta Karram and Lynne Macedo, *No land, no mother: Essays on David Dabydeen* (2007) Leeds, Peepal Tree, pp. 162-180.
2. Mark McWatt, "Self-consciously post-colonial: The fiction of David Dabybeen". In: Kevin Grant, *The art of David Dabydeen*. (1997) Leeds, Peepal Tree, p. 121.
3. Mark McWatt, *Suspended sentences: Fiction of atonement* (2005) Leeds, Peepal Tree, pp. 9-10.
4. McWatt, *Suspended Sentences*, p. 18
5. Mark Stein, "David Dabydeen with Mark Stein". In: Susheila Nasta, *Writing across worlds: Contemporary writers talk* (2004) London, Routledge, p 232.
6. David Dabydeen, *Disappearance*, (1994 [1993]), London, Vintage, p 48.
7. Gaiutra Bahadur, *Coolie woman: The odyssey of indenture* (2013) London, Hurst and Company, p. xx.
8. Dabydeen, *Disappearance*, p. 62.
9. Julia Kristeva, *Nations without nationalism* (1993) Columbia, Columbia University Press, p. 3.
10. Wolfgang Berg and Aoileann Ní Éigeartaigh, *Exploring transculturalism: A biographical approach* (2013 [2010]), Wiesbaden, VS Verlag für Sozialwissenschaften, p. 11

11. Julia Kristeva, *Strangers to ourselves* (1994) Columbia, Columbia University Press, p. 30.
12. Stuart Hall, "Cultural identity and diaspora". In: Jonathan Ruteford, *Identity: Community, culture, difference* (1990) London, Lawerence, p. 225.
13. Dabydeen, *Disappearance*, p. 7.
14. Dabydeen, *Disappearance*, p. 102.
15. George Lamming, *The pleasures of exile* (2012 [1960]). The University of Michigan Press, p. 214.
16. Dabydeen, *Disappearance*, p. 102; emphasis mine; MFD.
17. Homi Bhabha, *The location of culture* (2004) London, Routledge, p. 154.
18. Dabydeen, *Disappearance*, p. 104.
19. Dabydeen, *Disappearance*, pp. 81-82.
20. Shalini Puri, *The Caribbean postcolonial: Social equality, post/nationalism, and cultural hybridity* (2004) London and New York, Palgrave, p 8.
21. Dabydeen, *Disappearance*, p 102; emphasis mine, MFD.
22. Dabydeen, *Disappearance*, pp. 132-133.
23. Dabydeen, *Disappearance*, p 109.
24. Dabydeen, *Disappearance*, p 109.
25. Dabydeen, *Disappearance*, p 117.
26. Dabydeen, *Disappearance*, p 113.
27. Dabydeen, *Disappearance*, p 128; italics mine; MFD.
28. Kristeva, *Strangers to ourselves*, p. 13.
29. Kristeva, *Strangers to ourselves*, p. 133.
30. Dabydeen, *Disappearance*, p 177.
31. Dabydeen, *Disappearance*, p 179.
32. Dabydeen, *Disappearance*, p 15.
33. Samuel Selvon, "Three into one can't go – East Indian, Trinidadian, Westindian". In: David Dabydeen and Brinsley Samaroo, *India in the Caribbean* (1987) Hertford, Hansib Publications, p. 24.

CHAPTER FOUR

Spatial Transgressions and the Search for a Non-Identitarian Ethics in David Dabydeen's *Disappearance*

Sten Pultz Moslund

ABSTRACT

This article looks at the representation of place and spatial realities in David Dabydeen's novel *Disappearance* from 1993. The analysis takes up the novel's key concerns of migration, history, modernity, human–nature relations and ways of being in the world. While doing so, it traces two primary modes of spatial transgression – *discursive* and *sensuous* – that accomplish a post-structural as well as a phenomenological challenge to oppressive Western histories and narratives. The article finishes with a consideration of how Dabydeen's novel searches for a non-identitarian ethics of interhuman recognition that moves away from national and sometimes postcolonial identity ascriptions and demands for discursively clear subject positions.

KEY WORDS

Place, migration, Western metaphysics, modernity, human-nature relations, post-structural analysis, phenomenological sensuous analysis

* * * * *

David Dabydeen's *Disappearance* (1993) carefully uncovers a complex intertwinement of different productions of place – sociocultural, economic, historical, political, individual and bodily – some of which are interrelated, some of which are incommensurable (though all of them coexisting within the same place). The settings of the novel are the coasts of Guyana and England, and mainly the symbolically laden site of Hastings in West Sussex. The novel's anonymous first-person narrator is a migrant African-Caribbean engineer who builds dams to reclaim and protect land from the sea – once in Guyana, where he was born (like Dabydeen himself), and now, in the novel's present, in Hastings near the fictive village of Dunsmere. What is quite remarkable about Dabydeen's novel is how the book dramatizes different productions of spatial reality, or different modes of perceiving spatial realities as they are caused to *appear* and *disappear* at different levels of human experience, effecting different kinds of relations not only to the same place but also to various human histories.

The following reading will show how the novel uses the appearance and disappearance of these different, yet, in fact, *simultaneous* modes of relating to the same place to challenge subjugating discourses/histories from the two quite different strategies of *discursive* and *sensuous* transgression. *Disappearance* is explicitly about the metaphysics that determine our lives and the novel's settings are, in this regard, explored for all their discursive and sensuous dimensions. On the one hand, the novel performs a "careful teasing out of warring forces of signification", to quote Barbara Johnson's famous description of the post-structural method (Johnson, 1981, ix). As a piece of postcolonial resistance of the deconstructive kind, *Disappearance* challenges the ideology of empire, nation and modernity by the release of a plurality of disparate voices, meanings and perspectives – even within single words. On the other hand, the novel's spatial references often shift from their status as discursive/metaphorical vehicles (*topoi*) to manifestations of sensuous experiences of places and physical phenomena (*aistheta*). Places in the novel thus appear as materializations of meta-physical ideas and counter-ideas that control and direct our subjective destinies while at the same time, in a different mode of sensuous experience, the place world also reappears as an embodied dimension of human existence in which synaesthetic perceptions of reality more radically defy discursive territorializations of the world. The latter concretizes a sphere of life and reality that proves deeply incongruous with oppressive suprasensory regimes of thought.

Disappearance ceaselessly creates a great deal of unrest about the spatial references and metaphors that circulate within its narrative. A central noun like "landslip" signifies in several different ways. It deictically points to the physical crumbling of cliffs and land erosion caused by the sea, and, as a *metaphor* (standing for something other than itself), "landslip" figures as an image in nationalist rhetoric of an alleged need to defend the nation from the "loss of land" to immigrants and post-imperial decline (131-7). The novel thus exposes how nationalist discourse exploits the concrete fear of land crumbling into the sea, but the migration of the word's meaning does not stop at that. In the novel's postcolonial discourse, "landslip" comes to stand for a *celebration* of the fall of the empire: "they once ruled the seas" but now "the cliffs around Hastings were collapsing as the Empire had crumbled" and, in the novel's discourse of migratory movement, "landslip" plays on the metaphorical disappearance of ground beneath the migrant's feet, suggesting the kind of deterritorialization by migration that is also at work in, for example, Salman Rushdie's literature. Dabydeen's narrator describes the state of migration as a new restless state full of the potential for newness: as a state of "belonging nowhere and everywhere" and "having no uniform shape or colour" (108, 117). Yet, in keeping with one of the novel's central intertexts, V.S. Naipaul's *The Enigma of Arrival*, "landslip" also comes to signify an upsetting loss of touch with place and affective connections with local and familiar environments. The latter is mainly caused by the disembodied metaphysics of modernity that the novel quite explicitly unearths as the undercurrent of colonial territorializations and oppressions.

Closely intertwined with the motifs of *appearance*, *disappearance* and *landslip*, the novel operates with the trope of *digging* in very much the same way. Histories of places are buried, dug up and re-buried, by human hand, historical narratives and natural forces that all change the perceptible surfaces of places. Imperial and Amerindian histories are buried, or half-buried, in Guyana. Literally, the sea and the sand bury human records and inscriptions on the land – such as remnants from the Dutch colonial presence and bones, relics and written records of slaves rotting away in tropical dampness – and by the practices of everyday life which hold no conscious commemoration of slaves or Amerindians, and by the hundreds of thousands of indentured Indians who have completely reshaped the landscape with canals, rice fields, huts and Hindu flags on bamboo poles. Songs and stories in Guyana may derive from Amerindians and slaves, "but they were ours now", the narrator says with reference to contemporary communities inhabiting the same historical space, "we shaped our mouths differently when we sang or told them" (21-2). In Hastings the migrant narrator is prompted by his landlady, Mrs. Rutherford, to dig up other realities and place relations long covered over by English national and imperial history (which is where my analysis below of the novel's discursive mode of transgression will begin).

It follows that the many different modes and histories of relating to the same place also cause different perceptions of self and the other to appear and disappear in the novel's narration of identity, which the article will illustrate, along with illustrations of how the novel also causes narratives of identity (and self versus other) to disappear altogether by radical non-narrative interruptions of historical ascriptions of identity. The latter, it will be argued, constitutes a vital source of life affirmation in *Disappearance* as well as a search for a human ethics that does not reject the need to contest negative identity ascriptions and build assertive self-ascriptions, but nevertheless attempts to reach even deeper for a non-identitarian human connectivity.

The Machinery of Modernization and the Naturalization of the Nation

In "The Age of the World Picture" Heidegger equates "the essence of modern metaphysics" with "the essence of modern technology" (Heidegger, 1938, 57), and this is, in a nutshell, the analysis of modernity's territorialization of reality that Dabydeen's novel performs, while depicting and challenging the empire and nation as central vehicles in all of it. As I will show, the novel exposes a spatial territorialization that is conjointly produced, concretely, by modern machinery and, discursively, by a naturalization of the narratives of the empire and the nation, which has significant consequences for the ways in which human life is understood and recognized. In step with the advance of metaphysically engineered space (by modern utilizations of space and imperial/national territorializations), the liberating potential of alternative human relationships to any stretch of natural space is shown to dwindle or disappear in Dabydeen's novel.

To accentuate this development, the novel consciously dramatizes the degree to which it is almost impossible to perceive space as something else than a *national* space. The conquest of physical spaces by the narrative of the nation (and its powerful metaphysics of *heritage*, *border* and *defence*) is so forcefully present mentally and materially when the narrator arrives in Hastings that it is hard to sense the place without the idea of the nation. The natural scenery along the coast, for instance, is literally strewn with "plaques, statues, public inscriptions" (66), which are all physically manifested signs and marks of the national narrative that turn this stretch of nature into a socio-political text to be read and sensed in a certain predesigned way. The novel exhibits how time, too, is nationalized in Hastings. The histories of the place are turned into the history of the nation. Museums gather things from the coastal area and exhibit them as part of the nation's history. The stories of ancient flint and pottery, daggers and axe heads, even the story of dinosaur bones, are claimed by the voice of the nation as "part of our heritage" (92). Accordingly, the *setting* in Dabydeen's novel is less Hastings-the-*place* than

Hastings-the-*history*, Hastings-the-national-*discourse*, Hastings-the-*symbol* – the symbol of the English empire, the symbol of the strength, defence and perdurance of the English nation and its excluding myth of Englishness. Added to that is Hastings-the-*reclaimed-symbol* in the novel's migratory discourse that rewrites the history of Hastings as a history of successive waves of foreign invasions, breeding cultural heterogeneities and fusions (I will return to this in a little while).

The novel dramatizes how in a thoroughly engineered space like this, human subjects become subjects within the national picture of the world: the novel's characters become characters in the narrative of the nation, acting out roles in its reality script. People who are born in the place and fit the idea of the national character as offered by the script perceive themselves and each other as belonging *naturally* to the place. Everyone else is made to stand out as a stranger and to represent homespun national images of Other, foreign spaces and identities. Within this *storied space*, it is virtually impossible for the "English" characters around the narrator to perceive a human being with a black body without spontaneous associations of foreign intrusion and disturbance.

In the Guyanese parts of the text, the modern colonial engineering of space also centres on questions of belonging "naturally" to a place or not, but to a distinctly different effect. Shortly before Guyana's independence, Americans arrive in the narrator's village with all the modern machinery of floodlights, generators, electricity, oil and smoke, and a bulldozer which "dug its steel teeth into the soil" and made "the greatest noise ever heard in the village" (41). As an image of the colonized world's "irruption into modernity" (Glissant, 1989, 144), the bulldozer deafens the usual sounds of cows and long bouts of stillness. The bulldozer screamed and screamed, "no sound was louder or more cruel" (41), and it banged its mouth in the ground again and again, ripping earth and vegetation in a snap. This is how the Americans grant the village a basketball pitch, "leaving behind a perfect rectangle in the bush" (41). The Euclidian geometry of this rectangle creates an unprecedented distance to the natural environment of the place: suddenly trees and bushes are caused to appear as "crooked" and "unruly" (41-2). The appearance of the perfect rectangle (after a violent construction process) initiates the disappearance of a more immediate and spontaneous relation to the local place. The moment the perfect rectangle emerges, a cognitive and emotional displacement emerges along with it: it is an inaugural moment of coloniality/modernity after which the narrator comes to judge the place by the standard of foreign ideas and ideals of development and modernization. Subsequently, an adult friend posits the idea in the young mind of the narrator that "This place here is bush, just look around, is only bush your eye behold", that "Real life is abroad and big-big stories...not like we people", "tall buildings, a mile high in the sky, made of glass and concrete" (51). Soon this is all the narrator sees: "There was truly *nothing* here, only sea and sky, a wild tract of earth and courida bush growing before a ragged shore" (51, emphasis added). Hence, in Dabydeen, the central story of how colonialized and neo-colonialized subjects suffer from being "disconnected with the spot they inhabited" and are always "dreaming of other places of superior value" (114, 52) is a narrative that runs deeper than self-defeating attitudes caused by the internalization of imperial images of non-white cultures and identities. Displacement is entwined with the drama of how the metaphysics of modernity can cause our embodied and affective relations to reality to disappear.

Deconstruction and Historical Revisionism

As a postcolonial migration novel, *Disappearance* unfolds mainly as a story of how the colonized subject, the mimic man, discovers the constructedness of identities and the constructedness of places whose nationalist/imperialist narratives exclude him as a subject. The narrator arrives from Guyana with the anticipation of finally meeting "the true nature of England"; that is, finally to experience the physical materialization of the ideal image of England from the English story-books he was brought up with (75). Yet, the initial feeling of being "in the presence of venerable England" soon gives way to a sense that "nothing exists in England", that everything is "reported story" (15, 138). The landscape appears less than ideal, along with all the characters who people it. Such denaturalization of the English nation – the exposure of the nation as a discursive construction only – opens the way for all sorts of rediscoveries and re-narrativizations. Replacing the narrative of a superior race growing from roots in the soil, the novel digs out a history of migration as the true "heritage of England", an island produced by successive invasions by "barbarian" hordes of difference and waves of intercultural mixture and ambiguity – and this is how the migrant narrator may eventually "carve" his name in local history (154, 155). The laboured nationalist history of Hastings is defeated by its insistent silencings and self-contradictions. With the slightest deconstructive manoeuvre, Hastings no longer commemorates a history of national defence and cultural sameness but a history of difference and diversity. The governing notion of collective identity and culture – locally and nationally – is *re-membered* as produced by historical tides of immigration spawning a mixture of races, cultures and ethnicities, the latest historical surges of immigration just adding to historical layers of mixture and immigration. Within the narrator's, and, even more so, his landlady Mrs. Rutherford's migratory world picture, Hastings ceases to be told as a territorial story of *Blut und Boden*. Even Mr. Curtis, the right-wing nationalist who runs the local anti-immigration campaign, is revealed by this deconstructive feat to be a second-generation immigrant – of German origin like the Queen Mother (136).

Despite this recognizable storyline in migration literature, Dabydeen's novel distinguishes itself from a large part of other postcolonial novels at its time in interesting ways. It certainly subverts English nationalist/imperialist history written and perceived as a series of past triumphs and victories in postcolonial fashion (writing back to the centre and pluralizing it with a migratory perspective in the wake of the nation's denaturalization), but the sense of everything being "reported story" is also directed at a postcolonial re-subjectification of identities. Hence, the novel's primary challenge to history encompasses more than a pluralization of perspectives and a rewriting of the world in terms of a postcolonial migrant history. This level of the novel's historical criticism is scaffolded on the Rutherford figure. Rutherford hails her tenant, the narrator, in a different way than the other inhabitants in the village. After spending several years in colonial Africa, witnessing the grinding down of African culture and identity, she has become estranged from the English imperial narrative and its colonization of human time, space and identity: "The history of England is a nasty business.... It's the English sickness. We carried it all over the world" (86). As if some returned modern Marlow, Rutherford wants the narrator to *re-tell* the story of England to challenge the way the English have represented "his" lot throughout the course of history. To Rutherford, England is "all order on the surface" and she has longed for "an African to arrive and disrupt the place" (140). As if in imitation of the rise of postcolonial studies in European academia, she wants him to take part in reclaiming a silenced history from behind the dominant history. Rutherford teaches, encourages and pleads the narrator to deterritorialize the imperial narrative of the English nation by digging up the history of slavery and colonial brutality.

But Rutherford's self-castigating appeal to revisionist activism does not liberate the narrator. It effects a re-territorialization. He is now expected to identify with the African slaves transported to the Caribbean, with Africa and the African masks plastered on her whitewashed wall. In Rutherford's gaze, the narrator feels as if turning into, or, rather, *disappearing* into a subjectification produced by yet another distant history long predating his own life, which is alleged to fundamentally determine who he is as well as his relations to everyone else. "I'm *me*", he protests, "not a mask or a movement in history. I'm not Black, I'm an engineer" (93).

A few scholars have already identified a Nietzschean critique of history in Dabydeen's novel: a view of history as the opposite of freedom in the sense that history prevents the present from coming into being (e.g., see Falk, 2007 or Nietzsche, 1887, 39, 45). Although wielded as a challenge to imperial history, the narrator's interpellation by postcolonial revisionism territorializes the present in similar ways. The demands on the world, by English and postcolonial histories, effect an incapacity for the narrator to connect with the living world right here and now. In response to this, Dabydeen's narrator expresses a desperate desire to "assert [his] substantialness, [his] indissoluble presence, without reference to colour, culture or age", to "connect ... with something real and solid .... something fleshy ... even if it stinks .... So long as it exists" (118, 138). The narrator's desperation is of crucial importance. It emerges from a deeper epistemic questioning in the novel, which Dabydeen alludes to with a few remarkable and mutually incongruous epigraphs on the opening pages of the book.

The Post-structural and the Phenomenological Challenge to Imperial Metaphysics

Before the story of *Disappearance* begins, Dabydeen entices the reader with a brief quote from Jacque Derrida's *Of Grammatology*: "What opens meaning and language is writing as the disappearance of natural presence" (7), which is made to scurry against a quote from Wilson Harris' *The Secret Ladder*: "All at once he leaned down and splashed the liquid extravagantly on his face to clear away all doubt of concrete existence" (7).

The post-structural meets the phenomenological challenge to hegemonic metaphysics here and the novel's deeper epistemic inquiry may be said, accordingly, to revolve around the two philosophies of reality that inform these modes of criticism. We have already seen how the novel opens meaning and language by causing the "natural presence" of the nation and the ideology of the empire to disappear. The novel challenges the homogenizing ideologies of Englishness, Africanness, etcetera, by opening language and meaning to the forces of diversity, multiplicity and heterogeneity – "writing" emerges as an unveiling of all the meaning-games produced by interpretations and re-interpretations of reality.

In accord with this, the novel unravels the ways in which our relations to reality rest on mediations of reality: on the textuality of socio-cultural positions and constructions, meanings endlessly challenged by other meanings or a plurality of meanings. Or, perhaps more to the point, the novel discloses how the construction of identities and realities comes down to *narrative accounts* of identity, the self, the other and reality. Judith Butler has reflected on narrative in this sense in an essay that criticizes both post-structuralism and the kind of opposition to post-structuralism that strongly asserts identity positions based on the belief that "a subject who is not self-grounding" will undermine "the possibility of responsibility" (Butler, 2001, 22). To Butler, narrative accounts of identity are informed by retrospective accounts of the world, a large part of which are long predating our individual lives. These retrospective accounts are typically centred on *self-sustenance*, generating so many normative fames for "seeing and judging" in order to uphold and justify a particular identity (Butler, 2001, 23). Accordingly, the assertion of identity – of *self-identity* – within this mode of interhuman relation is an assertion of an assumed complete and unambiguous *self-knowledge*. Butler theorizes how, in a larger perspective, this can be seen as a kind of "ethical violence": "the demand for self-identity or, more precisely, for complete coherence" is "a certain ethical violence that demands that we manifest and maintain self-identity at all times and require that others do the same" (Butler, 2001, 27). In this light, the assertion of identity easily becomes an act that "moralizes itself" by purging itself of difference and of its own inner unclarity, uncertainty, incoherence and unknowability (Butler, 2001, 31).

Viewing *Disappearance* through Butler's theory, the novel exhibits how identities are formed by narrations, by the narrative accounts we give of ourselves, building reality with stories and how these narratives are centred on identitarian self-sustenance (Butler, 2001, 34). The narrator discovers how he appears and disappears, how aspects of reality appear and disappear, depending on which narrative is granted the power to represent the world. Dabydeen's novel then interrupts any singular narrative by other narrative accounts of the world, by a multiplicity of narratives, each with their specific demands on the self, the world, the other. Difference and heterogeneity are invited into the story in this way to disturb any isolated narrative, to *unsettle it* by multiplying the accounts of the world. The migrant narrator, a narrator shaped by multiple conflicting narratives, can be said to alleviate the ethical violence of self-sustaining accounts of self-identity, the world and the other by migrating across a multiplicity of narrative accounts of the world and shaping himself not according to a single narrative but according to a variety of incongruent and unstable narratives – sometimes knowingly, sometimes unwittingly, sometimes hesitantly, half-heartedly, sometimes ambiguously. As the narrator's plural and shifting accounts of the self come to stand out as "divided, ungrounded, or incoherent" (Butler, 2001, 22), the novel creates an opening for a wider scope of human interconnection which builds on the recognition of the ceaseless becoming of selves rather than on the invention and sustenance of a knowable and coherent identity.

In *Disappearance*, as in migration literature writ large, difference and heterogeneity come to form a migratory aesthetic and ethic produced by movement, restlessness, ambiguity, hybridity, rootlessness and indeterminacy, in close affiliation with the liberating practice of post-structural thought (see e.g. Boehmer 2010 for a similar argument). Yet, as we have already seen, the disappearance of "natural presence" (Derrida) does not pertain only to the deconstruction of naturalized discourses or worldviews in Dabydeen's novel. The disappearance of "natural presence" also pertains to something that happened with the metaphysics of modernity (e.g., the perfect rectangle in the bush). The technology and metaphysics of modernity, which includes the engineering of spatial existence by nationalism and imperialism, can cause us to exile the human into an outside of nature, to a new spatial relation determined entirely by the logic of human self-creation and mastery of the world. Post-structural thought, for all its liberation of man from naturalized metaphysics and essentialisms, also seems, in this regard, to become a symptom and further intensification of the narrator's "doubt of concrete existence". As much as "writing" causes the "natural presence" of Englishness, or Africanness, to disappear, reality also comes to appear only as an endless proliferation of semantic ambiguity and difference – an endless proliferation of all the heterogeneous meaning-effects of language which contributes to the feeling that "nothing exists in England", that everything is "reported story".

In response to the possible absoluteness of an endless textual/discursive mediation of everything, the narrator's desire for "substantialness", a sense of "indissoluble presence", "something real and solid" works as an echo throughout the novel of Harris' image of a splash of water in the face – with all the connotations it harbours of sensuous *touch* as clearing the doubt of "concrete existence". As with the sensations of a splash of water, this way of challenging oppressive territorializations in the novel does not release a multiplicity of unsettled and unstable narratives as much as it momentarily disrupts narrative altogether.

Dabydeen's narrator is not only a narrator of multiple narratives; he is also a narrator who, paradoxically, *interrupts narratives*: he interrupts the narrative of the nation, the narrative of history, the narrative of things and phenomena, the narrative of modernity, and the narrative of movement and migration that usually give shape to the identity of the migrant hero. The narrator in *Disappearance* tells the story of how all of the world is storied, how we are all storied, but he also disrupts the storying of all identities with moments of unstoried intensities of sensuous experiences of objects and phenomena in the physical place world.

Weighing an old leather-bound book in his hand, the narrator at one point reflects on how he feels able to

> look through the tunnels made by the termites which bored through the whole text, and beyond, through the board covers, even into the substance of the desk or shelf that held the book, always making space, clearing space (17).

This *clearing of space* involves a ripping away of the narrated interrelations of things. It is a clearing, a making space that seeks to renew our experience of and relation with the physical world. When history recedes in an instantaneous experience of the sensate presence of a thing or another human being, the world may momentarily re-appear in its perpetual newness: "futures" are no longer "bound to the past like pages in a book following each other" (16). It is in this non-narrative mode of relating to reality that the narrator is able to assert a feeling of being in the world in other ways than being a subject produced by history: "I was always present, always new" (16-7). The sensate connectivity with reality in a moment cleared of historical narratives is specifically concentrated in a single small scene. Mrs. Rutherford gives the narrator a lecture on the flowers in her garden which are all narrated as "rooted in English history .... evoking some episode in the life of the nation": Dane's Blood, Turkish Domes, etc. – which are of course also symbolic references to the long migrant history of the English isles (67, 68, 65). Rutherford draws particular attention to the poppy which, to the English, is inseparable from the national commemoration of those who died in Flanders in defence of the nation. Dabydeen's narrator, arriving from an outside to the history of the English nation and its narration of things, notes how the thing, the flower as a sensed object, completely disappears the moment it is overwritten by the patriotic sentiment it has been "designed" – or "re-*signed*" – to stir (even if patriotism be mixed with sentiments about Flanders as a historical tragedy of modernity). In response to Rutherford's lecture, the narrator reflects on how he "wished she could see them for what they were, sizzling with life ... not tired symbols of some monumental stupidity" (65). The sensuous presence and the life of the flower disappears the moment it is made into a symbol or caused to represent or stand for something else, but in a passage like this – connected, as it is, with the intense presence-effects of water splashed in the face (Harris' image) – Dabydeen's novel deterritorializes (or defers) meaning by opening language in other ways than Derrida's notion of "writing". Language changes from a narrative vehicle to a vehicle that can convey sensuous intensities: "sizzling with life" the poppy is no longer a metaphor, no longer a referent to something beyond itself, no longer a representation of something else; it presences itself as an object that has an intense effect on the body and mind of the narrator, drawing the narrator into a condensed moment in the present. This is not a deterritorialization that replaces one historical or identitarian narrative with another (flowers as national symbols replaced by flowers as symbols of hybrid identities or idealizations of roots replaced by idealizations of rootlessness). This is a deterritorialization of a thing that shifts from a register of narrative and identitarian meaning to a non-narrative register of sensuous experiences of reality. Within this sensate mode of being, it is not the disappearance of presence, but the disappearance of discursive meanings, narrative accounts and multiple textualizations that destabilizes dominant representations of the world. To put it differently, Dabydeen's novel does not only destabilize established discursive meanings with more discursive meanings, it also attempts to destabilize meaning with embodied sensations that do not rest on discursive meaning-ascriptions at all. The aesthetic perception of the poppies constitutes a spatial transgression not by migrant movement, but by immersion, not by other representations and translations but by their momentary disappearance within another mode of being in the world.

Balancing on the Edge of History

Compared to a lot of other novels dealing with global migration, *Disappearance* is quite explicitly "planetary" (Spivak) in its thinking – and it is closely affiliated with *The Enigma of Arrival* in this regard as well as with Wilson Harris' migration novels, such as *Da Silva Da Silva's Cultivated Wilderness* from 1977. Amidst all the global movement and histories represented by the migrant narrator, the novel gives us a "view of the Earth" (Spivak, 2003, 94) as a radical Other to human history and its production of socio-cultural identities. A "planet-thought" (Spivak, 2003, 73) is emerging in minute non-narrative geographies such as in the colours of the poppy, but also in geographies on a massive scale that mock "the records of human effort inscribed in the land" (23): the sea could not be:

> confined by the dogmas of history. It was older than any measurement that man could make and it negated even recent events which sought to give it history. Each new wave was a previous page turned over and forever dissolved (118).

Dabydeen's migrant engineer is thus quite explicitly "interpellated by planetary alterity", in Spivak's terms, a "planetary creature" rather than a "global agent" (Spivak, 2012, 347; 2003, 73).

Yet as much as planetarity holds open a mode of reality in which being-in-the-world is freed not only from dominant political histories and the history of the nation, but from coloniality/modernity altogether, the narrator's desire to escape being defined solely by the roots to which he feels involuntarily bound (slavery and the history of the empire) – all the holds on the present by the past – also involves a highly problematic disappearance of history. To a critic like Gilroy, the disappearance of history is incongruous with the essence of "diasporic identity": "diasporic identity" is "defined by a strong sense of the dangers involved in forgetting the ... origin and process of dispersal"; that is to say, the danger of forgetting the histories of slavery, indenture, pogroms and genocides (Gilroy, 1997, 318). We are left with the problem of how the narrator's sensuous deterritorialization of reality can cause the history of wrongs to disappear. Dabydeen's planetarity – the sand, the waves, the weather as well as the sensuous intensity of the poppy – causes both the history of human slaughter in Flanders and the history of slavery to disappear: the sea "kept no archive of the ships that brought us from Africa. We existed and then never existed, giving way to other peoples and other disappearances" (118).

However, Dabydeen's novel contrasts this kind of disappearance with a decidedly oppressive kind of historical erasure, i.e., the historical erasure of atrocities effected by the kind of imperialist/nationalist narratives that made the atrocities possible in the first place. The novel explicitly points to the erasure of historical atrocities by the narratives of modernity/coloniality. We catch glimpses of the oblivion produced by late capitalist consumption, as when the slavery that financed a "splendid mansion in the Georgian style" is made to disappear by guidebooks and by the awe of gaping tourists who "think it's the best of English heritage" (155). And, like Conrad's Marlow, the narrator at times seeks refuge in the daily work routines that are part of the system that unmade him: "the screaking of the bulldozers distracting me from my humanity: drowning any feeling of remorse for past cruelties, any memory of shame or unfulfilment" (95). In contrast, the disappearance of history within the experience of a moment of sensuous intensity is not a disappearance caused by a logic that *distracts* the narrator from humanity but a disappearance that *returns* the narrator to humanity: the momentary intensity of the narrator's sensuous experience is precisely the kind of aesthetic and affective human-world relation that coloniality/modernity ultimately needs humans to efface for its territorializing logic to take hold on reality – its biopolitics hinges on policed definitions of the sensible through a deep regulation of sensing and feeling (e.g. see Mignolo, 2011, 139-144, 178).

Yet, even so, Dabydeen does not allow history to disappear as much as he causes it to stand out as a life-negating contrast to the appearance of a life-affirming presence of things. As in the scene of the poppy, history disappears and reappears in Dabydeen's story right at the border of intense experiences of being alive. We might also say that Dabydeen's novel is in this way always *on the edge of* things and *on the edge of* history.

The *edge*, as place philosopher Edward Casey points out, is where things cease to be and where they come into being (Casey, 2010, 2). Things and objectifications, humans and identities, nature and culture – histories and presences – appear and disappear at the edge of things. At one point the narrator in *Disappearance* is told that he lives "at the edge of a ruler" (139). This of course points to the double meaning and entanglement of the ruler as master and the ruler as a geometric instrument, but, in light of the edge, it also points to how rulers (masters and technological instruments) make things appear as much as they cause things to disappear. As mentioned, Heidegger equates "the essence of modern technology" with "the essence of modern metaphysics", the instruments through which "the subjectivism of man reaches its highest point" (Heidegger, 1938, 57, 84). But Dabydeen's engineer is not Heidegger's "rational being of the Enlightenment" or "technically organized man" who "empowers himself as lord of the earth" (Heidegger, 1938, 57). Rutherford calls him "a new breed of animist" who has "managed to master the science and still retain a sense of nature" (95). Throughout the story, the narrator shows how the application of modern science has caused us to lose sight of nature, but he also shows how modern science has caused the Otherness of nature to become visible. It is the ruler that creates a detachment from nature – as in the appearance of the suddenly displeasing crookedness of the trees around the basketball pitch, but it is also this Euclidian space that makes the Otherness of nature stand out – an Otherness we are entangled with and to which we belong *vis a vis* our bodies as the nature we are ourselves. Likewise, on the coast of Hastings, it is the *science of geology* that causes the force of nature's Otherness to appear from its disappearance behind "the dogmas of history" (118): the engineer produces a chronicle of *natural* events, a "narrative of the coastline", of weather records and the texture of rock and stone, etcetera (27). The science of geology (in this case) is specifically "placing history itself in the forces of nature and ... away from the specificity of nations" (Spivak, 2003, 94).

Human history, too, appears and disappears on the edge of things, and on the edge of such phenomena as intense sensuous experiences of the place world. However, when past atrocities are caused to reappear from another side than their usual representation in historical narratives and identity-based discourses (that is, when the history of human atrocities is caused to *appear alongside the Otherness of nature* and thus "away from the specificity of nations"), by a voice balancing on the edge to the Otherness within our own humanity, the history of human atrocities takes on a radically different interpellation. It no longer hails specific subject identities as either insiders or outsiders of the experience of that history. The histories of slavery, Flanders, Holocaust, etcetera, become *human histories*, the heritage of all humanity: crimes against *humanity*. When understood as the tragic heritage of humanity, historical atrocities no longer lock interhuman relations in particular patterns of warring identities.

* * *

Dabydeen's novel performs an ethics that interrupts our narrative accounts of the world and each other. The narrator does not allow himself – or the novel's narrative – to be recognized by Rutherford's identitarian accounts of the past. Nor does he allow himself, or the novel's narrative, to be recognized by the logic of modernity/coloniality that erases the darkest chapters of its own history. In fact, the sustained anonymity of the narrator leaves a stunning gap right in the centre of every reference to a finally knowable identity. The novel's interruptions of all the narratives it takes up – the sensate now-hereness of its aesthetic reconnection with things – its non-narrative/ non-identitarian moments and gaps – cause non-identitarian human connectedness to arise from within the unknowability that implicates us all as beings made of an unaccountable Otherness – the Otherness of life itself, the Otherness of nature, the Otherness of the planet.

Hence, a reading of Dabydeen's *Disappearance* may say with Butler that, if the limits of knowing who we are is "the predicament of humanity itself", it is on the edge of our registers of meaning and explanation and knowable identities that "the sign of humanity" emerges (Butler, 2001, 37). In that way, the novel's interruption of identitarian narratives with phenomena and events that resist narrativization (life itself, nature, the flower, bodily presence, the violence in Flanders, on the slave boat, on the plantation and in the concentration camp) neither causes history to disappear nor prevents the present from coming into being. In fact, it is precisely the memory of past atrocities as a non-identitarian *human* heritage that compels humans to commit to a *different* present and future. In this region, no justification of violence or violent retaliation can happen "under the sign of 'self-defence'" (Butler, 2001, 39) as there is no separate identity of the self to defend.

REFERENCES

Boehmer, E. (2010) 'A Postcolonial Aesthetic. Repeating Upon the Present', in Wilson, J., ªandru C. and Welsh Lawson, S. (eds) *Rerouting the Postcolonial: New Directions for the New Millennium*. London, Routledge, pp. 170-81.

Dabydeen, D. (1993) *Disappearance*. Leeds, Peepal Tree.

Falk, E. (2007) 'How to Really Forget: David Dabydeen's "Creative Amnesia"', *Cross/Cultures – Readings in the Post/Colonial Literatures in English*, 89, pp. 187-203.

Glissant, É. (1989) *Caribbean Discourse. Selected Essays.* Charlottesville, University of Virginia Press.

Gilroy, P. (1997) "Diaspora and Detours of Identity" in Woodward, K. (ed.) *Identity and Difference*. London, Sage, pp. 299-346.

Harris, W. (1977) *Da Silva Da Silva's Cultivated Wilderness*. London, Faber and Faber.

Heidegger, M. (1977) 'The Age of the World Picture' in *The Question Concerning Technology and Other Essays*. New York and London, Harper and Row, pp. 115-136.

Johnson, B. (1981) 'Translator's Introduction' in Derrida, Jacques *Dissemination*. Chicago, University of Chicago Press, 1981, pp. vii-xxxiii.

Mignolo, W. D. (2011), *The Darker Side of Western Modernity. Global Futures, Decolonial Options.* Durham and London, Duke University Press.

Naipaul, V. S. (1987), *The Enigma of Arrival.* New York, Viking Press.

Nietzsche, F. (1887), *On the Genealogy of Morals*. Oxford, Oxford University Press, 1996.

CHAPTER FIVE

'Telling it how *I* want': Reading the Liminality of David Dabydeen's *The Counting House*

Mark Tumbridge

ABSTRACT

This chapter reads David Dabydeen's *The Counting House* with a number of aims. Dabydeen has for some time been interested in Naipaul's work and the relationship between the characters in the novel and V.S. Naipaul are discussed. Connected with this discussion is an analysis of the relationship between two major characters in the work, Rohini and Vidia. The discussion not only extends that connection with Naipaul, but also takes into account the frank manner in which Dabydeen's work addresses sexual issues. The article also engages with John Edward Jenkins' work *Lutchmee and Dilloo*, assessing the extent to which Dabydeen's work "writes back" to Jenkins in the form of implied intertextuality. A comparison of the positions taken up by the characters in the two novels shows how Dabydeen equates his characters nominally but shifts the ideological spaces between the characters. Taking into account Jenkins' strong sense of an implied British audience, the article reveals Dabydeen's response to this, his complex representation of the nation (both British and Guyanese), and his use of language as a tool of cultural translation. Before moving to a conclusion, the overarching theme of death in Dabydeen's work is assessed.

KEY WORDS

The Counting House, Lutchmee and Dilloo, John Edward Jenkins, Rohini and Vidia, V.S.Naipaul, Writing back, Indentureship, British Guiana.

* * * * *

"Her dazzling form sweet bliss did bring,
Like Rati 'midst Kamadeva and spring.
Or like amidst Budh and the moon,
Was lovely Rohini, Beauty boon." (Tulasidasa 109)
Ramayana

"Vidia was off to Zaire, following obliquely in the footsteps of Joseph Conrad seeking his own heart of darkness..." (French 361)
Patrick French

Dabydeen's text aims to visualize, in a broad way, the East Indian indentureship experience ranging from the small details of life in the portraits of his subjects – both Black and Indian – through to the globalising propensities of Empire. Reading Edward Jenkins' *Lutchmee and Dilloo* and David Dabydeen's *The Counting House* against each other allows one to visualize or place these novels within the field more clearly; this also reveals the degree of play opened up in the space between the texts. Some writers of the postcolonial world have concerned themselves with 'writing back' to earlier foundational texts of the 'Western' canon. The aim of 'writing back' according to Ashcroft, Griffiths and Tiffin is to restructure "European 'realities' in post-colonial terms, not simply by reversing the hierarchical order, but by interrogating the philosophical assumptions on which that order was based" (Ashcroft et al. 32). J.M. Coetzee's *Foe* (1986) addressed Daniel Defoe's *Robinson Crusoe* (1719) or, in a similar way, Jean Rhys' *Wide Sargasso Sea* (1966) can be read against Charlotte Brontë's *Jane Eyre* (1847); the connections between these novels are made rather more explicitly than in the case of Jenkins and Dabydeen's works. One has to be much more tuned in to the finer subtleties of the connections between the latter pairing (for example, by paying close attention to how the network of power relations between the subjects in the two narratives play out) because Dabydeen does not announce any direct link in the manner that, for example, Coetzee does with the title of his novel. While the connections are much more subterranean, Dabydeen's text not only lends itself to comparison with Jenkins, bringing that narrative to the point of crisis, but also manages to be relatable yet distinct. *The Counting House* retains much more autonomy and intellectual distancing from *Lutchmee and Dilloo* than perhaps the above examples of Coetzee or Rhys.

When writing his novel, Dabydeen's view of indentureship from a twentieth century perspective allowed him a broader contextual vision than Jenkins; the latter was in and of his colonial times with all the romanticising of his subject's milieu that that entailed. Even so, Dabydeen includes only just enough contextual backdrop and background on his protagonists – the reader is given sufficient detail, which is distributed across the text, to allow an imaginative reconstruction of both the Indian and British Guianese social and historical settings. This is apparent, for example, when considering the prologue, which provides only the highest level of historical information on indentureship. Similarly, the date of the opening scene is unclear until much later in the novel; it is not until references to history appear that the reader can date the text with more precision than the 1838 to 1917 context that the prologue suggests. Two examples of references to historical events are the recruiter referring to the 1857 Mutiny in India and to the "British free[ing] nigger slaves long ago" (*The Counting House* 47). The Mutiny becomes the backdrop for the first part of the novel, which witnesses two of the main protagonists, Rohini and Vidia, beginning their lives in India under British rule. They enter the indenture system during the 1857 Mutiny, a critical point in the history of the British occupation of India. The prologue makes the first explicit reference to the rebellion saying that "the Indian Mutiny of 1857 [...] led to mass migration" (xi). In the main body of the text, the unnamed recruiter or *arkatia* functions as a trope of British presence in India and represents the British to the would-be migrants of Rohini and Vidia's village. Although there is a recruiter in Jenkins' novel, perhaps one may consider the function of Hunoomaun in *Lutchmee and Dilloo* as not only a foil for Drummond, but also to mask over the darker side of recruitment. The recruiter in *Lutchmee and Dilloo* rather too easily appeals to the subjects conditions of existence in India in a fairly reasonable fashion without needing to tell stories. It is the recruiter in Dabydeen's novel that announces that "everything own by British" and "law is British" (*The Counting House* 46). When in the village, he says that "Less than one hundred miles from here, [...] war going on, Muslim slaughtering and British fighting back, killing everybody, they don't care who is sow-keeper from Hindu, who Brahmin from hill-coolie" (46-47). He also threatens the elder's authority by publicly suggesting that he "will be put to work to grease British bullets in pig-fat" (50). This issue was one of the triggers for the 1857 Mutiny; the bullets were used with a particular weapon that required the ammunition to be lubricated with animal fats, and both "Muslims and Hindus alike were convinced that the cartridges were proof of an insidious plot to defile them and force their conversion to Christianity" (Wolpert 240). Dabydeen distributes the contextual detail of his novel across the text sparingly and allows the reader to draw these together imaginatively. These references to Emancipation and the Indian Mutiny anchor the text historically for the reader – this stops the text from becoming isolated from its historical moorings.

In addition to comparing *The Counting House* with Jenkins' work, any analysis should take into account the novel's relationship with another seminal Indo-Caribbean author. Dabydeen grapples with the influence of V.S. Naipaul in the text, but also, perhaps as a condition of tackling him, includes Joseph Conrad as well. According to Patrick French, the critics often compared Naipaul to Conrad (350), and yet the former's attitude to the latter's work underwent a sea change over time. In 1961 Naipaul included Conrad in a list of authors that he did not like; the list includes "Jane Austen, Hardy, Henry James, Conrad, and nearly every contemporary French novelist" (French 196). By 1974 Naipaul's position had softened; at the time he said, "It has taken me a long time to come round to Conrad" (French 350).

Clearly, it is a complex relationship. Compared to Naipaul, the less accentuated references to Conrad in *The Counting House* are perhaps due to Dabydeen's sense of a need to move literature on to newer, fertile ground; as long ago as twelve years, when the idea was still perhaps in vogue with some authors, Dabydeen is recorded as saying that "we no longer 'write back' to Conrad and Defoe, but to the likes of Naipaul, and in doing so, we create a sense of living literary tradition which is distinctly West Indian" (*Pak's Britannica* 87).

At least one, possibly two, allusions to Joseph Conrad's *Heart of Darkness* (1902) appear in *The Counting House*. One is during a disturbed and disturbing dream sequence when Rohini falls into "a temple of bone" (*The Counting House* 73), a building which seems to resemble the one that Marlow encounters made of human bones: "for near the house half-a-dozen slim posts remained in a row, roughly trimmed, and with their upper ends ornamented with round carved balls" (Conrad 80). Conrad's text seems to confirm that these orbs are skulls supported by femurs. With more certainty over provenance, a veiled reference to one of Marlow's enigmatic pronouncements on empire is made by Dabydeen's narrator while filling in the story of old Gladstone, the father of Gladstone, the manager of the plantation during the 'present-time' of the narrative: "It was neither greed nor guilt which motivated old Gladstone but the *idea* of endeavour, the *idea* of making a structure in the bush" (*The Counting House* 117) [Dabydeen's italics]. Perhaps the major difference between Conrad's text and Dabydeen's engagement with it at this point is that the ideology behind old Gladstone's motivations in *The Counting House* can be deconstructed with clarity; the text seems to offer or encourage this position. The unmasking of Old Gladstone's idea occurs through his effort to impose order ('structure') on the supposed chaos of 'the bush', but he is unable to believe in his slaves – "They were incapable of order" (*The Counting House* 119) – and so he has them killed en masse. Later in the narrative during an account of a slave rebellion in the eighteenth century, the text, once more, invokes the order/chaos dialectic – Dabydeen notes that the slaves recognised "their power to damage the psyche of the English"

(138). The common soldiers are brutalised by the massacre they inflict on the rebellious slaves, and the violence and chaos of the colony pose a serious threat to the metropolitan centre if or when those same soldiers returned to Britain:

> Such evolution could not be tolerated for it represented a threat to England itself. The soldier would eventually return home with the habits of a spontaneous brute. The crime and disorder of the colony which he carried with him like a virus, would sicken England (138).

Perhaps Conrad's text does not offer such a clearly damning vision of the return of violence from the colonies to Britain – *Heart of Darkness* seems much more preoccupied with destabilising the referent and the critical position of the less-well-prepared reader.

In Dabydeen's novels and elsewhere, references to Naipaul and his work are rather more easily identified or open and direct. In 2000, four years after *The Counting House* was published, Dabydeen said, "The novels I've written so far are forms of wrestling with Naipaul, the revered and despised Indian, and the revered and despised father figure" (*Pak's Britannica* 87). With such strong opinions being expressed about Naipaul in literary circles, one might expect him to be on the receiving end of a good deal of criticism, derision, and lampooning from an author such as Dabydeen. In *The Counting House* Dabydeen calls one of the main protagonists Vidia whose mother's name is Droopatie – this seems to correspond with the shortened first name of Naipaul (in full, it is Vidyadhar (French 8)) whose mother's name is Droapatie (French 7). Dabydeen makes a number of more veiled references to Naipaul's work, particularly *A House for Mr. Biswas*. For example, when Kampta, a rebellious indentured labourer on the estate in the novel, is speaking with Vidia, and the latter asks if the former can count, Kampta replies that "You gotta learn fast that you can only count what belong to you, and here you is nothing, nought, bruk-up calabash and rusty gill, you is o. O plus o is o." (*The Counting House* 79) For anyone who has read Naipaul's novel, this is a passing allusion to the scene in *A House for Mr Biswas* where Lal is teaching his students (one of which is Biswas) their times tables by rote. Lal begins with "ought oughts are ought" (Naipaul 44), and he goes on to associate it (like Kampta) with a person who will amount to nothing; this is comical because 'ought' is an archaic reference to nought (Ought, n.2." *Oxford English Dictionary*). Dabydeen use of "O plus o is o" (*The Counting House* 79) seems to strip away what now reads like affected language – though perhaps this usage of ought was widespread during Biswas' day – and represents the numbers in an everyday manner. Connected to Kampta and Lal's equations is Naipaul's sense of being a small man, a feature which is reinforced in *A House for Mr Biswas* (for example, "Mr Biswas was astonished at his own smallness" (Naipaul 34)) – Dabydeen reflects this in *The Counting House*: "He felt small and shameful again"(17). However implied or explicit these 'intertextual' references maybe, overstressing the connections would be an error – these are very different novels after all, and Dabydeen's work, as suggested above, establishes a relationship yet remains distinct.

The impotence that Dabydeen writes about can be framed within a wider set of issues that affected the relationships of Indian women and men. In 1857, the very year in which Rohini and Vidia's story begins, the ratio of women to men was 35:100 respectively (Mangru 211); Clem Seecharan confirms that this was the mandatory proportion (Seecharan 28). Indian women's newly found independence in the creolised communities of the Caribbean, a shift away from the patriarchal values of India, was a transformation that many men found difficult to accept or adjust to. Overseers often formed "temporary connections with Indian women", and this not only compounded the problem of the disparity in the ratio, but also "produced considerable tension in the immigrant camp" (Mangru 217). Men, enraged that their women were being taken from them and emasculated by a system which disarmed them, often reacted and turned to violence. In *The Counting House*, Vidia is initially frustrated by lack of opportunity to sleep with Rohini, and he is mocked for his ineptitude: "'So you not fuckie-fuckie the child fully yet?' Kumar said in a tone verging on laughter. Vidia shuddered [...]" (*The

Counting House 25). On one occasion when Dabydeen plunges into Vidia's consciousness he is "dwelling, as usual, on goats"; this is during an intimate moment with Rohini, Vidia having "retracted from his excitement and misery" (29). Linked to this inability and emasculation is the brutal domestic violence meted out by Vidia. At one point Vidia accuses his wife of sleeping with a Black man, for which he punishes her with violence: "'Nigger man digging in your belly for gold that belong to me,' Vidia screamed, hitting Rohini in the face" (97). Rohini clutches Vidia's feet "in case he kicked her in the stomach" (99); Mr Biswas kicks Shama in the stomach in *A House for Mr Biswas* (Naipaul 277). Between 1859 and 1864 – this would include the period during which Vidia violently attacks his wife – "23 murders of Indian women by their husbands or reputed husbands" (Mangru 217) occurred. When considered against the total population, such a high proportion suggests that the violence of the plantations was transferring into familial relationships.

Although Dilloo raises his hand to Lutchmee in *Lutchmee and Dilloo*, the way in which Dabydeen characterizes Rohini as a subject of his text differs significantly from Jenkins' portrayal of Lutchmee. Although Rohini is described as a "low-caste, dark-skinned, barefooted girl" (*The Counting House* 22), which would seem similar to Lutchmee, many of the other details surrounding Rohini are altogether different. For example, the romanticized landscape of the opening scene in which Lutchmee appears is contrary to the altogether more grounded representation of Rohini's childhood:

> Goats wandered through the litter of excrement, rags, balls of straw, eating everything, even sniffing at the children put out to play in the dirt. Rohini was born in such circumstances, and her mother and grandmother before her. Her inheritance was secure until the day the recruiter came and filled her head with fable (4).

This uncompromising vision of the reality of many of the migrants' experience of India, whether lived or merely viewed from better-off positions, would certainly test the purest of Brahmin's notions about contamination. Perhaps this is also a view of India that became lost to the migrants who, having spent so much time in the Caribbean, began to idealize India; the so-called "Queen of Sheba" in W.H. Angel's text[1] certainly seems to reveal the Indian migrant's imagined India to some extent. If Jenkins had written such a scene into his novel, with the conditions represented realistically, one wonders what the effect would have been on a nineteenth-century British public's view of Empire.

In stark contrast to both Jenkins and Naipaul's work, *The Counting House* tackles sexual issues and the body in a direct and frank manner from the opening pages. For example, when Rohini encounters the recruiter after he has surprised the village by firing a gun, he asks the shocked crowd who Rohini belongs to, and she thinks that he wants to buy her (it is "as if he wanted to offer money for her"). The narrator then tells the reader that "she could see his eye looking at her nipple." Her response to the male gaze is significant: "She hated this man. Nasty money-minded bitch!". Rohini's strong feelings are written in short sentences which help represent the force of her attitude; the second sentence seems to allow the reader access to Rohini's consciousness. She is given agency to act in her own defence as well: "she would bite him if he touched her bubby" (6). This scene mounts a challenge to the stereotype of the passive Indian woman, which Jenkins so thoroughly utilized in his portrait of Lutchmee. Dabydeen allows Rohini the freedom of sexual agency, too, and this is written into a number of scenes in order to provide Rohini with a spectrum of attitudes; she can be sensual ("she stares at the movement of his lips"); tentative (she asks Vidia "just in case I kiss you, what you will do?" [sic] (14)); or, alternatively, provocative (again, speaking with Vidia she asks, "'You want do with me what you see ram-goat do?' she asked"[sic] (18)). Rohini is therefore given an initiative and responsibility for her actions that Lutchmee is denied.

In writing his text Dabydeen created spaces and correlations between the power relations of the key figures in his text. Reading these associations between *Lutchmee and Dilloo* and *The*

Counting House provides a productive comparison between the two texts. This is because three important subjects in each text respectively, who nominally but not ideologically occupy the same position in the estate hierarchy, are involved in a love triangle. Both texts contain intimate encounters, in varying degrees, between a Black 'housekeeper' (Missa Nina and Miriam, respectively), the leading Indo-Caribbean female protagonist (Lutchmee and Rohini) and the manager of the estate (Drummond and Gladstone). The foregoing analysis suggests that these are very different texts, but part of Dabydeen's project seems to have been to read Jenkins and then reconfigure the power relations of the love triangle in his novel so as to incorporate a greater sympathy towards the interiority of the subjects while maintaining enough objective distance to allow them to flourish. The following comparison works through these issues.

To a much greater extent than in *Lutchmee and Dilloo*, the relationship between the love triangle is foregrounded in *The Counting House* – particularly Miriam and Rohini, with Gladstone relegated to the shadows and periphery of the text, a position which is perhaps 'other' or antithetical to Drummond, Jenkins' plantation manager. As such the women in Dabydeen's text are much stronger than Lutchmee or Missa Nina are ever allowed to be, as the above analysis of Rohini suggests. Miriam's status and power on the plantation is not left uncertain at all by Dabydeen, and she is distributed across the text rather than being condensed down to a few pages like Missa Nina. Miriam enters the text early in the second part, where she is described, as if focalized from Rohini's position, as "the nigger maid in Mr Gladstone's house" (*The Counting House* 71), and her presence in the narrative only becomes greater as the story continues. Miriam begins working for Gladstone at a young age – she is "twelve years old" (87) when her mother leaves home, and she starts work in the Great House; these details are very similar to Missa Nina in Jenkins' work. During the present-time of the narrative, Miriam is a thirty-year-old woman, who is altogether conscious of her power and position in the hierarchy of the estate: "She knew her status among them [the plantation "niggers and coolies"], as someone who could roam among the master's possessions and throughout his estate with the freedom they lacked" (109). The effect of Miriam's presence on the community during the scene in which Kampta is whipped embodies the impact of her power – on Miriam's entrance, "the crowd fell silent" (82). There are moments of vulnerability for Miriam in the text, but more often than not she speaks strongly; on one occasion she says that the "Next time you call my man coolie is the last time you preserve teeth and tongue in your mouth, you hear?"(86). Perhaps she is most vulnerable over the issue of childbirth because when Rohini asks "'How come you get thirty years and never make baby?'" the "question hurt[s] Miriam" (114); later in the narrative Miriam says that she "done drop many babies for Gladstone" (163). Her children do not seem to be a part of Miriam's life in the novel – there is no sense that she is surrounded by a large family of her own. Kampta's view of Gladstone's attitude to his offspring seems to suggest that the children would have been torn away from Miriam to avoid Gladstone's relationship with her coming to light:

> [...]What matter is that the factory run perfect, and that's why coolie and nigger and whiteman got to stay clear of each other. God make things so, and you have to accept that the most that can happen is a little secret fucking in the dark and hope that God don't see you, like Gladstone doing it to Miriam late at night, when no other whiteman around to shame him, or charge him for exposing the colony to the danger of half-caste breed, or for putting ideas into nigger people head that they beautiful – that's why whiteman desire them [...] (142).

Kampta recognizes the economic realm is the determining factor in the last instance – the factory must run. Kampta seems to have internalized that this is dependent on the 'racial' division of labour; he says that Black, East Indian and white people have to 'stay clear of each other'. And yet this does not apply to Gladstone's 'secret' meetings with Miriam, which are shrouded in shame for the manager – there is a danger, for him, that his children from

Miriam will be discovered. There is a sense in which the two women bond as Miriam shows Rohini how to put curls in her hair and gives her "pieces of bright African cloth with which to make headbands" (71), but all the overt sentimentality of feigned hand kissing that Lutchmee was put through in Jenkins' text is gone. The animosity expressed by Black people on the arrival of indentured labourers, who they saw as usurping their position on the plantation, is examined in the relationship between the two women; for example, Miriam tells Rohini that "Coolie can't just come and inherit we kingdom" (163). The relationship between the two women becomes affected, perhaps to the point of being irreparable, by Gladstone's relationship with Rohini.

Many of the elements in Jenkins' work – such as the structure and form, his writing strategies, the way the implied audience is constructed – are realigned in *The Counting House*; Dabydeen has calibrated his text not only to address his contemporary audience, but also perhaps with a view of 'writing back' to the inadequacies of Jenkins' view of things. In the introduction to *Lutchmee and Dilloo*, Dabydeen had opined that Jenkins would not allow Lutchmee "her own voice, her own emotional and intellectual control over the narrative of her experience" ("Introduction" 19), and, similarly, that the other non-Europeanized subjects such as Missa Nina were "denied the capacity to fictionalise their own world" (20). One example of the ways in which Dabydeen responds to texts such as Jenkins' in *The Counting House* is by introducing a radical difference into the text through switching the narrator's voice. In addition to Rohini's consciousness bearing its own narrator, there is another shift at the beginning of part III, which is entitled Miriam. Changing the narrator's voice to one of the subjects of the text in a novel introduces a radical discontinuity into the text; only novelists that are completely in charge of their material successfully try this strategy because it threatens to collapse the coherence and continuity of the themes and distribution systems set up before the break. One is aware of a difference in *The Counting House* almost immediately by the presence of not only personal pronouns attached to the narrator's voice, but also of the audience being interpellated again: "*I* did suspect already [...] because when *you* live among coolie *you* have to conspire to survive all their errors" (*The Counting House* 159). This perhaps constructs the hailed subject as a Black person like Miriam because she seems to set them up alongside herself in opposition to the 'coolie'. However, on the very next page this position changes. In the scene that covers Kampta's courtroom appearance Miriam says: "And if I did talk Creole sense, who will listen? If I say that it is not Law and God but Gladstone who make Kampta behave like crocodile and mongoose and snake, not even *you* will believe, you blasted no-face no-tongue coolies". While Miriam could be addressing the audience of the court room in this quotation (she has just curtseyed to the "coolie crowd" (160)), this could equally be directed to the reader of the novel, who, in a sense, does not have a face-to-face relationship with Miriam ('no-face') and cannot speak to her or the rest of the audience as she can ('no-tongue'). Perhaps this is why Miriam says later in the novel that "is only me talking but still I can't hear the echo of myself" (178). This suggests that Dabydeen wants his readers to realize Miriam as a strictly textual subject – he seems to be highlighting the fact that, unlike 'Gladstone', Miriam is a fictional creation. As such Dabydeen's text foregrounds a contradiction that Jenkins endeavoured but failed to suppress; Dabydeen's readers are prompted to recognize the text's own fictionality – this was not a writing strategy that Jenkins incorporated, and he only ever did this in error. These quotations above do have the potential of placing any reader into a position where they are aligned with or must consider the Black or 'Coolie' subject, whether that reader is Black, East Indian, Chinese, white, or however else they identify themselves. While reading Dabydeen's text, the particular configuration of audience that Jenkins had in mind – white, metropolitan, bourgeois, and specifically British – is therefore placed in position where the text has some power over them. They are forced to assume a location that seems to answer Miriam's question 'Who will listen?' Around the reading subject, multiple perspectives are constructed as opposed to Jenkins' much more exclusive notion of his audience as white, British, and bourgeois.

The artifice of Dabydeen's text goes further when one considers how these ideas above dovetail into the idea of 'nation'. The name of the plantation, Plantation Albion, that Rohini, Miriam, Vidia and the other subjects of *The Counting House* toil upon has particular significance and is loaded with meaning. One of the legacies of the plantations in Guyana is that many of the towns still bear the names of the estates today. Although Albion was a plantation back in the nineteenth century, today the town is associated with and recognized for its cricket grounds by the Guyanese. In Jenkins' day, Plantation Albion belonged to the Colonial Company (*The Coolie: His Rights and Wrongs* 52) and is described as being one of "two great estates" (197). Albion, as a word, has a long history of usage and etymology that stretches back through Old English and Latin – it has a poetic and rhetorical aspect to it and is associated with the colour white through the Latin word *albus,* "the allusion being to the white cliffs of Britain". The *Oxford English Dictionary* continues to explain that the word refers to Great Britain through the phrase "*perfidious Albion*, rendering French *la perfide Albion*, a rhetorical expression for 'England,' with reference to her alleged treacherous policy towards foreigners" ("Albion, n." *Oxford English Dictionary*). So this means that not only did Albion exist as a plantation in British Guiana and still does as a present-day reality in independent Guyana, but it also refers to Great Britain and has presence in Dabydeen's novel *The Counting House*. Albion, as Cyril Dabydeen has observed, is "synonymous with a romantic England [...], but ironic in the sense of outpost and empire" (*Shaping the Environment* 18); because of this play of and between distance and time, its presence in the novel has both a wryly amusing effect and an emphatic seriousness about it as well. The above suggests that there is already some reconfigured correspondence to the nationalistic aspect of Jenkins' text and his writing strategies. So when Miriam assertively states a claim of ownership, the ground over which she declares her people's right is not to be underestimated: "Albion is *we* land, *we* man and *we* story and *I* tell it how *I* want" (*The Counting House* 170). The presence in this quotation seems to speak to the absence in one of

Dabydeen's poems that refers to "no land, no words, no community" (*Turner* 40). Albion can be read in this quotation as a condensed symbol of the 'nation' as it is '*we* land'; this can be thought of alongside the similar movement that is akin to synecdoche in the title of the book where the 'Counting House', as a building, is a part of the whole plantation – similarly, Albion appears to be standing in for British Guiana or more properly for the future Guyana. At this level, Miriam's claim can be read as a nationalistic assertion for the land of people ('*we* man') and the right to narrativise the nation's history ('*we* story'). And this is where *The Counting House* addresses Jenkins' idea that the 'nation' writes *Lutchmee and Dilloo* (Jenkins used the phrase 'we are writing') because Dabydeen's text has already handed the narration over to Miriam to "fictionalise [her] own world" ("Introduction" 20), and she accepts the role: 'I tell it how *I* want'. The 'I' of the text is Miriam not Dabydeen directly addressing his audience; at no point in the narrative does Dabydeen directly intrude into his narrative in the manner of Jenkins. Miriam's words also seem to correspond to the earlier scene between Rohini and Gladstone; the latter says that "Miriam is my maid, she do what *I* tell her," to which Rohini responds curtly "She do what *she* do" (*The Counting House* 128). Miriam and the other subjects are allowed to inhabit the text with Dabydeen ventriloquising them. The foregoing analysis configures the gap between the author, the audience, Miriam as a textual subject, and the 'nation', which contributes to a greater understanding of the form of *The Counting House*. While Gail Low analyses *The Counting House*, she briefly includes a productive discussion about Dabydeen's *Coolie Odyssey*. She isolates what she calls "the voice of old Dabydeen's wife" saying that this "shows the gap between the poet, his ancestors, the audience, and those 'fleshed' out in 'folk'." She does continues to say, insightfully, that "*The Counting House* can be seen as a response to this ambivalence about what the past means for the present, how the past is imagined by the present and for what ends" (Low 214).

    A number of the threads already discussed in this article continue to run through an examination of the use of language in

Dabydeen's novel. The ideas of circulation, of a literary tradition in the Caribbean, and of displacement are all present in the novel. From the opening pages a dislocation of language occurs which has a number of implications. This movement is apparent from the moment that the subjects in the Indian setting begin speaking. For example, the elder of Rohini and Vidia's village tells the recruiter "This is one stupidness you talking." (*The Counting House* 4), and "Shut your mouth, you mad-rass man" (5). David Dabydeen uses Creolese speech patterns and phrases for Indian subjects who have not even left India at this point in the narrative – the elder of the village is fundamentally against any of his fellow villagers leaving Indian soil and can see through the recruiter's strategies and curses him accordingly. This has the effect of 'translating' the elder's feelings into a language that a Caribbean audience would recognize immediately; indeed, Caribbean readers of Dabydeen's work are effectively interpellated because meaning is transmitted in Creolese – perhaps we feel the euphony of the words and that this literature speaks to and of us, allowing a greater sense of belonging than one would in W.H. Angel's text, for example. It is a much more intimate representation of the timbre of the Caribbean voice than the speech foisted onto the Black subjects of Jenkins' novel – Jeremy Poynting has said that Jenkins has "no great ear for dialogue" ("John Edward Jenkins..." 214). Gail Low eloquently observes the displacement of language from the Caribbean onto the Indian setting:

> Similar syntax, creolised and folk expressions (for example, 'boy-pickni' or 'bruk-down') are used deliberately for both before and after their journey. This has the effect of making the world of the village community echo the world of Plantation Albion, as if the latter has already been prefigured in the former, or the latter has corrupted – against apparent causal logic – even the temporal space of the former (Low 215).

The idea of transposing the creolized voice of the Caribbean onto the Indian subject (the movement seems to posit the closing of a geographic circle) is made possible only by the very fact of the displacement of indentureship, and by the acquisition and eventual mastery of the English language by the ancestors of the slaves and indentured labourers. On a number of occasions in the text, Dabydeen's position as a late twentieth/early twenty-first century writer emerges briefly – one such instance occurs when he writes about the acquisition of English and a broader education into the text:

> And they [the English] set up the odd school, to give the coolie English words, to link education with reward, so that the coolie believed that his illiteracy and ignorance were the cause of his backwardness. It took over a century to acquire the freedom and it would take another century to acquire the education that made Gladstone economically superior to him (*The Counting House* 139).

The second sentence above seems to shift the narrator from his place of telling the present-time of the story in the nineteenth century to look back through history from a mid-to-late-twentieth-century position; this seems to suggest a distancing of the past that gives way to a present located in the post-colonial which is dependent on the acquisition of the 'masters' language and education. Another displacement based around language can be seen in Vidia's view of a preacher at the depot in Calcutta who holds aloft a Bible and "told them in Hindi how English god made the universe in seven days". Vidia's reaction to this appears to be related, at least partially, to Dabydeen's wrestling with Naipaul, but it also seems to reorder a present-day situation, which has perhaps only been acknowledged by the literary establishment in Britain in the last twenty years or so: "He marvelled at how whiteman could speak their language so nicely, better than he did. It made him feel ashamed, tongue-tied and from an obscure village" (65). So, firstly, in a reconfigured way, Dabydeen may be getting at the roots of Naipaul's complete obsession and preoccupation with mastering the language. Secondly, the quality of literary production that has emerged from the Caribbean over the last forty years seems to indicate that the region is a cultural cross-roads – the multiple languages brought to these shores by colonialism appear to have made the area very sensitive to language. This can be demonstrated by pointing out that from the relatively small population of the Caribbean, four Nobel Prize winners have emerged – Arthur Lewis, Saint-John Perse, Derek Walcott, V.S. Naipaul – not to mention the huge achievements of a host of other authors such as Sam Selvon, Earl Lovelace, and Dabydeen himself.

Death is a constantly repeating presence in *The Counting House* – the death of the sacred cow is just one example – the novel seems unable to avoid returning to this theme. Jagnat, Rohini's father and husband to Finee, becomes a symbol of the constant return of death in the narrative – on more than one occasion, his death is written into the text. His actual death is followed by an uncanny re-enactment of his expiry by Finee who appears to be suffering from "nervous depression" (Gramaglia 84). The scene is focalized by Rohini: "Rohini watched her as she enacted the dying, the shuddering, the sporadic vomiting, the way Jagnat's mouth finally jolted upright to meet hers in a grotesque and involuntary romance" (*The Counting House* 17). This scene invokes an abject splitting of subjectivity into doubles – Finee seemingly replacing the position of Jagnat and being present herself simultaneously. This recalls Julia Kristeva's work: "Syntactical passivation, which heralds the subject's ability to put himself in the place of the object, is a radical stage in the constitution of subjectivity" (Kristeva 39). The scene is made all the more shocking by another double, a similar image that follows in the very next sentence. The narrative jumps to an intimate moment between Rohini and Vidia: "'Kiss me now,' Rohini demanded, and without waiting for a response ran her tongue along the side of Vidia's face" (*The Counting House* 17). Situating such a sensual scene alongside a similar one involving death delivers to the narrative another jarring shock of similarity juxtaposed alongside difference. The repeated return of death in the novel functions in a similar way to the ideas of slavery and racism, and the "repetition of the past in the present" (Low 204).

The vast majority of those who are seriously involved in the study or artistic treatment of these subjects would surely want them to go away – to die, so to speak – but the banishment of these aberrations from the collective consciousness of people, appears to lay in the path of discussing the issues to gain a greater understanding and enable them to be more fully processed. And herein lies the contradiction because that means that they do not go away. Perhaps this is why Jagnat's death remains unresolved – Finee "still owed the pandit five rupees for the prayers, so Jagnat's soul was frozen in space, unable to be reborn and marry a better woman" (*The Counting House* 24).

In conclusion, Dabydeen's text not only aligns itself radically in-between the novel form and criticism, but it can also be used to read Jenkins' text with the aim of cultural (re)appropriation. The fixed positions inscribed into thoroughgoing colonial texts such as Jenkins' work are untethered and allowed greater freedom in Dabydeen's text. Reading Dabydeen's text against Jenkins' allows a reading to be constructed that reveals the subtle use of and reconfiguration of the power relations between one of the love triangles in Jenkins' text. The article has begun to examine the positions of the Black 'housemaid', female indentured labourer, and manager of the plantation, and how these interact with the 'nation' and the narrator, for example, in a very complex light. Whereas Jenkins was prone to romanticising his subjects along a linear narrative in pursuit of his colonialist ideology, Dabydeen's text is stripped of sentimentality; he reveals the harsh realities of life in colonized India and his subjects' experiences of the New World. Romanticism is an idea mocked from a distance in *The Counting House*. Equally as challenging is Dabydeen's engagement with Naipaul.

NOTES

1. See Mark Tumbridge, "Networks of Empire and the Representation of the 'Queen of Sheba' in W.H. Angels *The Clipper Ship 'Sheila'*" in *Caribbean Review of Gender Studies*, Issue 6, 2012.

REFERENCES

"Albion, n." *Oxford English Dictionary.* 2nd ed. Online version December 2011. Web. 21 Jan 2012. <http://www.oed.com/view/Entry/4622>.

Angel, Captain W.H. (1923) *The Clipper Ship "Sheila" Angel – Master. 1921.* Boston, Charles Lauriat and Co.

Ashcroft, Bill et al. (2002) *The Empire Writes Back: Theory and Practice in Post-Colonial Literatures.* 2nd ed. London, Routledge.

Conrad, Joseph. (1995 reprint) *Heart of Darkness and Other Stories. 1902.* Ware, Herts, Wordsworth Editions.

Coetzee, J.M. (1987) *Foe*, London, Penguin.

Dabydeen, Cyril. (2009) "Shaping the Environment: Sugar Plantation or Life After," *ShiftingHomelands, Travelling Identities. Writers of the Caribbean Diaspora.* Eds. Supriya Agarwal and Jasbir Jain. Kingston, Jamaica, Ian Randle.

Dabydeen, David. (1988) *Coolie Odyssey.* Hansib, London.

— (2011) *Pak's Britannica: Articles by and Interviews with David Dabydeen.* Ed. Lynne Macedo, Kingston, Jamaica, U. West Indies Press.

— (2003) "Introduction" *Lutchmee and Dilloo.* Oxford, Macmillan.

— (1997) *The Counting House.* London, Vintage.

— (1994) *Turner. New and Selected Poems.* London, Jonathan Cape.

Defoe, Daniel. (1994 reprint) *Robinson Crusoe, 1719.* London, Penguin.

French, Patrick. (2009) *The World Is What It Is: The Authorized Biography of V.S. Naipaul.* London, Picador.

Gramaglia, Letizia. (2008) *Representations of Madness in Indo-Caribbean Literature.* Unpublished PhD thesis, University of Warwick.

Jenkins, Edward. (2003 reprint) *Lutchmee and Dilloo: A Study of West Indian Life. 1877.* Oxford, Macmillan.

— (2010 reprint) *The Coolie: His Rights and Wrongs. 1871.* Guyana, The Caribbean Press.

Kristeva, Julia. (1982) *Powers of Horror: An Essay on Abjection.* New York, Columbia UP.

Low, Gail.(2007) "'To make bountiful our minds in an England starved of gold': Reading *The Counting House*." *No Land, No Mother: Essays on the Work of David Dabydeen*. Eds Kampta Karran and Lynne Macedo. Leeds, Peepal Tree Press.

Mangru, Basdeo. (1987) "The Sex-Ratio Disparity and its Consequences under Indenture in British Guiana." *India in the Caribbean*. Eds. David Dabydeen and Brinsley Samaroo. London, Hansib.

Naipaul, V.S. (1992 reprint) *A House for Mr Biswas*. Harmondswort,: Penguin Books..

"Ought, n.2." *Oxford English Dictionary*. 3rd edn. December 2004; online version December 2011. Web. 6 Marc 2012. <http://www.oed.com/view/Entry/133335>.

Poynting, Jeremy. (1986) "John Edward Jenkins and the Imperial Conscience," in *Journal of Commonwealth Literature*. 21.1.

Rhys, Jean. (1968) *Wide Sargasso Sea*, Harmondsworth, Penguin.

Seecharan, Clem. (1997) *'Tiger in the Stars': The Anatomy of Indian Achievement in British Guiana 1919-1929*. London and Basingstoke, Macmillan.

Tulasîdâsa, Satya Prakash Bahadur. (1972) *The Ramayana of Goswani Tulsidas*. Bombay, Jaico Publishing House.

Wolpert, Stanley. (1999) *A New History of India*. 6th ed. Oxford, Oxford U.P.

CHAPTER SIX

Racial Capitalism and Racial Intimacies: Post-Emancipation British Guiana in David Dabydeen's *The Counting House*
Najnin Islam

ABSTRACT

Racial capitalism is a "technology of antirelationality", one that reduces collective life to a set of relations that benefits neoliberal capitalism (Melamed, 2015). Colonial capitalism, undergirded by racialization, similarly thrived on the annihilation of collective life. In the context of British plantation colonies in the Caribbean, this took the form of instituting plans and structures of governance that created friction among racialized labour populations. Turning a critical eye on the colonial production of antirelationality between Indians and Africans on post-Emancipation Caribbean sugar plantations, this essay asks how we might learn about its *effects* on these racialized groups. It explores the consequences of British colonial plans for racial separation in terms of the conflict it generated between Indians and Africans. More importantly, it tracks moments of empathy and intimacy among these communities. To this end, the novel speculates about the affective and potentially political solidarities they may have cultivated under shared historical conditions. Reading the novel appositionally with nineteenth-century accounts of plantation life and archival documents, this essay centres a narrative of intimacy and solidarity between Indians and Africans that has been rendered invisible not only by the colonial archive, but also by later cultural theory, which has tended to study these diasporic groups as separate, insulated units.

KEYWORDS
Racial capitalism; creolization; Afro-Indian relations; British Guiana; plantation.

* * * * *

INTRODUCTION

In an 1803 document entitled "Secret Memorandum from the British Colonial Office to the Chairman of the Court of Directors of the East India Company", colonial administrator John Sullivan declares the need to import Chinese labourers to the British West Indies. This was deemed necessary in the wake of the Haitian Revolution, in order to guard against the possibility of a similar uprising of enslaved Africans in the British plantation colonies. Sullivan hopes that this new class of labourers "could be kept distinct from the Negroes" and that they "would be inseparably attached to European proprietors" (as quoted in Lowe 2015, 22-23). In her discussion of this document, Lisa Lowe observes that the decision to experiment with a different form of labour was explicitly racialized and that "it framed the importation of this newly, and differently 'raced' Chinese labour as a solution to both the colonial need to suppress Black rebellion and the capitalist desire to expand production" (2015, 23). The Trinidad Experiment, as this plan came to be known, generated more conversations among British colonial officials about suitable methods to implement it. British planter John Gladstone's correspondence with the commercial firm Gillanders Arbuthnot and Co. in the late 1830s reflects the impulse and tenor of earlier documents. Writing close to the Emancipation of enslaved Africans, Gladstone expresses doubt about their continued service on the plantations once the period of apprenticeship was over.[1] As a solution to this problem, he requests the firm to send him information about Indian indentured servants that they had already been supplying to Mauritius.[2] Gladstone emphasizes the importance of procuring "a portion of other labourers, whom [they] might use as a set-off, and, when the time for it comes, make [them], as far as it is possible, independent of [their] negro population".[3]

These examples from colonial documents yield crucial insights about the mechanics of racial capitalism and its intended benefits for empire. They reveal the colonial need for a new racialized labour force that would not only make British planters independent of potentially rebellious or newly emancipated Africans but would also serve as a "racial barrier" between them. A careful study of the colonial archive of indentureship further reveals that the British positioned Indian, Chinese, and African labourers in a "field of racial positions", a flexible set of hierarchies where one group was valorised over others depending on the specific needs of the planters. (Kim 1999, 106). While an extended discussion of this comparative racialization is beyond the immediate scope of this essay, of particular importance is the recognition that colonial governmentality relied on the active production of racial hierarchies not just *between* the planter class and the labourers but also *among* different racialized labouring groups.

The survival of the plantation complex depended not just on the expropriation of indigenous lands and the exploitation of African and Asian people, but also on the activation of what Jodi Melamed (2015, 78), in dialogue with Ruth Wilson Gilmore's scholarship, describes as a "technology of antirelationality". In her discussion of racial capitalism, Melamed argues that beyond the expropriation of labour, land, and resources, accumulation under capitalism is also "a system of expropriating violence on collective life". She insists that we need "to name and analyse the production of social separateness – the disjoining or deactivating of relations between human beings (and human and nature) – needed for capitalist expropriation to work" (2015, 78).[4] The British colonial plan to deploy a group of people as a "racial barrier" between European planters and African labourers sought to institute a structure that would heavily circumscribe social and political intercourse between those who were to serve as this safety valve (Chinese and Indians) and those who were to be dispossessed again, especially post-Emancipation, under the conditions of the plantation economy. In other words, the capitalist expansion of production entailed the dissolution not only of social relations between individuals, but also of collective life on the plantation.

Sullivan's insistence on keeping Chinese labourers "distinct" from enslaved Africans, Farquahar's delineation of various methods to facilitate that, and Gladstone's plan to "use" Indian indentured servants to make planters "independent" of emancipated African labourers, point to this very fact.

The documents discussed above testify to the expectations that scaffolded the organization of plantation labour. They also illuminate the mechanisms through which the British sought to institute a racialized and hierarchical society in their Caribbean colonies. What is absent in these records of colonial bureaucracy are the perspectives of the labourers, people who were brought across the Atlantic and Indian Ocean worlds to do empire's bidding. How might we learn about this racialized regime, not from the perspective of the planter, the absentee owner, or the British colonial official, but from that of the enslaved and the indentured? What might this reveal about the social effects of the colonial production of this racial hierarchy? In other words, how was this hierarchy inhabited, and how did it inflect social relations between racialized groups? The colonial record's inability to fully represent the voices of the enslaved and indentured makes it an inadequate source for such inquiry. In contrast, contemporary fiction continues to serve as a productive site that engages with the quotidian and affective effects of colonial policy, especially from the perspective of those who rarely find voice and representation in official records. Moving beyond the narrative of a "racial barrier", it imagines the possibility of new social formations facilitated by the coexistence of people from different racial backgrounds on the plantation. Indo-Guyanese author David Dabydeen's novel *The Counting House* (1996) attends to these questions through its engagement with the perspectives of the archive's dispossessed.

Set in 1857, *The Counting House* tells the story of Vidia, an upper-caste man, and Rohini, a woman who hails from a poor, lower-caste family, who indenture themselves in search of a better life in British Guiana. The first section, set in an Indian village called Kandeera, narrates how the villagers, including Rohini, are lured by the extravagant promises of the recruiter. The second and third parts are set in Plantation Albion in British Guiana, and are named after an Indo and an Afro-Creole character in the novel – Kampta and Miriam – respectively. Together they narrate the story of Vidia and Rohini's arrival in Plantation Albion, their encounter with the racialized regimes of labour control, their gradual disillusionment with the colony, and the unravelling of their relationship.

Whereas scholars have engaged with various aspects of this novel, relatively less has been said about the specific ways in which it engages with the racial geography of post-Emancipation British Guiana.[5] Alison Klein notes that the relationships between the central characters are "eroded by the power of capital", and thus, the "potential for solidarity between the races is eventually wasted" in the novel (2018, 122-123). Keith Jardim observes that the novel reveals the classic colonial situation: "Massa, the African and Indian servants, their estate work, and the petty rivalries – in short, the classic, defining dynamic of West Indian society" (2011, 61). Rather than the "petty rivalries" that, according to Jardim, triangulate the relationship between European planters, emancipated Africans, and Indian indentured servants, I argue that *The Counting House* illuminates the social effects of colonial governmentality that activated race as its defining principle. The history that the novel seeks to illuminate is not an individual's or a single group's narrative, but one that draws within its purview the plantation's multiple racialized populations. To this end, the novel engages with the troubled and often tenuous intimacies that these racialized groups cultivated among themselves – political and affective intimacies that offer a counterpoint to the systematic destruction of collective life under colonial capitalism. Even though the novel is unable to articulate a radical vision of life beyond the plantation, it affirms the possibility of interracial solidarities under shared historical conditions.

"All you come to steal we work and wages": Antirelationality on the plantation

The Counting House offers a sustained account of how the different racialized groups on Plantation Albion respond to each other's presence. On the one hand, the novel probes the antagonisms arising out of the colonial ordering of the plantation's racial landscape. On the other hand, it productively speculates about moments of mutual empathy and solidarity between Indians and Afro-Creoles. Vidia's reflections on the colony's Afro-Creole community offers interesting insights. Newly arrived in British Guiana, Vidia sees the plantation as rich with opportunities for personal advancement through the performance of physical labour. He observes,

> Only nigger people slept where there was so much work to do. So much riches to be got by piece-work or day-wage, however Buckra-boss chose to pay, and for chopping, weeding, manuring, pan-boiling and seven hundred other tasks each giving seven cents. In Plantation Albion you could work till you dropped. Nigger people turned Christian so they could mimic English god and laze on Sunday. (63)

Vidia's obliviousness to the violent conditions of servitude and the relentlessness of the work day under slavery is evident here. His accusation that Afro-Creoles neglect opportunities to amass wealth, or that they "turned Christian" so they could "laze" on Sundays, further reveals that in his worldview, one's disposition towards work determines one's value as a productive subject and, by extension, as human. The text leverages Vidia's perspective to rehearse a staple of nineteenth-century colonial racial discourse – the opposition between "the thriftless African/the thrifty Indian" or "the lazy African/the hard-working Indian" (Puri 2004, 173). His enterprising nature and his calculations of profit are, thus, juxtaposed against those who ostensibly waste their time. This criticism, however, is reserved only for the Afro-Creole community, and not all Christians in the colony. Vidia's interpellation into the hierarchy of races, and the expectations of labour built into it, exonerates white European planters from the same critique.

The novel counterbalances this scene with instances of how the Afro-Creole population perceives Indian indentured servants. The scene where Kampta is publicly flogged for stealing from the planter's stores is particularly relevant here. While recently arrived "coolies" are brought in to be disciplined by the spectacle of the flogging, emancipated African peoples also turn up "in increasing numbers to witness the beating" and bring "mischief to the scene":

> 'Coolies! Welcome to the colony!' One called out between whiplashes, 'all-you come to steal we work and wages but scab will form instead on your arse.' 'Chastize the heathen, cleanse him of iniquities', another sang to a Christian tune, satirizing his own progress yet delighting in the sonorousness of the words. Others took the opportunity of doing hard business. (76)

Kampta's punishment becomes an occasion to air grievances against Indian indentured servants. Further, the absurdity of people "doing hard business" on site speaks simultaneously to the routinization of violence on the plantation and the rationing of empathy in a racially charged social context. The sentiments expressed by these anonymous voices, particularly the phrase, "all you come to steal we work and wages", points to the primary source of antagonism between Africans and Indians. Brought in as a replacement labour force, Indians were perceived by emancipated Africans as a group that usurped opportunities for work that could have benefited them. Whereas the British colonial government maintained that the system of indentureship was necessitated by labour shortage after Emancipation, historians such as Madhavi Kale (1998) have suggested that this was an artificial justification. Kale argues that the employment of indentured servants was an effective means of sourcing a labour population that would work for the kind of low wages that emancipated Africans were no longer willing to accept. Thus, while this transition to the use of indentured labourers fixed the apparent problem of labour shortage for British planters, it also disenfranchised the previously enslaved population, fostering antagonism between Africans and Indians. Reflecting on such antagonisms in the context of colonial Trinidad, anthropologist

Aisha Khan explains that Afro-Trinidadians perceived Indians in the nineteenth century as economic threats as well as "cultural oddities in their garb, languages (primarily Bhojpuri, but others as well), their cuisines, their forms of social organization (kinship, marriage) and their cosmologies". In response, "Indians could turn to the discursive weapons at their disposal too: the extant forms of colonial racism against Afro-Trinidadians" (2004, 170). The two sections from the novel that I juxtapose here illuminate key aspects of this dynamic.

In his non-fiction, Dabydeen writes about Indian indentured labourers being perceived by the Afro-Guianese as scab labour – a derogatory term for someone who continues to work despite organized efforts to strike; in other words, a strike-breaker (Introduction of the 2003 reprint of *Lutchmee and Dilloo*). Historian Walton Look Lai explains that Indians were perceived "as instruments of planter politics directed against Black workers and as threats to their newly won bargaining power in the labor market" (1993, 165). Such perceptions were confirmed by events like the 1848 general strike by Black workers in British Guiana, which failed because of the lack of support from Indian and Portuguese labourers, who refused to desert the plantations (112-113). Dabydeen's use of the word "scab" in the extract above performs a dual function, in that it speaks directly to the violence of plantation work on the one hand and, on the other, underscores the fraught relationship between Indians and Africans arising out of the pressures of economic survival in the colony.

This is emphasized in the novel through a poignant exchange between Miriam and Rohini, an Afro-Creole and Indian woman respectively, who are both servants in Gladstone's house and objects of his sexual desire.

> 'If whiteman order, you run fast-fast to serve. But nigger is nothing, eh? I is nothing?' she stared accusingly at the girl. 'Don't think I don't realize that all-you coolie people come to Guiana to enslave we. And everything we build up, all the dams and all the canals we dig and all the cane we plant, you people greed for and conspire to inherit.' (108)

Miriam's words express a deep recognition of the racial hierarchy into which Indian indentured servants are introduced, and the position they occupy within it. The fear of being superseded, of being rendered dispensable as a community articulates with a renewed fear of dispossession, not at the hands of the European masters this time, but at the hands of the new working class. Dabydeen explains elsewhere, "Indians were seen as stealing [the African's] rightful inheritance, newcomers and interlopers accorded legal protections and material privileges denied to slave and ex-slave population" (2003, 4). Miriam's apprehension finds its fullest expression in her use of the words "enslave" and "inherit". Indian indentured servants are accused of wanting to enslave Africans and inherit or usurp the products of their labour. For Miriam, this fear extends into the sexual economy of the plantation, particularly for her relationship with Gladstone, for whom she performs both domestic and sexual labour. She sees Rohini as a rival who would conspire against her and "gather up Gladstone and all his gifts", thus leaving her and her brothers destitute (108).

The anxiety that Miriam's conversation with Rohini reveals must be accounted for in any efforts to unpack race relations in Caribbean plantation colonies. In her scholarship, Shona Jackson (2012) discusses the significance of the discourse of labour for claims of creole belonging in the Caribbean. Jackson explains the usefulness of this discourse to both Afro and Indo-Guyanese populations in that the physical act of investing labour in the land became grounds for claiming indigeneity and eventually, political belonging in the postcolonial context. Miriam's words, while establishing the crucial connection between labour, land, and belonging, also underscore how, in the post-Emancipation era, the colonial project of replacement (of the enslaved by the indentured) fostered racial tension by activating fears of dispossession in a community that had, after centuries of servitude, hoped to find some degree of autonomy.[6] By offering an account of the fraught relations between Africans and Indians, Dabydeen's novel illuminates the social *effects* of the colonial plan to leverage one group as a racial barrier against another. In particular, the narrative highlights the toll this plan took on the possibility of collective life for these racialized groups.

The novel, however, turns to the quotidian lives of its characters as a site where sympathy and solidarity are cultivated through an understanding of the shared historical circumstances that marked the existence of Indians and Africans in the colony. This comes across in a significant textual moment that registers a shift in Vidia's outlook. Sitting under a calabash tree, he is described as sharing space with the spirits of the enslaved, "with whom he was now familiar". He listened to the voices of the dead "fluting through slit throats", unafraid of being harmed "because he came from a land that bore no malice to niggers". He also thinks of how, before coming to Guiana, "he had never known that there were people like niggers" (90). Vidia, an indentured servant sharing space with the spirits of the enslaved with whom he is "now familiar", renders the geography of the plantation palimpsestic in terms of the histories that it holds. The text deploys the idea of spirits to highlight the past of African peoples in Guiana, which continues to haunt the present. Vidia's "encounter" with the spirits is the narrative's way of emphasizing his growing acknowledgement of the violent history and afterlife of slavery.

This is further emphasized in the scene in which he learns about a mound of earth in Plantation Albion where "fifty men and women slain by old Gladstone were dumped" (90). Vidia wonders why Gladstone would "squander his wealth so freely" by killing "healthy and productive people" who were not rebellious. This moment bears testament to how cheaply the lives of the enslaved were bought and how painfully dependent they were on the whims of the powerful. Here, the narrative tracks a shift from Vidia wondering why Gladstone chose to dispose of productive bodies, to him arriving at an understanding of slavery as an enterprise of sourcing "an endless supply of victims" and turning human beings into chattel. Further, regardless of its factual accuracy, Vidia's declaration that he came from a land that was unaware of the existence of African people performs the critical function of suggesting that the racial antagonism between Africans and Indians was a product of the workings of colonial capitalism.

Even as the novel uses Vidia to chart the possibility of empathy through greater understanding, it does not romanticize the idea of Afro-Asian solidarity. Vidia's growing awareness of the history and material conditions of enslavement does not radically alter his perception of African people, whom he continues to deem "beyond disinfection", set in what he sees as idle and unproductive habits. Instead of offering a neat, linear narrative of intimacy, the novel uses Vidia's perspective to enact a minor shift, a growing acknowledgement of the presence of a people who were sacrificed at the altar of colonial capitalism and have now been replaced by people like him. In doing so, it offers the hope that such affirmations can pave the way for stronger affective and potentially political solidarities.

One of the significant shifts that the novel charts is in the relationship between Miriam and Rohini. Although Miriam considers Rohini a rival for Gladstone's favours, she tends to her bruises when Vidia batters her, and goes as far as to offer counsel about the fate of women on the plantation. After losing her child with Gladstone, Rohini is nursed back to health by Miriam, and by the end of the novel, she takes up residence with Miriam and adopts a maternal role towards her brother, Thomas. The complicated nature of their relationship marked simultaneously by affection, malice, and disgust gives pause to any interpretation of absolute solidarity. Their status as gendered and sexualized subjects within the plantation economy, however, plays a significant role in their ability to build affective alliances across racial lines.

The novel is also deeply attentive to new modes of interaction, and the attendant social formations, between Afro and Indo-Guianese peoples that the colonial government may not have expected or foreseen, given their intentions to keep them separate. This is evident in the way the text foregrounds alternative arrangements of labour relations. For instance, to supplement his income, Vidia contemplates working "unlawfully" in the nearby villages where his Afro-Creole employers would pay him in corn or sheepskin to clean ponds and canals (66). This instance suggests the operation of an alternative economy of exchange unmediated by the white master. Such a brief, potentially one-off example acquires traction when read in conjunction with similar traces elsewhere. In his 1877 text, *Lutchmee and Dilloo*, Edward Jenkins offers one such instance. Jenkins describes an Indian "coolie" Achattu who had amassed a lot of wealth through his hard work and thrifty living. Having done so, he "became the owner of three or four cows: he paid a Negro man to look after them – a change of race relations not unknown in British Guiana" (100-101). The latter part of this sentence is of particular interest. The "change in race relations" might refer to the fact that, in this instance, it is the Indian who adopts the role of the employer to Afro-Creole people. To this extent, it is a commentary on the articulation of race and class, whereby the Indian brought to the colony as a wage worker, acquires the means to employ others in his service. More importantly, the "change" emphasized here might refer to a shift from antagonism or insulation to one where African and Indian peoples forged new social and economic relationships with one another. I am cognizant of how Jenkins risks reifying the dominant narrative about the upward mobility of Indians through their hard work as opposed to their African counterparts. Further, I do not suggest that this one instance gives us definite insight into the consolidation of a new social and racial hierarchy that would remain unchanged in the way the position of the planter class did. However, taken together, the two instances from Dabydeen's and Jenkins' novels suggest the possibility of a more fluid social structure in which subjugated groups cultivate their own modes of engaging with one another.

Creole intimacies on the plantation

The novel's attention to new social formations and possible intimacies between different racialized groups finds its most sustained elaboration in the character of Kampta. In characterizing him, the text is attentive to the limits of colonial racial knowledge and how, it is at these very limits, that new identities and interracial alliances are forged. When he makes his first appearance in the novel, we see Kampta showing his birth certificate, his "born-papers", to Vidia:

'Here it say "Name", beside which whiteman write "Kampta". Father's name: Unknown deceased." "Mother's name: Unknown, deceased." Grandmothers name: Unknown, deceased." "Date of birth" Unknown." "Distinguishing marks: None." Everything is none or unknown or deceased, except my name in big-big writing, K-A-M-P-T-A.' (73)

Amidst staccato repetitions of "deceased" and "unknown", what stands out is Kampta's name. Initially presented here as a cipher, one whose biography is filled with too many gaps, Kampta is gradually revealed to readers as the novel unfolds. After being apprehended for stealing food from Gladstone to take to a bacchanal, Gladstone describes him to the magistrate in the following terms:

'Through birth and rearing in the colony he has taken on nigger values to add to his Madrasi instincts for troublesomeness; he is indolent, thievish and cunning, and seeks the company of lewd and faithless Creole women in preference to the sobriety of a settled relationship. He has no sense of the rights of ownership and in stealing from his fellow coolies – a crime to which he is habituated – he creates a web of accusation and counter-accusation among them, which is detrimental to the welfare of the Plantation.' (74-75)

Here, the text leverages Gladstone's perspective to reveal colonial stereotypes about people of African and Indian descent and anxieties about racial mixing. Interestingly, and perhaps crucially, Kampta is presented not as a mixed-race character, but instead, as one who indexes a certain kind of cultural intimacy. His East Indian ancestry is indicated through the use of the word "Madrasi". Kampta is an East Indian, who, according to Gladstone, has acquired "nigger values" while growing up in the colony. This manner of characterizing Kampta renders him simultaneously a racial outlier and a product of the processes of creolization, neither of which are desirable in Gladstone's outlook. The anxiety that he expresses about the "welfare of the Plantation" is fuelled both by the possibility of sexual intimacy between the races, and that of social and cultural miscegenation. His negative view of Kampta can find its strongest articulation only by underscoring racial stereotypes about Indians and Africans. In his testimony to the magistrate, "Madrasi instincts" and "nigger values" are treated as self-evident categories suggesting a world of shared racial knowledge between Gladstone and his audience.

Nineteenth-century accounts help to clarify the nature and terms of this racial knowledge. While "Madrasi" is a generic term used to refer to indentured servants from Madras in southern India – and, to that extent is, primarily a geographical referent – nineteenth-century use of this term suggests that it came to acquire a host of connotations over time. A sustained account of the "Madrasi instinct" is available in the writings of Wesleyan Missionary H.V.P. Bronkhurst. In *The Colony of British Guiana and Its Labouring Population* (1883), Bronkhurst discusses how "coolies" from the Presidency of Madras are "looked upon as worthless and everything that is bad" in British Guiana. He quotes from Immigration Agent-General J.G. Daly, who explains that the Madrasi is "very prone on occasion, but more particularly in times of festivity, to give way to drinking and quarrelling, and in domestic service adds the vice of pilfering and stealing" (140-141). These instances allow us to piece together one of the ways in which the Madrasi came to be characterized in the nineteenth century. Kampta's supposed indolence, cunning, and propensity for stealing seems to conform to this descriptive apparatus, and are combined with racial stereotypes about the African population, who, too, were persistently described as "indolent, docile and brutish" (Brereton 1979, 195). While discussing British perceptions about labouring populations in Trinidad, historian Bridget Brereton (1979) explains that attitudes towards Africans ranged from mild amusement at their difference to outright negative stereotyping, often couched in the rhetoric of scientific discourse. In the British imagination, the West Indian Black was perceived as "immoral, deceitful, unstable, capricious, dishonest, thieving, quarrelsome" (195). In Gladstone's worldview, Kampta's "troublesomeness", his apparent lack of respect for authority, cannot be explained away as individual character traits, but must be accounted for through racialized understandings of "Madrasi" and "nigger values". Kampta combines the worst of both "types" in him.

Kampta is "detrimental to the welfare of the plantation" because he unsettles colonial expectations regarding the nature of social intercourse between Indians and Africans. His relationship with Miriam fractures dominant narratives about the lack of sexual and affective intimacies between the races. Commenting on the improbability of intimate interracial relationships, Henry Kirke, who had served as the Sheriff of Demerara, said that it was "the rarest thing in the world for an Indian to take up with a black woman" (1898, 263). Other nineteenth-century commentators similarly insisted on the lack of interracial relations, sexual or otherwise, based on the mutual dislike harboured by Africans and Indians towards one another. Emphasizing the potential benefits for colonial governance of such dislike, a group of commissioners appointed to investigate the treatment of immigrants in British Guiana in 1871 declared that there "will never be much danger of seditious disturbances among East Indian immigrants on estates as long as large numbers of negroes continue to be employed with them". They based this conclusion on the understanding that the Indian "coolie" disliked the "negro, because he considers him a being not so highly civilized; while the negro in turn, despises the Coolie, because he is so immensely inferior to him in physical strength".[7] In affirming the utility of racial antagonism to the project of empire, these observations echo the intentions of the colonial government and the perceived success of the plan laid out in the early nineteenth-century documents with which I began this essay. Shalini Puri usefully reminds us that declarations like "the African and Asian will not mix", which James Anthony Froude made in *The English in the West Indies, or the Bow of Ulysses* (1888), ignores contemporary colonial legislations that were geared towards halting "processes of cultural hybridization that were generating a cross-ethnic imagined community at the popular level" (2004, 43). Kampta's sexual and affective intimacy with Miriam, and his identification with the Afro-Creole community bears testament to this possibility of cultural hybridization.

Kampta's characterization as racially ambiguous further frustrates neat classifications offered by nineteenth-century racial knowledge. As a child, he escaped from Plantation Fielding after his Indian parents died of malaria. In order to protect him from being sent back to the plantation, Miriam passed him off as her cousin. This invented biography, coupled with his appearance, "skin, darker than hers, and tightly curled hair" made it possible "for him to be taken as a half-caste" (82). The text offers a phenotypic inventory of Kampta – "dark skin", "curly hair", "negroid appearance" – aspects which, according to nineteenth-century racial discourse, should ideally distinguish him from members of other races, but which in this instance, conversely, end up facilitating his racial passing. Kampta literally embodies the perceived unique traits of multiple races, which makes others read him as a mixed-race person. By pulling apart racial codes and recombining them in Kampta, the text unsettles the standard "scientific" ways in which an absolutist idea of racial difference was signalled in the late eighteenth and nineteenth centuries. The text's repeated references to Kampta's skin colour – "black skinned coolie", "darker than [Miriam]" – ventriloquize the obsessive need to record even the slightest variation in skin colour as fundamental to determining one's racial identity.

In her scholarship on British ideas of race in the eighteenth century, Roxanne Wheeler (2000) argues that the third quarter of the century saw the consolidation of complexion as a significant visible human difference. Daniel Segal too discusses the processes by which authorities in colonial Trinidad engaged in the "racial accounting" of Black-white mixing. This process necessitated a complex array of race, colour, and hair distinctions ranging from "white", "Trinidad white", "so-called white", "near white", to "red", "brown", "light black", "black", and "black-black" (as quoted in Puri, 190). In the novel's representational scheme, Kampta's physiognomy and somatic features, instead of distinguishing him from the African population, facilitate his passing as a "half-caste". Here, the novel performs a double function. It employs the vocabulary of nineteenth-century racial knowledge, only to enact its failure through Kampta. In doing so, it also draws attention to him not as a racial miscegenate but as a cultural hybrid or a creole subject. Kampta's involvement with the African population in the colony and Miriam's insistence that he is part of the community reveals him as a peculiar product of the plantation complex. Neither just "Madrasi", nor just "Indian" or "coolie", he is a creole subject. Paying attention to discourses of creolization as they pertain to the Caribbean allows us to engage more fully with the specificity of the multiracial plantation complex and the social formations facilitated by it. Further, it enables us to apprehend the critical function of a character like Kampta in a way that is responsive to theorizations about social formations in multiracial plantation colonies.

Within Caribbean critical discourse, the concept of creolization has had multiple trajectories. Scholars have used the word to describe the formation of a new cultural identity that derives from the encounter between Europeans and enslaved Africans. Kamau Brathwaite (1974), for instance, defines creolization as a cultural process that can take two distinct forms. The first, which he calls ac/culturation, refers to the "yoking (by force and example, deriving from power/prestige)" of the culture of the enslaved African to the European. The second, inter/culturation, "is an unplanned, unstructured but osmotic relationship from the yoke". The creolization that results from this, he suggests, "becomes the tentative norm of the society" (6). Others, such as Edouard Glissant (1989), approach creolization as the outcome of a "forced poetics", one that necessitated linguistic and cultural invention in the face of decimation by European colonists. Verene Shepherd and Glen Richards have noted the debates between scholars who "see creole cultures as almost entirely new creations which seek to adapt to new social and geographical environments", and those who "stress cultural continuity between Africa and the Caribbean and advance Afrogenesis as an explanation for many of the cultural patterns described as Creole" (2002, xiii).

The concept of creolization has gained traction primarily in relation to Europeans and Africans, and occasionally, so-called "mixed blood" people of the Caribbean, but less legibly in relation to the Indian population (Khan 2004; Mohammed 2002; Shepherd and Richards 2002). Lincoln Shlensky suggests that, as a specific theory of social development and identity, creolization exhibits deep association with "Afro Caribbean nationalist ideology while excluding other cultural projects or political histories (2011, 307). Offering a historical perspective on the question of creolization, anthropologist Aisha Khan explains that when Indians arrived in Trinidad in the mid-nineteenth century, it was already a society structured by race and class hierarchies. The Indian immigrant community was deemed culturally foreign and completely separate from the local creole culture, which was shaped by the "ideological foundations of a race-color continuum, where Euro/white and Afro/black and their various, ranked combinations, formed the basis of creole society" (2004, 172). Racial mixing among Afro-Creoles and Indians, however, has been significant enough "to produce a distinctive Creole variant identified as 'Douglas' in local lexicon" (Hintzen 2002, 99).

The novel's characterization of Kampta cannot be understood sufficiently through dominant models of creolization or "douglarisation". Kampta's identification with the Afro-Creole community, and his relationship with Miriam illuminate practices of intimacy that extend beyond the sexual to encompass the affective and the cultural in all its quotidian iterations. His very being is, thus, an elaboration of the "interstices where people and practices cross boundaries and mix" and which, as Aisha Khan insists, are much harder to track when studying social and cultural transformations in the Caribbean (2004, 182). Similarly, nineteenth-century colonial accounts whose descriptive apparatus is driven by the desire for neat classifications would read Kampta's existence as an aberration and therefore, as a threat, as Gladstone puts it, to the "welfare of the plantation" (75). The representation of this hidden, unaccounted for, "hybrid" character is the novel's way of unsettling what Aisha Khan (2004, 168) describes as "the finality of colonial representation", and of making possible "the emergence of an 'interstitial' agency that refuses the binary representation of social antagonism" (Bhabha 1996, 58). Kampta exemplifies an emergent consciousness that is attentive to the shared histories of labour, trauma, and dispossession between people of African and Indian descent on the plantation. In a particularly revealing scene, Kampta imagines killing Gladstone and risking a riot the same way that the first slave rebels in the colony had. He thinks to himself, "it is time coolie learn what nigger gone through". Even though this thought does not find its fullest or even its clearest articulation in Kampta's mind, when he emphasizes the need for indentured servants to learn that the clearing of the bush was no miracle but the product of the labour of enslaved people, or that eventually indentured servants will realize that "each penny Gladstone pay them make from the same metal as the bullet that bore into nigger backside long-time", he expresses not just an awareness of the history of slavery but also the possibility of solidarity that arises from that shared knowledge (121).

CONCLUSION

In the prologue, Dabydeen offers three vignettes that do not relate directly to the plot of the novel but collectively comment on the colonial archive as a site of absence. In one of these vignettes, colonial official, Henry Fielding describes his encounter with a group of Indian and African labourers. He characterizes them as voices "vying against each other to tell a story, like crabs in a sack seeking escape by clambering over each other". Even though Fielding promises to give "each story equal weight and benign consideration", he ultimately abandons them, leaving behind only his account of the encounter, rather than the stories the labourers wanted to tell (9). Dabydeen's novel is a response to this absence. The incompleteness of the colonial record necessitates that Dabydeen look into the scraps of letters and documents that "survive as the only evidence of the nineteenth-century Indian presence", that he create characters like Kampta who "never existed" and Miriam whose presence, like that of thousands of enslaved and indentured peoples, remains unacknowledged by the colonial archive (9).

In the epilogue, Dabydeen returns to the mound where some of the events of the novel unfold. He writes that the mound was excavated by a team of English anthropologists and archaeologists in 1911. No skeletons were found, and the mound is now "believed to be an Amerindian (Carib) ceremonial site back to pre-Columbian times" (157). The act of excavation supplements an earlier reading of the site as a burial ground for enslaved Africans with the possibility that it was an Amerindian ceremonial site. The suggestion of a history that is palimpsestic and multivalent, and that invites "excavation", reads as a productive metaphor for the task Dabydeen undertakes in the novel. Pushing beyond predominant discourses of racial antagonism – "crabs clambering over one another" – the novel imagines the possibility of intimacy between Africans and Indians. Although Kampta may not have existed as a historical figure, in Dabydeen's novel, he embodies the racial and social formations that were simultaneously engendered and disavowed by the realities of the plantation complex. The cultivation of cross-racial alliances, the novel suggests, is a challenge to the foundational premise of racial capitalism, "a technology of antirelationality" that thrives on the annihilation of collective life (Melamed 2015, 78). *The Counting House* does not propose the overthrow of Plantation Albion, nor is it able to imagine communal life outside the economy of the estate. Its radical potential lay, instead, in its imagination of a life where Africans and Indians, "racial barrier" and antagonists in the theatre of empire, cultivate social, political, and affective affiliations.

NOTES

1. Immediately after their emancipation, Africans were made to serve as "apprentices", with their labour supposed to offset the cost of their manumission. Kris Manjapra describes this as a process by which emancipated Africans were "made to compensate their enslavers for the slave-owners loss, instead of the other way round" (2018, 363).

2. Mauritius, which came to be known as the site of the "Great Experiment", was the first among British colonies to employ indentured labourers after emancipation.
3. John Gladstone to Messrs. Gillanders, Arbuthnot and Co., 4 January 1836, BPP, 1837-38, LII (180 232).
4. Scholarship on racial capitalism has a rich intellectual trajectory. See Cedric Robinson, *Black Marxism: The Making of the Black Radical Tradition* (1983); Eric Williams, *Capitalism and Slavery* (1944); and W.E.B. Du Bois, *Black Reconstruction in America* (1935). More recent scholarship includes works by Jodi Byrd, Alyosha Goldstein, Paula Chakravarty, Denise Ferreira da Silva, Glen Coulthard, and Chandan Reddy, among many others.
5. Abigail Ward comments on the ways in which Dabydeen seeks to ameliorate the "insubstantial portrayal of Indian indentured people" by adapting historical facts and creatively imagining what their lives may have looked like (2011, 90). Elizabeth Jackson (2015) attends to the novel's representation of gendered violence, the conditions that aggravate it, and women's responses to such violence.
6. Structural impediments to the transition of emancipated Africans out of the plantation economy are evident in the fact that, whereas Indian indentured servants were given land in lieu of a return passage at the end of their indentureship to encourage retention of their labour, emancipated Africans had to purchase Crown lands, the cost of which was prohibitively high.
7. Commissioners William Edward Frere, Esquire, Sir George Young, Baronet, and Charles Mitchell, Esquire were appointed to enquire into certain statements made by George William Des Voeux, a Stipendiary Magistrate in British Guiana, regarding the treatment of immigrants in the colony. "Report of the Commissioners Appointed to Enquire Into The Treatment of Immigrants in British Guiana," June 1871, BPP, 1871, XX (C. 393).

REFERENCES

Bhabha, Homi K. (1996) 'Culture's In-Between', in Hall, S. and du Gay, P., eds., *Questions of Cultural Identity*. London, Sage, 53-60.

Brathwaite, Edward Kamau. (1974) *Contradictory Omens: Cultural Diversity and Integration in the Caribbean*. Jamaica, Savacou Publications.

Brereton, Bridget. (1979) *Race Relations in Colonial Trinidad, 1870-1900*. Cambridge, Cambridge University Press.

Bronkhurst, H.V.P. (1883) *The Colony of British Guiana and Its Laboring Population*. London, T Woolmer.

Dabydeen, David. (2005) *The Counting House*. Leeds, Peepal Tree Press.

Glissant, Edouard. (1989) *Caribbean Discourse: Selected Essays*. Translated by J. Michael Dash. Charlottesville, University Press of Virginia.

Hintzen, Percy. (2002) 'Race and Creole Ethnicity in the Caribbean', in Shepherd, V.A. and Richards, G.L., eds., *Questioning Creole: Creolisation Discourses in Caribbean Culture*. Jamaica, Ian Randle, 92-110.

Jackson, Elizabeth. (2015) 'Voyeurism or Social Criticism? Women and Sexuality in David Dabydeen's The Intended, The Counting House and Our Lady of Demerara', *Women: A Cultural Review*, 26(4), pp. 427–442. doi: 10.1080/09574042.2015.1106256.

Jackson, Shona N. (2012) *Creole Indigeneity: Between Myth Nation in the Caribbean*. Minneapolis, University of Minnesota Press.

Jardim, Keith. (2011) 'Welcome to the Plantation: Three Novels by David Dabydeen', *The Arts Journal: Critical Perspectives on contemporary literatures, arts and cultures of Guyana, the Caribbean and their Diasporas*, 6 (1 and 2), pp. 61–68.

Jenkins, Edward. (1877) *Lutchmee and Dilloo: A Study of West Indian Life*. Reprint, ed., Dabydeen, D. Oxford, Macmillan Education, 2003.

Kale, Madhavi. (1998) *Fragments of Empire: Capital, Slavery and Indian Indentured Labor Migration in the British Caribbean*. Philadelphia, University of Pennsylvania Press.

Khan, Aisha. (2004) 'Sacred Subversions? Syncretic Creoles, the Indo-Caribbean and "Culture's In-between"', *Radical History Review*, 89, pp. 165–184. doi: https://doi.org/10.1215/01636545-2004-89-165.

Kim, Claire Jean. (1999) 'The Racial Triangulation of Asian Americans', *Politics and Society*, 27(1), pp. 105–138. doi: https://doi.org/10.1177/0032329299027001005.

Kirke, Henry. (1898) *Twenty-Five Years in British Guiana*. London, Sampson Low, Marston and Company.

Klein, Alison. (2018) *Anglophone Literature of Caribbean Indenture: The Seductive Hierarchies of Empire*. Cham, Switzerland, Palgrave Macmillan.

Lai, Walton Look. (1993) *Indentured Labor, Caribbean Sugar: Chinese and Indian Migrants to the British West Indies, 1838-1918*. Baltimore and London, Johns Hopkins University Press.

Lowe, Lisa. (2015) *The Intimacies of Four Continents*. Durham, Duke University Press.

Manjapra, Kris. (2018) 'Plantation Dispossessions: The Global Travel of Agricultural Racial Capitalism', in Beckert, S. and Desan, C., eds., *American Capitalism: New Histories*. New York, Columbia University Press, 361-387.

Melamed, Jodi. (2015) 'Racial Capitalism', *Critical Ethnic Studies* 1(1), pp. 76-85. doi: 10.5749/jcritethnstud.1.1.0076.

Mohammed, Patricia. (2002) 'The 'Creolisation' of Indian Women in Trinidad', in Shepherd, V. and Richards, G., eds., *Questioning Creole: Creolisation Discourses in Caribbean Culture*. Jamaica, Ian Randle, 130-147.

Puri, Shalini. (2004) *The Caribbean Postcolonial: Social Equality, Post-Nationalism and Cultural Hybridity*. New York, Palgrave Macmillan.

Shepherd, Verene A. and Glen L. Richards, eds. (2002) *Questioning Creole: Creolisation Discourses in Caribbean Culture*. Jamaica, Ian Randle.

Shlensky, Lincoln. (2011) 'Splitting the Difference: Hybridity and Subalternity in the Postcolonial Caribbean', in Bucknor, M.A. and Donnell, A., eds., *The Routledge Companion to Anglophone Caribbean Literature*. London, Routledge, 304-313.

Ward, Abigail. (2011) *Caryl Phillips, David Dabydeen and Fred D'Aguiar: Representations of Slavery*. Manchester, Manchester University Press.

Wheeler, Roxanne. (2000) *The Complexion of Race: Categories of Difference in Eighteenth-Century British Culture*. Philadelphia, University of Pennsylvania Press.

CHAPTER SEVEN

Slave Narratives and (Black) British History in David Dabydeen's *A Harlot's Progress*

Sofía Muñoz-Valdivieso

ABSTRACT

David Dabydeen's *A Harlot's Progress* (1999) establishes a dialogue with William Hogarth's engraving series of the same title produced in 1732, as it re-imagines the life of a minor character in Plate 2, a Black boy servant who is now a destitute old man in late eighteenth-century London. An Englishman significantly named Thomas Pringle, after the editor of Mary Prince's 1831 autobiography, is attempting to mine his memories of Africa, enslavement and servitude in Britain to ghost write a slave narrative that may contribute to the cause of abolition. Mungo is reluctant to tell his story to this prospective editor-mediator, but the novel presents his own idiosyncratic autobiographical account. This narrative is thus connected to actual memoirs by former slaves within the British Atlantic trade, most famously those of Olaudah Equiano in 1789 and Mary Prince in 1831, but also to the slave narrative as a genre, which was mostly fashioned by former American slaves who in the nineteenth century conveyed their stories to editors or put them in writing themselves. By choosing to place him in Britain, instead of the plantation colonies of the Caribbean, Dabydeen is anchoring his fictional African in the history of the metropolis and providing a new angle into it, as he rewrites British history by weaving Black history into it.

KEYWORDS

African diaspora, Black British, *A Harlot's Progress,* slave narratives

* * * * *

A Harlot's Progress was published almost a decade before the 2007 Bicentenary of the Abolition of the Slave Trade brought the involvement of Britain in transatlantic slavery into open public discussions. Some of its commemoration activities moved their attention away from the celebration of the country's humanitarian role as the leader of abolition, which had guided for two centuries Britain's understanding of this part of its national past, and they highlighted what the Victoria and Albert Museum exhibit at the time called the "Uncomfortable Truths" of the country's participation in slavery. It was a shift in perspective that focused on the commodification and exploitation of human beings as the enterprise that generated a significant part of the wealth that sustained Britain and the British Empire. In *A Harlot's Progress* Dabydeen envisions the life of one of the Africans who, like Equiano, found themselves living in Britain in the late eighteenth century, part of a minority that until the final years of the twentieth century had been practically invisible both in history books and in the public memory of the country. These Africans were the breathing embodiment on British soil of the uncomfortable truths of the slave trade and plantation economy; they were here because Britain was involved in slavery and the expanding British Empire was thriving on its profits.

The turn of the century in Britain was thus marked by two commemorations that provided different angles into the history of Black Britain. In 2007 the Bicentenary of the Abolition of the Slave Trade remembered the legal ending of the transportation of Africans to the Americas; in 1998 the fifty-year anniversary of the arrival of the liner *Empire Windrush* with Caribbean immigrant workers had commemorated a beginning – although both memorial years were much more complex, as slavery had continued in the British Empire for almost three decades after 1807, and some of its insidious damage is still present today; the long history of the Black population of Britain cannot really be encapsulated in this narrative of post-WWII migration. When *A Harlot's Progress* was published in 1999, the archaeological task of finding evidence and articulating a narrative of the pre-Windrush African presence in Britain was starting to take shape in what I would call its second wave of the nineties, which in turn has led to the present surge of academic work and prompted unprecedented non-academic dissemination. After the pioneers of the 1970s, Scobie (1972), Shyllon (1974 and 1977) and Walvin (1971 and 1973), and the highly visible volume by Fryer (1985), new voices of the nineties built on their work such as Braidwood (1994), Gretchen (1995), or Myers (1996). In the new millennium the number of studies on Black Britain's history has increased remarkably and its visibility extends from academic domains into popular culture and mass media, from BBC 2 series *Black and British* (2016) to blogs such as *Afropean* or films like *Belle* (2013), which transfers Dido Elizabeth Belle to the big screen from her traditional place as a footnote in history books as the daughter of an African slave and Lord Mansfield's nephew.[1] This is the context that Gerzina has in mind when, in the introduction to a volume based on her 2016 BBC Radio 4 series, *Britain's Black Past* (2020), she states:

> Television and radio, art exhibitions, blogs and websites: all are keeping this past alive and bringing to wider audiences this growing sense that Black people have been in Britain far longer than they knew, and that this is not just a Black past but a shared one. (Gerzina, 2020, p. 3)

Among the recent volumes devoted to the archaeology of the Black past of Britain, some are collections of articles by different authors devoted to varied moments of history, such as Adi (2019) or Gerzina (2020). Others focus on a particular period, such as the retrieval of the Black presence in Medieval and Renaissance Britain by Habib (2017), Kauffmann (2017) and Onyeka (2013 and 2019), the eighteenth century by Chater (2011), Hanley (2018) and Schama (2005), or moments of war, such as Bourne (2012,

2014 and 2020). Other authors provide a narrative of Black history in Britain from Roman times, as for instance Olusoga (2016), whose volume appeared as the companion to the BBC2 documentary, while in others the history of Black Britain is the context for discussions of ethnicity and contemporary identities, such as Akala (2019) and Hirsch (2018).

In *A Harlot's Progress* most of the actions are focalised from the perspective of the African Mungo (also briefly called Noah; and later Perseus, as the servant of the aristocratic Montagues). The novel nevertheless interweaves passages focalised by other characters like the washerwoman Betty, who cares for Mungo in the days prior to his auction in London, or Lord Montague at the moment when he buys him in a coffee house as replacement for his wife's dead pet monkey, or even characters that appear briefly in the text, such as the Black servant of the Cardews, a figure who seems to have been inspired by Joshua Reynold's portrait "A Young Black Man" (ca. 1770) – with Mungo's memories of his African village occasionally focalised from the ghosts' perspectives, as in Part IV those of Ellar and Kaka. Beyond these moments of polyphony, there seem to be two parallel narrative acts going on, with the disordered memories in fits and starts that Mungo provides giving way at times to what Mr Pringle could be thinking and/or attempting to write. Sometimes Mungo calls attention to the doubling up of narratives, typically defending his version as the true story, as when he commends Betty to readers: "Recognize her by *my* testimony, and not by the descriptions of thief and sinner that Mr Pringle will furnish of her" (Dabydeen, 1999, p. 168; emphasis in the original).

Mungo's narrative is disjointed but he claims ownership to this disarray, his life story on his own terms, and Mr Pringle's entrance into his memories is for him a defilement that he envisions as sexual violation: "Mr Pringle will nail [me] down with the nib of his pen and [I] will struggle to wriggle free from his page, as from Captain Thistlewood's bed, and Betty's solicitations" (156). The horror of his past cannot be easily captured in words; his narrative cannot possibly fall into the neat structure that Mr Pringle would wish for clarity and persuasion, the kind of structure that slave narratives would come to follow in their attempt to convince readers of the iniquities of slavery and the humanity of the enslaved individuals. Mungo's narrative is chaotic, a jumble of false starts and multiple versions of events. "I envy Mr Pringle his quest for tidiness, but the truth is otherwise" (Dabydeen, 1999, p. 111), he states, as he admits that his mind combines, eliminates and transfigures elements. When dealing with the horrors of slavery, "Dabydeen's novel suggests the difficulty of telling the untold" (Wallace, 2006, p. 108). The original slave narrators filtered their memories to make their stories palatable for their white readership and match the expectations of what was proper writing. Thus, as Toni Morrison points out, these former slaves "were silent about many things, and they 'forgot' many other things" (Morrison, 1987, 110). When considered within the framework of the original slave narratives, *A Harlot's Progress* hints at some of the issues those writers had to face "to write themselves into existence, since their 'truth' had to be presented in a stylized manner that would fit white readers' expectations of what constituted 'authentic' slave experience" (Muñoz-Valdivieso, 2012, p. 51).

Their personal narratives were complemented by different paratextual elements written and provided by respected white citizens, which served to reassure readers of the honesty of the authors and the truthfulness of their accounts – the large number of letters and other materials, such as notes, that Thomas Pringle added to the first-person narrative in *The History of Mary Prince* (1831) takes up almost as many pages as the autobiography itself. The paratextual component in Equiano's volume was not as extensive, yet it was also felt to be necessary, from the subscribers' list to letters by relevant white figures that attested to the honourable character of the writer, or the famous portrait in the frontispiece that cast him as an elegant Christian gentleman holding the Bible. In the American tradition, paratextual interventions were also very important. The original slave narratives included varied texts to support the author, and they commonly closed with documents such as "bills of sale, details of purchase from slavery, newspaper items, further reflections on slavery, sermons, anti-slavery speeches, poems, appeals to the reader for funds and moral support in the battle against slavery" (Olney, 1984, p. 51). Slave narratives are the only testimony that the victims of slavery left behind, but the context in which they were written should be considered when reading them. Mungo's ambition is to provide an unmediated story without the common intervention of an editor.

Dabydeen's novel responds to this tradition of paratextuality in slave narratives, and it is quite significant that, as we will see, it opens with a Prologue that sets English editor and African narrator face to face; however, it reverses the power relations between them, making the African reluctant to tell his story while the Englishman waits impatiently by his side. Instead of the common frontispiece that provided a portrait of the author (Olney, 1984, p. 49), *A Harlot's Progress* uses as paratext for each of its nine parts a fragment from one of the plates in Hogarth's engraving series, which visually connects with important developments in each one – mostly from plate 2, which provides the Black boy servant for Part I, a shattered teapot for Part II, a white mask and a mirror for Part IV, Moll hiding her lover for Part VI, the pet monkey for Part VII, and the tea-holding Jew for Part VII; from plate 5 the novel uses dying Moll's face for Part VIII, and Moll with another inmate in Bridwell prison for Part IX; a cleaning maid in Plate 3 introduces Part V, the beginning of Mungo's narration in Britain. *A Harlot's Progress* is a fictional response to these Black authored texts that could be so heavily mediated by white editors and publishers. The paratextual interventions in the novel are appropriately fragments of the engraving series that connect with Mungo's fragmentary narration. Instead of attesting to the honesty of the fictional narrator, these fragments ground his story in British visual art and link Mungo's life as an African in Britain to eighteenth-century British culture.

The novel consists of nine parts and a Prologue, which distils the essence of the whole text and is one of the most suggestive sections. Parts I and II present Mungo's evocation of his African village, a place far removed from the pastoral Africa of Equiano's childhood. Parts III and IV take place on Captain Thistlewood's slaver in the course of "three years or thirty days" (Dabydeen, 1999, p. 47), as he exerts atrocious physical and sexual violence while he teaches English language and culture to Mungo, who finds himself surrounded by the ghosts of his fellow Africans and has constant flashbacks to the obliteration of his village.[2] Parts V to IX are located in Britain, first in the days prior to his auction after returning from his life at sea, then as the Black servant Perseus in the mansion of Lord and Lady Montague, and finally in Dr Gideon's house, where he lives tending dying prostitutes after he escapes the Montagues' household.[3] All in all, two thirds of the action take place in Britain. These nine chapters correspond in number to the structure outlined in the Prologue by Mr Pringle in his notebook, when he sketches Mungo's life while he waits for an answer to his insistent request that "something must be said ... A beginning, Mungo" (Dabydeen, 1999, p. 1). The similarity between Mr Pringle's envisioning and what Mungo provides to the reader is restricted to the number of chapters. Mr Pringle's plan includes a chapter on the voyage to the Americas and life on a plantation, which do not appear in Mungo's memoir, and a final chapter that fits his Christian objective of spiritual salvation "Redemption of Mungo by the Committee for the Abolition of Slavery" (Dabydeen, 1999, p. 6) after his "Descent into the Mire of Poverty and Disease" (Dabydeen, 1999, p. 6).

This ending does not correspond to what the novel presents, since the spiritual redemption that Pringle imagines is far from accomplished, and the old man appears uneasy about accepting the charity of the abolitionists that have been feeding and clothing him for months and "will not return their benevolence with the gift of confession" (Dabydeen, 1999, p. 1). The unfolding of Mungo's narrative does not advance in the clear straight line proposed by the prospective editor. The second chapter, for instance, does not move from Africa to the middle passage, since Mungo's memories return over and again to his origins, with conflicting versions of his African background and the destruction of his people, all somehow conveying the anguish of a survivor haunted by the ghosts of those left behind. There are then multiple narratives of his African childhood that only coincide in articulating the boy's guilt for the destruction of his "tribe" and/ or his "village" by some unclear trespass or disobedience. Similarly, the marks on his brow are variously explained in different moments as "the sign of evil on my forehead" that he was born with (Dabydeen, 1999, p. 33), the markings of the manhood ritual performed on him by the men of his village (Dabydeen, 1999, p. 65), the sign of evil that the Headman brands as punishment, for "I had trespassed in the spaces of the dead" (Dabydeen, 1999, p. 19), and the branding of the double T initials of Captain Thomas Thistlewood (Dabydeen, 1999, p. 66), left on his face as a stamp of his ownership.

The introductory paragraph in the novel sets up the scene with the contained tension between two characters, a former African slave that has joined the ranks of what the late eighteenth century would have called "the Black poor" in London,[4] and an impatient Englishman who wants to write down and print Mungo's story to help the cause of abolition. Mr Pringle is presented in *A Harlot's Progress* as the Secretary of the Abolition Committee, a fictional conflation of the Society for the Abolition of the Slave Trade (1787-1807) and the Anti-Slavery Society (1823-1838), the former focusing on the abolition of the slave trade in the British Empire and the latter on the abolition of slavery itself and the emancipation of the slaves – two issues that are also conflated in the novel. Even though in the late eighteenth-century the issue discussed in Britain was the abolition of the trade itself and not yet the emancipation of the slaves, the line between them is blurred in the novel, as when Mungo refuses to offer Mr Pringle "a sober testimony that will appeal to the Christian charity of an enlightened citizenry who will, on perusing my tale of underserved woe, campaign in the Houses of Parliament for my emancipation and that of millions of my brethren" (Dabydeen, 1999, p. 5).

A journal entry with an incomplete date, "22nd April, 17____" (Dabydeen, 1999, p. 1) opens *A Harlot's Progress*, and the third-person narrative in the present tense is focalised from Mr Pringle's perspective. He sits at Mungo's table with a wad of paper ready at hand as "[h]e jabs the nib of his pen into the inkwell and stirs nervously, awaiting word. This is the third visit, but at least he has made a start, if only to record the date of the meeting" (Dabydeen, 1999, p. 1). In this opening, Dabydeen explicitly reverses the power balance between Englishman and African, with the former anxiously waiting for a narrative and the latter reluctant to proceed with it. Mr Pringle is "a dog with imploring eyes" and Mungo "master of the situation" (Dabydeen, 1999, p. 1), who willingly restrains from full dialogue and only proffers a few vague words about his origins, so that the Prologue closes with a repetition of the dog-master image, as "[Mr Pringle's] face twitches like an excited poodle twitching its tale, working up sufficient rage for an intimidating growl" (Dabydeen, 1999, p. 9). It is their third encounter, and this journal entry brings to mind Dorothy Wordsworth's April 15th 1802 annotation in her Grasmere Journals. Here she records the walk that inspired her brother to write 'The Daffodils', the iconic poem that several postcolonial writers have reacted to as a trope of imperial control and an emblem of the Englishness they were forced to learn as children.[5] These are the flowers that for both the Romantic poet and for Mr Pringle embody the renewal of nature:

> [Mr Pringle] doodles over the date, drawing a series of ears, some drooping and mutilated, others like the heads of daffodils that he had seen by the wayside on his way to the garret; daffodils bright against the blackened frost of the city, defiant in their proclamation of survival into newness, a new season, a new beginning (Dabydeen, 1999, p. 2).

Mr Pringle's hope for a parallel beginning of Mungo's tale is thwarted by his silence, although his jumbled memories and meandering narrative will unfold in silence, even as in this encounter with his future editor he communicates little – indeed when the novel closes Mr Pringle continues with "the doodles he makes on his paper as he waits for my confession" (Dabydeen, 1999, p. 276). The Prologue shifts focalization between Mr Pringle and Mungo, which shows the contrast between what the former can perceive about Mungo's "responses, which are brief to the point of uncouthness" (Dabydeen, 1999, p. 2) and the African's own mind, which retorts "No, I am not uncouth, I can write the story myself" (Dabydeen, 1999, p. 5). Mungo feels that he has the skills to write his own life narrative, for he has "imbibed many of your mannerisms of language, and the King James Bible is at hand to furnish me with such expressions as could set you aglow with compassion for the plight of the Negro" (Dabydeen, 1999, p. 5). In fact, Mungo can quote the classics at will in his own silent argumentation (Dabydeen, 1999, p. 7), and his narrative is full of references to Western books that he has read, from the literary works of the English canon to "Adamson's *Voyage to Africa*" (Dabydeen, 1999, p. 41) – a reference inspired by the actual volume *A Voyage to Senegal, the Isle of Goree, and the River Gambia* (1759) by Michel Adanson (1727-1806).

He chooses not to show his dominion of the English language and European culture to Mr Pringle, but his is a cultivated mind into which spring the Greek and Roman classics ("*Radix malorum est cupiditas*, as the ancients put it" [Dabydeen, 1999, p. 7; emphasis in the original]), as well as quintessentially English works by Shakespeare that he plays with – as a defiant Caliban, to whom the captain "taught me language" (Dabydeen, 1999, p. 57), he rebels, for instance, by adopting and distorting Ariel's song in *The Tempest*: "Where the bee sucks there suck I. Let me talk like dis and dat" (Dabydeen, 1999, p. 5). When narrating his tribe's myth about a camboue rat that has sex with a woman, Mungo uses Latin, as the planter Thomas Thistlewood did in his Jamaican journal entries: "It slid into the lake and corpus feminae intravit" (Dabydeen, 1999, p. 38). Dabydeen ironically engages with Thistlewood's atrocious text by having Mungo openly declare that in retelling "the origins of our tribe, [it is] so shameful an event that you will excuse me, gentle reader, if I abbreviate it and secrete its obscenity in the elegant shell of Latin" (Dabydeen, 1999, p. 38).

From the little that he knows about him as the Black page boy captured in Plate 2 of William Hogarth's *A Harlot's Progress*, Mr Pringle imagines how Mungo has moved from servant of the high ranks in eighteenth-century British society to the fringe location of the destitute Black poor that prompted the actions of the

Committee for their relocation to Africa. In Mr Pringle's mind he is a composite of these two extreme social positions that his vision links by alliteration: "[H]is presence greeted with equal excitement in seedy **b**agnio and **b**aroque gallery. **B**eggars and no**b**ility were his equal friends, and they flocked to him as he made his entrance in **wh**ore-house and **H**igh church" (Dabydeen, 1999, p. 4; emphasis added). Mungo indeed has lived in mansions and slums, and his experiences capture two distinct groups of Africans in Britain in the eighteenth-century. As Perseus he stands for the exotic servants of the upper classes, who were integrated into their households and even sometimes highly educated. Lady Montague's choice of costume for him captures his nature as a colourful ornament that has come to replace her pet monkey: "He is to be remod-elled into a fantastic land creature, part Indian (his turban), part English coxcomb (his suit), part Chinese (his slippers), with a small Arabian scimitar strapped to his side" (Dabydeen, 1999, p. 207).[6] In fact, in eighteenth century urban life the liveried Black slave became a "sought-after possession and […] a form of social currency" (Molineux, 2005, p. 498), and indeed

> [i]n the early eighteenth century large numbers of Blacks were kidnapped from Africa as boys and flaunted as prized young servants who were ornaments to their masters and especially to their mistresses […] It is the Black boy rather than the Black man who prevails in English high culture of the period, a child who is converted to an *object d'art* and a status symbol who represents colonial wealth (Nussbaum, 2003, p. 198).

On the other hand, in the last decades of the century cities like London, Bristol or Liverpool saw rising numbers of disenfranchised Africans, some of them coming as former slaves from the North American colonies after helping the British side in the war, who found themselves free yet destitute and became, as we have seen, so visible in London that the Committee for the Relief of the Black Poor in 1786 organized their transportation to settle in a free community in Sierra Leone. Mungo-Perseus appears to be one of them after he escapes the Montagues' household to join Dr Gideon the Jewish physician, and as an old man his situation deteriorates as he struggles to survive and is forced to accept the charity of the Abolition Committee. These two groups of Africans constituted the extremes of the Black population in Britain at the time, for which there is no definite figure, with Fryer speaking of 10,000 or so (1984, p. 72), Carretta mentioning a figure of 14,000-20,000 in 1771 (1995, p. 283), and Schama referring to around 7,000 in London (2005, p. 31). The definite number will remain a matter of speculation, but recent research of British newspapers in the eighteenth century has found over 800 advertisements for Black runaways and sustains the claim that "[e]nslaved people were far from unusual in Georgian Britain" (Mullen et al., 2020, p. 81) – with studies on London concluding that "[b]etween 1691 and 1776, at least 222 advertisements for Black runaways were placed in the London papers" (Corlett, 2019, p. 38). Contrary to what the image of the eighteenth century may have been until recent decades, it was not unusual to see Africans in cities, particularly in London,

> some living in fine town houses where, suitably got up in embroidered coats, powdered wigs and silk breeches, they served, ornamentally, as footmen or body servants to the quality. Some, like Dr Johnson's Francis Barber, were minor celebrities, sketched and painted as charming "sable" curiosities. The less fortunate made a living as musicians and waiters in the taverns and brothels of Covent Garden, and went home to a bare, verminous room in neighbouring St Giles, where they were called "blackbirds". More congregated in the dockland parish of St George in the East, in the filthy streets that led from Nicholas Hawksmoor's eccentric basilica. Many of them were sailors, bargemen, haulers, carters and stevedores; and some for a few pence boxed bare knuckle or played on drums and fifes to crowds in the streets and piazzas. The "blackbirds," then, were mostly poor, and were known for flitting in and out of trouble. (Schama, 2005, p. 31)

Mr Pringle's planned biography of Mungo is motivated by his plan to agitate against slavery by provoking guilt in the reader, but Mungo is uneasy about this: "It is your love that I greed for, not the coinage of your guilt" (Dabydeen, 1999, p. 71). Mungo seems to distance himself from the intent of original slave narratives to make readers feel sympathy and pity for the enslaved individual ("I feel sorry for you"), into a more equalitarian relation of empathy ("I feel your sorrow"). It could be argued that Mr Pringle aims to produce a slave narrative that fulfils the structure and objectives of such a text in its political intent as it came to develop in the States in the nineteenth century: to make readers feel pity for the enslaved protagonist of the story, see the iniquity of the institution and take actions against it – at the end of the eighteenth century in Britain, the attempted change was, as mentioned before, the abolition of the trade. Mungo wants to write his individual story as a human being who happened to be a slave for many years, but who is not necessarily a type or a representation, even though his confused and nightmarish account is inevitably an articulation of the uprooting and violence of the trade and slavery, and the description of his origin can apply to the millions of people displaced and tortured through the centuries: "I had many beginnings, all of them marked by a long and futile wailing" (Dabydeen, 1999, p. 27). The blending between his individual and collective story is captured in the use of an all-encompassing "I" as he describes the newspaper clips that he has been collecting:

> In the faraway plantations of the West Indies, in the barracoons of the African coast, *I* have rebelled, stabbed, poisoned, raped, absconded, and sought escape by killing *myself* and *my* offsprings. In return *I* have been strangled, flogged to death, roasted alive, blown away and lynched. Truly *I* have made havoc in the hearts and minds of white people, compromising their civility, sharpening their Christian principles to breaking-point" (Dabydeen, 1999, p. 244; emphasis added).

Mungo seems to be initially against self-expression in books, which in Mr Pringle's society are "deemed the highest achievement of man", but for him are "no more than a splendidly adorned memorial and grave" (Dabydeen, 1999, p. 34). He thus maintains the ownership of his story by keeping "silence before the nib and gravedigger's spade of Mr Pringle" (Dabydeen, 1999, p. 34). Despite this rejection of books, the tale that we encounter after the Prologue is sensed to be not just Mungo's rambling thoughts and memories but at points his very act of writing: "And *if my hands become stained with ink as I now compose this tale for you*, it is because my mother['s] frantic silent gestures compel my pen to describe her suffering. I write for Moll, not for Mr Pringle's money" (Dabydeen, 1999, p. 45; emphasis added).[7] Throughout the nine parts of the novel Mungo frequently conveys the sense that he is writing with an audience in mind, as he addresses the reader several times as "dear reader" (Dabydeen, 1999, p. 40, 206, 248), "gentle reader" (Dabydeen, 1999, p. 38, 168), "valued reader" (Dabydeen, 1999, p. 175), "my sympathetic reader" (Dabydeen, 1999, p. 75), or "grateful reader" (Dabydeen, 1999, p. 186). At points he sounds proud of his intellectual accomplishments, but the African ghosts that haunt him nevertheless keep him humble, as when one of them bluntly tells him "Just because you are making a book of fancy words [...] don't make you better than us" (Dabydeen, 1999, p. 258).

The harlot in the novel title is not primarily Moll Hackabout, the woman whose life journey, or progress, is presented in Hogarth's engravings. She only appears at the end of Mungo's narrative when she is terminally ill, her life parallel to that of other innocent young women that came to London from the countryside, like Mary or Betty in the novel. After being sexually, physically and psychologically abused by Thistlewood, Mungo feels he has been the captain's harlot – and the voices of the African ghosts on the ship accuse him of having become "the whiteman's wife" (Dabydeen, 1999, p. 59). If the word harlot is understood metaphorically, Mungo feels that in telling his story to Mr Pringle he would be prostituting himself, selling his past in exchange for money: "He makes me feel like a strumpet whose performance is undeserving of his coin" (178). It could be argued that Mungo "struggles with the ethics of narrating his story and, in so doing, arguably trades places with the harlot of the title" (Ward 2011, p. 114). Overall, at certain moments in his narrative there is the suggestion that the whole country has become a kind of harlot who is willing to trade in human dignity for the sake of profit. This metaphoric adscription is encapsulated in Lady Montague, when Mungo describes her as Britannia figure in an Archimboldo-like portrait that combines the shapes of trade goods to form her figure, "skin of bleached sugar, bales of cotton her breasts, veins of gold tinning along her arms, her lap a mine of inexhaustible ores, and yet all the cargoes of Empire but a trifle compared to the effort that went into her creation, the centuries and centuries of constant *progress*" (Dabydeen, 1999, p. 184-85; emphasis added).

Intertextuality with painting goes beyond these and other references. It determines the conception of the novel both as a dialogue with Hogarth and his characters and as a crucial reversal of eighteenth-century portraits in which a Black figure appears as an exotic sable addition that highlights the wealth and high social standing of the aristocratic and upper-class sitters.[8] *A Harlot's Progress* places the Black character centre stage and writes against the representations of Africans in these portraits as adornments in wealthy mansions, but also against another common vision in the late eighteenth century in the context of abolition. It is the view of the African as victim that Mr Pringle wants to project and which Mungo rebels against. This conception was most likely best represented in the final decades of the century by the well-intentioned iconic image of the kneeling slave in chains of the medallion that was designed by Wedgwood in 1787 for the Committee for the Abolition of the Slave Trade – and became the most frequently reproduced image of a Black person by the end of the century.

Before the present explosion of studies on Britain's Black past and its high visibility in a variety of media, *A Harlot's Progress* used fiction to rescue "Black eighteenth-century England from the formerly neglected margins of social and cultural history" (King 2004, p. 163). Dabydeen's novel is steeped in eighteenth-century visual culture and he weaves into it his reimagining of contemporary figures. The Montagues in whose household Mungo becomes Perseus had been in fact the employers of the African writer, activist and businessman Ignatius Sancho. The Jewish Gideon, who seems to have been the wealthy merchant in Plate 2 of the series, is envisioned in the novel as a physician. The planter Thomas Thistlewood is transformed in Dabydeen's fiction from vicious planter into atrocious slaver – although Mungo argues that he will find redemption: "Was not Revd. John Newton whose hymns honey your throat every Sunday once a slaver?" (Dabydeen, 1999, p. 73), thus also bringing in the well-known minister, who is mostly remembered as the author of the lyrics to the hymn "Amazing Grace" but who had spent fourteen at sea as a slaver captain. The novel also echoes some well-known events of the time like the *Zong* scandal, which fell within the jurisdiction of the famous Mansfield judge ten years after his ruling in the Somerset case – in the novel it takes the name of the actual slaver captain and is thus discussed as the Collingwood case. The novel creates a vision of eighteenth-century society as an ethnically varied community with Jewish and Black population that is beginning to experience the cultural complexity that continues today. Mungo's story is an antidote to the eighteenth-century belief that Britain's treatment of slaves was mainly a civilizing action and the society reimagined in the novel includes the aristocratic owners of slaves but also servants, whores and socially excluded people like the Jew, and "gives them complex characters and lives" (King 2004, p. 163).

In *A Harlot's Progress* Dabydeen re-imagines the life and opinions of one of the Africans that fell prey to European greed in the eighteenth century, and it provides "a comprehensive picture of British society in the eighteenth century [including] the dispossession of a former slave, who is yet granted the power and freedom of saying and unsaying, of knitting and knotting memories" (Pagnoulle, 2007, p. 200). Mungo's struggle to find a voice in which to tell his story pulls him in different directions – and different vernaculars, from Equiano's sophisticated and elegant phrasing to Creole language to a mingling of Indian languages in the presence of his ghosts. In his old age he still is haunted by the spectres of the Atlantic, as one of them states: "he bears all of us, all our griefs" (138). Mungo is now a destitute old man in late eighteenth-century London, and his wealth is his own story, which he presents in a kaleidoscopic fusion of versions from disordered memories – or memories that have been transfigured so that he is able to deal with them. He defends his right to own his narrative and refuses the mediation of an editor, so that he establishes a dialogue with the slave narrative as a form of writing by the Black subject, calling attention to their possibly mediated nature. After having been a slave for many years, Mungo defends his freedom to remember as he wishes, and to recreate his past on his own terms. Dabydeen's novel predates the explosion of historical studies on the Black British history in the new millennium. Like other fictions by British writers such as Caryl Phillips, Fred D'Aguiar, Andrea Levy and Bernardine Evaristo, *A Harlot's Progress* highlights the participation of Britain in the exploitation of human beings as it shows slavery not in the faraway lands of the Caribbean but in the parlours of the upper classes in Britain in the late eighteenth century. Dabydeen creates a vision of Britain that reflects Gerzina's view that, if we refocus the lens to look back, "the London of Johnson, Reynolds, Hogarth and Pope – that elegant, feisty, intellectual and earthly place of neo-classicism and chaos – becomes occupied by a parallel world of Africans and their descendants working and living alongside the English" (Gerzina, 1995, p. 2). By recreating Britain in the eighteenth century as a crisscrossing of cultures and ethnicities, Dabydeen contributes to the recognition that Black history is part of British history, so that the fictional reimagining of the past in *A Harlot's Progress* can facilitate the inclusion of all Britons within Britain's imagined community in the present.

NOTES

1. Lord Mansfield famously ruled in 1772 over the Somerset case, determining that a master could not forcibly remove a slave from England – a decision that was misinterpreted as meaning that slavery was not allowed in the country, which was not the case.
2. The name of the captain positions Mungo's story within eighteenth-century British history, as this character is a composite of two historical figures, the infamous planter Thomas Thistlewood (1721-1786), who kept a detailed record of his atrocities on his Jamaican plantation in a diary, and Luke Collingwood (c. 1733-1781), the captain of the slaver *Zong* who was responsible for the massacre of 133 enslaved Africans, thrown overboard into the sea to collect insurance money in 1871.
3. Dabydeen chooses a different spelling for his reimagining of the actual eighteenth-century Montagu family that were involved in the life of Ignatius Sancho (c. 1729-1780), an African who worked as a butler with the Duchess of Montagu for two years in the early 1750s and was later a valet for another member of the family. Sancho became a writer and a composer, and *The Letters of the Late Ignatius Sancho, an African* were published in 1782.
4. The situation of the Black population of London prompted the creation of the Committee for the Relief of the Black Poor in 1786, which offered health care, clothing and jobs to destitute Black people, and developed a plan to transport them to the west coast of Africa, to start a settlement on land bought from local African authorities to be called Granville Town after the abolitionist Granville Sharp. The situation of the Black Poor is discussed, among others, by Myers, Gerzina, Braidwood and Schama. Schama's volume became a TV documentary for BBC 2 in 2007 and moved onto the stage in a 2008 play by the Black British writer Caryl Phillips.
5. The Caribbean protagonist of Jamaica Kincaid's *Lucy* (1990), for instance, had to memorize this poem at school to deliver it in a public performance for parents. When she migrates to the US to work and she sees daffodils for the first time, the flowers bring back memories of an oppressive English education: "a scene […] of conquered and conquests […] [N]othing could change the fact that where she saw beautiful flowers I saw sorrow and bitterness" (Kincaid, 1990, p. 30). For postcolonial reactions to the poem see Welberry (1997). Wordsworth's text also embodies the English refinement that Hortense hopes to achieve when she migrates from Jamaica to the homeland in Andrea Levy's *Small Island* (2004).
6. "This conflation of Arabic, African and Indian origins is typical of eighteenth-century representations of Black servants. What seems to matter is not that these servants are African, Muslim or Indian, but that they are exotic" (Tobin 1999, 27).
7. In *Hogarth's Blacks* Dabydeen establishes a connection between the Black boy in plate 2 and Moll's boy in plate 6, since "the two boys are identified by their similarity of dress" (Dabydeen, 1987, 110). This is a connection that the novel enacts in the several moments when Mungo thinks of Moll as a mother figure.

8. In one of the notes to his autobiographical narrative, Equiano shows his awareness that having a Black servant was a mark of high social standing: "She felt her pride alarmed at the superiority of her rival in being attended by a Black servant" (Equiano, 1996, p. 267). Dabydeen indeed started his academic career with a study of the Black presence in eighteenth-century British culture and he considered how "the wealthy were accustomed to having themselves and their families painted with their Black servants, the Black presence being a ready means of indicating their affluence ... and in some cases their colonial connections" (Dabydeen, 1987, p. 85). In his work he highlights the links between slavery and painting, since at the time "some of the outstanding connoisseurs and collectors of the age were heavily involved in the slave trade" (Dabydeen, 1987, p. 88), and he mentions the significant examples of the Duke of Chandos and William Beckford.

REFERENCES

Adi, Hakim (2019) *Black British History: New Perspectives*. Exeter, Zed Books.

Akala (2019) *Natives: Race and Class in the Ruins of the Empire*. London, John Murray Press.

Bourne, S. (2012) *The Motherland Calls: Britain's Black Servicemen & Women, 1939-45*. Cheltenham, The History Press.

— (2014) *Black Poppies: Britain's Black Community and the Great War*. Cheltenham, The History Press.

— (2020) *Under Fire: Black Britain in Wartime 1939-45*. Cheltenham, The History Press.

Braidwood, S. J. (1994) *Black Poor and White Philanthropists: London's Blacks and the Foundation of the Sierra Leone Settlement 1786-1791*. Liverpool, University of Liverpool Press.

Carretta, V. (1995) "Explanatory and Textual Notes". *The Interesting Narrative and Other Writings*. By Olaudah Equiano. Ed Vincent Carretta. Harmondsworth, Penguin. Pp. 237-305.

Chater, K. (2011) *Untold Histories: Black People in England and Wales during the Period of the British Slave Trade, c. 1660-1807*. Manchester, Manchester University Press.

Corlett, M. (2019) "Between Colony and Metropole: Empire, Race and Power in Eighteenth-Century Britain". *Black British History: New Perspectives*. Ed. Hakim Adi. London, Zed Books. pp.37-

Dabydeen, D. (1987) *Hogarth's Blacks: Images of Blacks in Eighteenth Century English Art*. Manchester, Manchester University Press.

— (1999) *A Harlot's Progress*. London, Jonathan Cape.

Equiano, O. (1996) *The Interesting Narrative and Other Writings*. Ed Vincent Carretta. Harmondsworth, Penguin.

Fryer P. (1984) *Staying Power: The History of Black People in Britain*. London, Pluto.

Gerzina, G. (1995) *Black England: Life before Emancipation*. London, John Murray.

Gerzina, G ed. (2020) *Britain's Black Past*. Liverpool, Liverpool University Press.

Habib, I. (2017) *Black Lives in the English Archives, 1500-1677*. London, Routledge.

Hanley, R (2018). *Beyond Slavery and Abolition: Black British Writing c. 1770-1830*. Cambridge. Cambridge University Press.

Hirsch, A. (2018) *Brit(ish): On Race, Identity and Belonging*. London, Jonathan Cape.

Kaufmann, M. (2017) *Black Tudors: The Untold Story*. London, Oneworld.

Kincaid, J. (1990) *Lucy*. New York, Farrar, Straus and Giroux.

King, B. (2004). *The Internationalization of English Literature*. Oxford, Oxford University Press

Molineux, C. (2005) "Hogarth's Fashionable Slaves: Moral Corruption in Eighteenth-Century London". *ELH* 72, pp.495-520.

Morrison, T. (1987) "The Site of Memory." *Inventing the Truth: The Art and Craft of Memoir*. Ed. William Zinsser. Boston, Houghton, 1987, pp.103–124.

Muñoz-Valdivieso, S. (2012) "Neo-Slave Narratives in Contemporary Black British Fiction," *Ariel: A Review of International English Literature* 42, 3-4, pp.43-59.

Mullen, S, N. Mundell and S. P. Newman. "Black Runaways in Eighteenth-Century Britain". *Britain's Black Past*. Ed. G. Gerzina. Liverpool, Liverpool University Press, pp.81-98.

Myers, N. (1996) *Reconstructing the Black Past: Blacks in Britain 1780-1830*. London, Routledge.

Nussbaum, F. A. (2003) *The Limits of the Human: Fictions of Anomaly, Race and Gender in the Long Eighteenth Century*. Cambridge, Cambridge University Press.

Olney, J. (1984) "'I Was Born': Slave Narratives, Their Status as Autobiography and as Literature," *Callaloo*, 20 (Winter), pp.46-73.

Olusoga, D. (2016) *Black and British*. London, Macmillan.

Onyeka (2013) *Blackamoores: Africans in Tudor England, their Presence, Status and Origins*. London, Narrative Eye.

— (2019) *England's Other Countrymen: Black Tudor Society*. London, Narrative Eye.

Pagnoulle, P. (2007) "*A Harlot's Progress*: Memories in Knots and Stays." *No Land, No Mother: Essays on David Dabydeen*. Eds. Lynne Macedo and Kampta Karran. Leeds, Peepal Tree Press.

Schama, S. (2005). *Rough Crossings: Britain, the Slaves and the American Revolution*. London, BBC Books.

Scobie, E. (1972) *Black Britannia: The History of Blacks in Britain*. Chicago, Johnson Publishing Company.

Shyllon F. (1974) Black Shyllon F. (1977) *Black Slaves in Britain*. Oxford, Oxford University Press.

— (1977) *Black People in Britain, 1555–1833*. Oxford, Oxford University Press.

Tobin B. F. (1999) *Picturing Imperial Power: Colonial Subjects in Eighteenth-Century British Painting*. Durham & London, Duke University Press.

Wallace, E. K. (2006) *The British Slave Trade and Public Memory*. New York, Columbia University Press.

Walvin J. (1971) *The Black Presence: A Documentary History of the Negro in England, 1555-1860*. London, Orbach and Chambers.

— (1973) *Black and White: The Negro and English Society 1555–1945*. London, Allen Lane.

Ward, A. (2011) *Caryl Phillips, David Dabydeen and Fred D'Aguiar: Representations of Slavery*. Manchester, Manchester University Press.

Welberry, K. (1997) "Colonial and Postcolonial Deployment of 'Daffodils'". *Kunapipi* 19.1, pp.32-44.

CHAPTER EIGHT

Infinite Worlds: Eighteenth-Century London, the Atlantic Ocean, and Post-Slavery
John Clement Ball

ABSTRACT

In four novels of slavery and emancipation published in the 1990s and 2000s, the interconnected spaces of eighteenth-century London and the Atlantic Ocean are associated with infinity and unboundness, and with relational identity and transnational worldliness. While narrative modes vary from detailed social realism (Martin and Hill) to speculative postmodern metafiction (Dabydeen and Wharton), the authors' shared interests in exploring travel, dislocation, and unbelonging – and related experiences of struggle, violence, and freedom (however limited) – reveal possibilities for Black identities after slavery that are frustratingly finite for some, tantalizingly infinite for others. Collectively, the novels suggest that the binary itself needs unshackling, because if the infinite can represent the hope of possibility to the ex-slave, to the newly enslaved it can prompt the dissolution of the self; and if the finite signifies the shackled, immobilized self of slavery's commodification and social death, it also points to the rooted, grounded self that was first lost to slavery and whose recovery is sought thereafter. These historical novels echo and anticipate the oceanic London still haunted by the legacy of slavery and racism that subsequent generations of Black Londoners have documented in their fictions of the twentieth-century metropolis.

KEYWORDS

London, transatlantic slavery, historical novel, eighteenth century, infinity, ocean, postcolonial, transnational

* * * * *

In *Black London: Life before Emancipation,* Gretchen Holbrook Gerzina writes of how, on discovering that 15,000 people of African descent were living in London in 1768, she was struck by a vision of her present-day London as 'suddenly occupied by two simultaneous centuries' (1995, p. 2) – an eighteenth-century city of Black pageboys and entertainers, of Black beggars and prostitutes and autobiographers, overlaying the late twentieth-century one like a ghostly palimpsest. In the same decade as Gerzina was articulating these spectral imaginings, four prominent Black British novelists were similarly looking back to the eighteenth century – to the final decades of the British slave trade, to the Atlantic Ocean across and around which it took place, and to London, where the abolitionist cause was advanced. Caryl Phillips, S.I. Martin, David Dabydeen, and Fred D'Aguiar all published novels in the 1990s that have Black protagonists and are set entirely or partly in the eighteenth-century metropolis. In the subsequent decade, two Canadian novelists did likewise: Thomas Wharton and Lawrence Hill both published historical novels featuring female ex-slaves that end up in London after long and circuitous ocean journeys.[1] Since historical novels are always prompted by present-tense obsessions and therefore frequently gaze at two centuries simultaneously, how does this outpouring of eighteenth-century-oriented narrative reflect and enhance our contemporary understanding of slavery, the Atlantic world, and London? What geographies and identities, what forms of mobility and dwelling, what personal quests and local or global communities do these novels imagine for the imperial capital's Black inhabitants at a time when the prevailing winds were blowing abolition and revolutionary political change across the Atlantic world? And how do these texts' transhistorical, transnational, circum-Atlantic visions of London echo – or anticipate – other postcolonial writings about the world city of our time and the Black person's place in it?

The four novels examined in this essay – Martin's *Incomparable World* (1996), Hill's *The Book of Negroes* (2007), Dabydeen's *A Harlot's Progress* (1999), and Wharton's *Salamander* (2001) – collectively offer a rich set of correspondences and contrasts in their portrayals of the Black urban subject. Two of these texts are by Black British authors (Martin and Dabydeen), and two are by Canadians (Hill and Wharton); two are written in a traditional realist mode (Martin and Hill), and two are postmodern metafictions that generate dizzyingly speculative ontologies (Dabydeen and Wharton); two are individual life stories modelled after the slave narrative genre (Hill and Dabydeen), and two are adventure novels about small groups of people, with no single protagonist or focalizing consciousness (Martin and Wharton). However, none of those six pairings matches any of the others: a foursquare arrangement of the texts reveals multiple and complex similarities and contrasts between every possible pair. What does unite them all is that to varying degrees in all four books travel is constant: dislocation prevails over settlement (or unbelonging over belonging) and characters' affiliations are intercontinental and transoceanic rather than local or national – though slavery being what it was, their internationalism is not by choice.

These relational aspects of narrative and identity are reinforced by three central elements common across the novels that become identified in them with such interrelated concepts as the boundless, the endless, the inclusive, and the infinite. First of these common elements is London itself; the port city and international gathering-point not only presided over a global empire on which the sun shone *ad infinitum*, but in the eighteenth and nineteenth centuries London was seen to contain, in Peter Ackroyd's words, 'the great world itself' (2000, p. 544): the city Addison called 'an aggregate of various nations' (quoted in Ackroyd, 2000, p. 701) included, it was imagined, 'no less than everything' (Ackroyd, 2000, p. 3). London's perceived infinitude was a function not just of its physical size and the variety of peoples it contained but of the economic and political power that the empire's intricate web of international affiliations brought to it; London was as global a city as the eighteenth century had to offer, and this idea of the metropolis as infinitely expansive, inclusive, and diverse has been a persistent trope ever since. For many ex-slaves going to London in the eighteenth century, as for their twentieth-century postcolonial counterparts, it seemed to offer the infinite hope and possibilities associated with freedom, opportunity, and access, even if the reality when they arrived was a far cry from any utopian imaginings.

The second image of the infinite central to the four novels is the sea on which their itinerant characters journey – the endless, boundary-defying oceans that separate but also connect their continental 'worlds,' which variously include Europe, Africa, the Caribbean, North and South America, and Asia. If London is a key site and symbol of imperial power, the ocean is another: the waves Britannia ruled, the literal 'space-of-flows' that enabled London to become a metaphorical 'space-of-flows.'[2] Laura Brown, in an elegant survey of oceanic imagery in seventeenth – and eighteenth-century poetry, shows how the ocean was often employed, along with the River Thames that flows into it, as a figure for Britain's expansionist destiny and benevolent global power, rhetorically figured as power over the unpopulated salt water rather than over inhabited lands. The popular image of 'the empire of the sea,' Brown argues, denoted

> a providential system of distribution and a proxy for British global power. Indeed, ... the claims for the benevolence of that system depend on that movement of superimposition of sea and land that generates the displacement of power from the 'solid space' of the globe to the nonspace of the flowing, gliding, foaming ocean. The representation of the solid *imperium* cannot be so pacific. By displacing imperial violence in this way, the fable of torrents and seas performs an essential service to the ideology of the Pax Britannica, sanctioning its assertion of the peaceful imposition of empire on the world. (Brown, 2003, p. 116)

The ocean was, of course, the space across which were borne many of the actors in the imperial drama, the goods that generated imperial wealth, and the ideas, images, and knowledges the imperial encounter produced. And as Derek Walcott's poetry (e.g., 'The Sea is History') and D'Aguiar's *Feeding the Ghosts* (whose first sentence is 'The sea is slavery' [1997, p. 3]), among other texts, remind us, the sea has a particular resonance for those who have experienced slavery. Indeed, the sea's infinitude is symbolic, for slaves and former slaves, of the boundless, disorienting infinity into which slavery plunges them, unmooring and uprooting their identity and often prompting them, on acquiring literacy, to look to narrative as a way to ground their identity – to make it finite and defined – once again.

It is paradoxical, therefore, that the third image of infinity, present in different forms in three of the four novels examined here, is a valorized book, a textual object of desire that promises to represent the seemingly unrepresentable or access the previously inaccessible, and that is either produced in London or leads to its supposedly endless possibilities. The infinite book that Wharton's protagonist is challenged to create is the most obvious of these, but Hill's historical *Book of Negroes* and Dabydeen's multiplicitous postmodern text point to their own apparent infinities. Popular science writer John D. Barrow begins *The Infinite Book*, his fascinating account of humanity's efforts to conceptualize infinity, with the following observation:

> There is something about infinity and books. Never-ending stories, libraries that contain all possible books, books that contain everything that has ever happened, and everything that hasn't; books that write themselves, books about themselves, books about there being no books and books that end before they've begun. (Barrow, 2005, p. 1)

And while he goes on to examine the mathematical, philosophical, and religious implications of unbounded or never-ending numbers, temporalities, spatialities, lives, and more, he acknowledges that 'infinity' is also used as 'a shorthand for "finite, but awfully big"'

(2005, pp. 2-3). The latter, looser, everyday meaning is at least as relevant to the books discussed here as the more elusive literal one.

The three spaces and objects that, I argue, are associated in these novels with infinity, unboundedness, or a kind of hyper-inclusive transnational worldliness – London, the sea, and the book – are important keys to their visions of eighteenth-century Black identity. All four authors render London, and the inhabitation of the city by their Black characters, in relation to an interconnected eighteenth-century Atlantic world, a world that historians and cultural theorists have advanced as an alternative to nation-based framings of history and identity. Most well-known of these is Paul Gilroy, whose influential (if controversial) *Black Atlantic* articulates a transnational, intercultural, triangulated Black cultural history for which the ocean is a conjoining centre, a defining space, rather than a yawning emptiness between the more consequential continents. Gilroy's organizing image of ships crossing the Atlantic stands for a mobile, mutable, hybrid, fluid Black identity characterized by its infinitely variable 'double consciousness,' a concept he adapts from W.E.B. Du Bois as a legacy of 'the intimate association between modernity and slavery' (1993, p. 53). Also relevant is the work of Atlantic historians such as Bernard Bailyn, Thomas Benjamin, and many others who gather the Americas, Europe, and Africa into an integrated and mutually constitutive (if Europe-dominated) Atlantic World that began with Columbus, ended when slavery ended, and reached its peak of interconnection and cross-pollination in the eighteenth century.[3] In the words of Peter Linebaugh and Marcus Rediker, a 'many-headed hydra' of separate but intimately linked peoples emerged as a result of 'the circular transmission of human experience from Europe to Africa to the Americas and back again'; all this movement created, 'in the seventeenth and eighteenth centuries, … a new transatlantic economy' (2000, p. 2). In the same spirit, Felicity Nussbaum's *The Global Eighteenth Century* suggests adding to the established concept of 'a *long* eighteenth century' that of a geographically '*widened* eighteenth century' in which the origins of contemporary globalization can be traced (2003, p. 1). In making her case for a global and less Eurocentric view of the century, Nussbaum lists 'the increased mobility of commodities and ideas, the unprecedented expansion of global trade, improved navigational techniques, and cultural and racial mixture' that included 'the period's well-known diasporas of the Black Atlantic' (2003, p. 8). For Bailyn, such historic interactions are best understood within an 'inter-hemispheric, transnational perspective' (2002, p. xvii).

These scholars all articulate relational models of the Atlantic and the lands, peoples, activities, and ideas located around its rim, including, of course, in London; sometimes their purview extends beyond the Atlantic to incorporate Mediterranean, Indian Ocean, or Pacific worlds as well. The final scholarly text that frames this essay's readings is Ian Baucom's *Specters of the Atlantic: Finance Capital, Slavery, and the Philosophy of History*. Meticulously teasing out the implications of the notorious British slave ship *Zong* and its captain's deliberate drowning of slaves for insurance purposes in 1781, Baucom places London and Liverpool at the heart of what he calls 'the oceanic trade that had become fundamental to Britain's prosperity even as it linked the nation's capital culture to an extranational, circum-Atlantic geography of exchange' (2005, p. 52). London's role as a dominant 'space-of-flows' – where ships, capital, commodities, and people continuously came and went – became, over the eighteenth century, diluted and multiplied; it was superseded by a decentralized 'archipelago of flows' scattered around the ocean, Baucom shows. His complex theory of finance capital underpins his concept of a long twentieth century that repeats and subsumes key elements of the long eighteenth century. Indeed, when Baucom talks about 'a late-twentieth and early-twenty-first-century "now" that houses within itself an eighteenth-century "what-has-been"' (2005, p. 32), and when he argues that 'the late twentieth century inherits, repeats, and intensifies the late eighteenth' (2005, p. 41), he articulates something like the correspondences established by these recent fictions about slavery, the Black Atlantic, and eighteenth-century London.

S.I. Martin's *Incomparable World*, set in 1786 among Black loyalists promised freedom for fighting in the American

Revolutionary war, focuses on a small community of male immigrants living hardscrabble London lives of poverty, danger, and grand schemes, criminal and benign. The novel, lauded by Sukhdev Sandhu as 'probably the best evocation of historic Black London to date' (2003, p. 302), uses detailed social realism to evoke a neighbourhood (St Giles and Seven Dials) where 'dark skin drew no second glances' (Martin, 1997, p. 4), but whose many African inhabitants risked re-enslavement or coerced resettlement in Sierra Leone as a result of growing ill-feeling toward the burgeoning Black population. A kind of eighteenth-century counterpart to Sam Selvon's classic novel about post-World War Two Black immigrants, *The Lonely Londoners* (1956), Martin's novel looks explicitly forward in time in passages that question whether Black people would ever make London their own or instead remain, even two hundred years hence, 'hovering by closed doors, waiting for scraps from the master's table?' (Martin, 1997, p. 40). Together with passages referring *back* two hundred years to Queen Elizabeth I's proclamation against Blacks,[4] Leila Kamali reads such speculative, forward-looking visions as evoking a 'cyclical' history of 'hostility towards Black people' (2005, p. 144). In Martin's version of historical simultaneity and double-consciousness, then, 1596 echoes through 1786, which, in turn, echoes through a variety of late twentieth-century moments, from the Notting Hill riots of 1958 to Margaret Thatcher's Nationality Act of 1981.

Complementing this cyclical history is a circular geography; although *Incomparable World* is set almost entirely in London and, unlike the other novels discussed here, does not describe its characters' sea-voyages, its Black Londoners have been formed as much by the ocean as the city; they are denizens (if not exactly citizens) of the Black Atlantic as much as of Britain, and the indeterminate, unsettled nature of their identities is figured spatially in both urban and oceanic settings. Georgie George, King of Beggars, says he lives 'Nowhere. And everywhere' in London' (Martin, 1997, p. 109); William is described as feeling, in London, 'as cold and grey, as vague and as restless as the ocean that separated him from his kin' (1997, p. 59). The adjectives *cold*, *grey*, and *restless* could serve readily as descriptions of the metropolis, and indeed often do, but 'an even colder, whiter country than this' (1997, p. 60), William notes, is the Nova Scotia colony to which he will eventually commit himself in preference to London or the perpetual in-betweenness of a transatlantic identity. Indeed, a defining moment for William finds him relaxing in that ocean after he has escaped London for coastal Brazil; floating in the South Atlantic, he imagines himself dying there, his body 'drifting away ... at the mercy of the tides, floating forever between the Old World and the New, never sinking, never rising, and never touching either shore' (1997, p. 159). He sees himself suspended infinitely in between, belonging nowhere and everywhere, dead to the terrestrial world until he finally opts for family and agrarian stability in Canada. The man who has been singing 'London Bridge is falling down' throughout the novel decides that 'London Bridge could fall down without him' (1997, p. 170). Buckram, the other main character, also ends the narrative with hopes of leaving London for a reunion with family – in his case in Staffordshire, to which this 'Black man on a Black horse' rides 'through the white of winter' across Hampstead Heath (1997, p. 178). But his racial identity is hidden beneath his winter clothing, suggesting infinite possibilities for reinvention: 'With just his eyes visible,' the narrator says, 'he could have been anyone or nobody at all' (1997, p. 177).

Early in the novel, Buckram tells himself 'sadly, slowly, *This is home: London*' (1997, p. 42); by the end, he and William are seeking new rural homes and newly domestic family lives as an escape from indeterminacy, although the novel concludes without revealing whether these hoped-for futures will work out. It is significant, however, that their decisions and desired futures project William and Buckram into non-metropolitan space: in the overseas colony or the overland British countryside that, as Raymond Williams has shown, had comparable structural relationships to London (as peripheries to its centre) during the age of empire (1993, pp. 279-88). Kamali's reading of Martin's novel suggests that both William and Buckram ultimately turn their backs on the Black Atlantic cycle, seeking new positions outside 'the centre-stage occupied by the drama of slavery and racism' (2005, p. 158); but it is important to note as well that the infinite possibilities the men imagine for themselves as settled terrestrial subjects are located outside the spaces they have known that are most associated with infinity: the metropolitan city and the Atlantic Ocean. The infinitude of those two spaces – whether perceived or actual – is too tainted by, on the one hand, the alienation and drift of the unanchored, uprooted self, and by, on the other hand, images and realities of confinement. London is, for Georgie, a 'prison' (1997, p. 6), and the novel's earliest images of London architecture, the tenements of St Giles – with their 'numberless small chambers,' 'tidal waves of shrieks and coarse chatter,' and odour of 'human gong' (1997, p. 3) – look, sound, and smell remarkably like a slave ship, as if standing in for this otherwise unrepresented space.[5] The London of *Incomparable World* can bring like-minded Blacks together and provide a social and economic springboard to better worlds, but those worlds will not be found in the city itself. Through his detailed depiction of this previously little-known London history, Martin may hope to make the metropolis more habitable for Blacks in his own time. But two hundred years earlier, the metropolitan possibilities for his characters are finite.

Lawrence Hill's *The Book of Negroes* begins and ends in London – its narrative frame has the ex-slave Aminata Diallo writing her memoirs for abolitionists in 1802 – but from the outset, her first-person narrative frames her life as much through the sea as the city. She introduces herself as 'a broken-down old Black woman who has crossed more water than I care to remember' (2007, p. 3), then warns readers: 'Do not trust large bodies of water, and do not cross them' (2007, p. 7). The ocean, which she calls 'a bottomless graveyard' (2007, p. 7), generates consistently negative associations throughout her narrative; captured as a girl in her inland West African village of Bayo, she knows only rivers, and when she first sees 'the big water' (2007, p. 44), it therefore looks frighteningly as if a river has 'expanded into eternity' and 'water had taken over the world' (2007, p. 49). The slave ship is 'an animal in the water' with 'an endless appetite' (2007, p. 57), and as it sails she feels 'lost in a world of water' that resembles an 'endless desert' (2007, p. 68).[6] These images of infinity convey the disorientation of a locally rooted village life and identity violently displaced and, ultimately, unmoored into the vagaries of what the global meant to any eighteenth-century African unlucky enough to have it mean anything: a lottery of death or survival into enslavement, enforced mobility, and an unasked-for double consciousness. 'The ones who survive the great river crossing are destined to live two lives,' says the first African American that Aminata meets, echoing (or anticipating) Du Bois and Gilroy; but Aminata steadfastly maintains that she does not want two lives, just 'my real life back' (2007, p. 121). Hers is a tale of stubborn non-belonging, of disaffiliation, and although she becomes a shrewd and adaptive survivor, when she tallies up her successive identities, the list suggests not relational, hybrid accumulation of multiple selves so much as misidentification and out-of-placeness. She says, 'In South Carolina, I had been an African. In Nova Scotia, I had become known as a Loyalist, or a Negro, or both. And now, finally back in Africa, I was seen as a Nova Scotian, and in some respects thought of myself that way too' (2007, p. 385). Even there, in Freetown, she feels 'as lost as I had been across the ocean' (2007, p. 395); 'I felt that the colony we were establishing was neither one thing nor the other' (2007, p. 384).

In such passages, Aminata's narrative reminds us that what the Atlantic historian or theorist may see as additive relational interconnection the slave, that most reluctant of participants in circum-Atlantic modernity, feels as subtractive loss. The British may have optimistically identified the global oceans with Britannia's expansionist destiny to 'rule the waves,' but Aminata sees the ocean, London, and the lyrics to *Rule Britannia* (which she roundly critiques) rather differently. London, where she resigns herself to being buried to avoid further ocean crossings, she experiences as 'an assault on my senses' (2007, p. 450): a damp place of suffering and indignity to many, of tasteless food, acrid air, and a colour palate limited to grey, where her solicitous but self-serving abolitionist hosts initially keep her away from other Black people. (She does meet the King and Queen, but little comes of it.) However infinite and inclusive London may have seemed to many then and now, the city is limited and finite in its associations to the drained and disappointed Aminata. Reuniting with her stolen daughter, and writing her story to assist an abolitionist cause on the verge of success, are the most enabling things Aminata does in London, but even such positive developments bring less hope and possibility to this dying woman than reminders of the irrecoverable losses they both signify. It is no surprise, then, that *The Book of Negroes* she earlier helps write up in New York proves to be another tainted image of infinity and possibility. By presiding over this book of names and stories of those petitioning to emigrate, Aminata does feel newly connected to a community of Black people with pasts like hers, and doing so makes her feel less isolated. But the hope that *The Book of Negroes* is supposed to represent for its transnational Black Atlantic survivors proves severely compromised. The provision of liberty in return for loyalty that it represents is a will-o'-the-wisp: many listed in its pages are barred from leaving New York by prior claims of owners, including Aminata herself for a time; others will remain slaves in Nova Scotia or, if free, will struggle with racism, poverty, and betrayal on reaching the supposed promised land. Indeed, in a bitter irony, the parcels of land the freed slaves *are* promised by the British are never given, their delivery infinitely deferred.

Not surprisingly given its subject and narrator, then, Hill's novel affirms a local, rooted identity – one left behind in Bayo and endlessly longed for thereafter – over the violent exigencies of circum-Atlantic travelling routes and the transnational, relational identities they generate. It posits Aminata as a type, even an archetype, of the enslaved casualties of the eighteenth century's emergent Atlantic World, and her story as an antidote to any celebratory or complacently Eurocentric views of that newly globalizing world. Baucom suggests that there is a 'violence' in being seen as a 'type' – of person or nonperson, of commodity or property (2005, p. 11) – that the slave trade exemplifies and that the realist novel, whose stock-in-trade is character types, manifests in a figurative way. *The Book of Negroes* incorporates various kinds of violence – to the body, the psyche, the family, and the at-homeness of a rooted identity. In this realist novel, with its linear autobiographical narrative and debt to the slave narrative[7] (a genre that originated in the eighteenth century), the breaking of that wholeness is an ushering of the Black subject into the infinitely unsettled Black Atlantic life – here lived by a character conceived of as the epitome or aggregate of the beleaguered slave. London provides a satisfactory end-point for Aminata in a way it does not for Martin's characters, but only as a kind of last resort when other places and people have failed her — and particularly after she has aborted her journey from Freetown to Bayo upon realizing that her guide plans to betray her into slavery again. In contrast to Buckram and William's experience in *Incomparable World*, then, for Aminata London *is* the best place – the only place – to escape the perils and disappointments of the Atlantic world.

Aminata insists on writing her own narrative rather than telling it to an abolitionist scribe; having had little control over her life, she will control its public representation. Another way of putting this is to say that, like many slaves or ex-slaves who wrote their life stories, she is drawn to narrative as a way to make finite and defined what has hitherto been damagingly infinite. Mungo, the generically named protagonist of David Dabydeen's *A Harlot's Progress*, is also an elderly former slave living in London after a peripatetic life, and the abolitionists are attracted to his story too. But unlike Hill's heroine (as far as the reader can tell), Mungo asserts control over his narrative through highly selective editing and reimagining of his life experience. As he coyly says at the outset, 'I can change memory, like I can change my posture' (1999, p. 2), and it becomes clear that the polyphonic mix of first-person and third-person narrative that he shares with the reader exceeds and complicates what this 'oldest African inhabitant of London' tells the abolitionist committee's secretary, Mr Pringle (1999, p. 3). A confusing mélange of the told and the untold, the spoken and the silently thought, his narrative is full of irresolvable contradictions; it captures what Elizabeth Kowaleski Wallace calls 'the chaos of Mungo's consciousness,' which 'defies logic, linearity, and reason' as it freely blends 'past and present, here and there, living and dead, truth and lies' (2000, p. 239). Wallace's and Pamela Albert's detailed readings unpack these labyrinthine indeterminacies to support their similar conclusions that the novel 'implicates everyone equally in the brutality and exploitation that comprised the slave trade' (Albert, 2008, p. 134; cf. Wallace, 2000, p. 250). Indeed, the novel's speculative, unstable narrative so radically multiplies what happened or could have happened to Mungo that it becomes its own kind of infinite text. It seems that anything he or his abolitionist interlocutors or the reader can imagine is fair game for inclusion – a possible truth. Like the embedded narratives explaining the meaning behind the infinite number *Pi* branded into Mungo's forehead – relayed in multiple versions that suggest, in Wallace's words, that 'he is simultaneously the product of the Greek marauders, his African forebears, and white civilization' (2000, p. 249) – this parodic subversion of the slave narrative formula is a radically unstable, epistemologically flexible, oceanically fluid signifier.

As such, its relevance for the argument here is less in how it represents the eighteenth-century metropolitan scene – a conventional catalogue of smelly, noisy, visually overwhelming, and disorderly streets[8] – than its use of London, as in *The Book of Negroes*, as a final destination for its protagonist and framing location for narrative. The centre of empire, of the abolitionist movement, and of Britain's eighteenth-century Black community is also, as both novels are clearly aware, the centre of English-language textuality: of publishing and disseminating ideas. Mungo does not believe (as Mr Pringle does) 'that a single book will alter the course of history' (1999, p. 256), but his is not a single, unified book conveying a coherent truth any more than London is a single, unified city. A single text (a newspaper ad for a slave auction) may have prompted Mungo's purchase as a boy by Lord Montague, but as strong a factor in the aristocrat's impulsive decision to buy him is the completely contradictory accounts of the Thistlewood slave-drowning case (modelled after the *Zong* case) published in a dozen London newspapers. Concluding from those journalistic texts that 'truth itself was ... another commodity changing hands at a price' (1999, p. 199), Montague decides to rescue the advertised boy, Mungo, from his own commodification. It is one of the novel's cheeky ironies that Mungo's own text is as epistemologically slippery as the newspaper accounts, which purport to get at the truth of an oceanic event for a metropolitan readership coming to terms with the slave trade just as his own narrative will purport to do. The London coffee house where Mungo is sold he recalls as being 'as infernal as the slaveship's hold' (1999, p. 163), and when he meets Lady Montague, to whom he is a gift, this 'most esteemed hostess in London' is wearing 'blue clothes, ruffled like waves of the sea, little nips here and there like the beaks of fish' (1999, pp. 186, 184).[9] Not only is the ocean embedded in Dabydeen's London imagery, but Mungo describes the city as a 'cannibal region' (1999, p. 266); 'What I know of London,' he says, 'is a jungle of poor white beasts with savage looks who will eat me' (1999, p. 239) – playfully reversing a common colonialist trope.

Conflating the places and spaces of the Atlantic world and the slave trade as freely as he does times, stories, and contradictory 'truths,' Mungo unites his worlds and their peoples in a shared complicity with slavery's violence. That multiple located violence includes sexual violence; a shared implication in enslavement and abuse marks the otherwise separate locations of the African village (where Rima is a domestic slave in Mungo's house by day and 'giv[es] pleasure' to his father by night [1999, p. 35]), the slave ship (where the pederast Thistlewood frees Mungo from the infernal hold to facilitate his own pleasure), and Lady Montague's house near London (where the servants Lizzie and Jane chain Mungo down and have sex with him nightly). He escapes this final situation and his identity as a slave by fleeing the Montague estate for urban London, where he works with dying prostitutes and later tells his story (or rather, stories) to Mr Pringle. London thus provides for Mungo what it did for Aminata but not for Martin's characters: a place to escape from the oceanic indeterminacy and exploitive violence of Black Atlantic slavery, and to participate in a movement that will free future generations – potentially infinite numbers of fellow Africans – that would otherwise have faced similar fates.

Herb Wyile calls contemporary historical novels 'speculative fictions' because they so often foreground our partial and compromised knowledge of the past (Wyile, 2002, p. xii). *A Harlot's Progress* does this to the nth degree: determining the veracity of Mungo's contradictory and unstable text is a project of infinite and unverifiable speculation. Of course, 'speculative fiction' is more often used as a generic label for those close cousins of science fiction and fantasy novels that imagine alternative worlds in the past or present. Thomas Wharton's *Salamander*, the fourth and final novel to be examined here, is a speculative fiction in that sense, as well as an historical one. More magic than realist, *Salamander* inhabits an eighteenth century overlaid not just by ours but by an alternative, parallel version of its own era filled with impossible objects and experiences that imaginatively extend that century's technologies and curiosities. With its mechanical people, its castle with endlessly moving walls, its optically illusive ship, and the time-warping printing press with which its protagonist seeks to print 'an infinite book' (Wharton, 2002, p. 40), *Salamander*'s differences from the previously discussed books are as notable as its similarities. It differs from them further in being written by a white author and in being the only one in which the slave or ex-slave character is not the protagonist. While the experiences of Buckram and William, Aminata, and Mungo were variously positioned as typical or representative of eighteenth-century Black lives, their counterpart in *Salamander*, Amphitrite Snow, is as atypical and unlikely as most of what happens in Wharton's fantastic, layered tale. This female ex-slave's seafaring, swashbuckling ways may affiliate her more with Olaudah Equiano than Aminata Diallo, but she shares the latter's intelligence, cunning, and determination, and she too ends up living and apparently dying in London. And while both Canadian novels discussed here include a major event in Canada's eighteenth-century history – the 1759 Plains of Abraham battle in *Salamander*, the Black Loyalists' arrival in Nova Scotia in 1783 in *The Book of Negroes* – they subordinate Canadian settings and themes to what Baucom calls 'the geographies of circulation' of an increasingly global and relational modernity ushered in by the slave trade (Baucom, 2005, p. 36).

Purchased by a British navy admiral and renamed after a Greek sea goddess, *Salamander*'s Amphitrite Snow is shipped as cargo to the Bahamas but leads an all-female rebellion en route, taking over the ship and casting the crew adrift; introduced as a 'NOTORIOUS FEMALE BUCCANEER' (2002, p. 205), this unrooted Black woman is as global in her orientation, and as seemingly accepting of her enforced mobility, as Aminata is not. Although she appears over halfway through and in a supporting role, Amphitrite exemplifies the spirit of perpetual motion, transformation, and reinvention that infuses Wharton's novel, with its constantly moving bookshelves in the castle library and its magic printing press whose rippling 'gooseflesh type' generates new forms automatically and endlessly in pursuit of the infinite book (2002, p. 186). Set in Quebec, Slovakia, Venice, Alexandria, Macau, China, Ceylon, Cape Town, London, and the seas and oceans between, the novel abounds with images of the infinite and inclusive accessed through the solid and contained: 'the spiral of a seashell, for instance, which is itself only a fragment of a greater spiral of increase' (2002, p. 94); the tiny ship named the *Bee* that, like the castle, contains a vast and shifting labyrinth;[10] the cosmic 'web of connectedness' that allows the 'tiniest pebble' to reflect 'the entire Creation' (2002, p. 107); the description of books as 'fragile vessel[s] of cloth and paper' that take readers 'everywhere and nowhere' (2002, p. 221), 'wondrous box[es] of paper that could contain anything' (2002, p. 309); and the novel's final sentence describing the character Pica's last piece of blank metal type as 'infinity in her pocket, ... the beginning of a new collection' (2002, p. 368).

This idiosyncratic novel – which merges reality with fantasy, endings with beginnings, and eighteenth-century-novel conventions into a postmodern speculative fiction – also, like Dabydeen's, posits similarities between city and ocean. London, where most of its characters end their globe-spanning quests, has 'swampy heat' that is 'as suffocating as anything they had endured on their ocean crossing' (2002, p. 304). Full of marvels, 'London was every place they had been: the crowds and the murkiness of Venice. The heat of Alexandria. The many-tongued babble of Canton' (2002, p. 292). It is a smoky, spectral place that has been transformed over time into something almost unrecognizable to the Londoner Nicholas Flood, its few familiar landmarks 'like beckoning islands in an unfamiliar sea' (2002, p. 291); 'This was a city extending not so much in the familiar directions of the compass as in sundered zones of fortune and desolation, with hidden passageways that could transport you from one to the other in an eyeblink' (2002, p. 287).

These various passages convey something of *Salamander*'s ontological fluidity, its obsession with infinity and with correspondences between the tangible and intangible, the materially contained and the expansively all-embracing. As a speculative metafiction, its genre facilitates such dizzying linkages and shifts between the minute and material local and the infinite, cosmic global in a way the other novels cannot. As it imagines an alternative, parallel, possible/impossible eighteenth century, Wharton's novel generates characters and incidents, philosophies and technologies that cumulatively reinforce its vision of a relational, global world – a 'limitless world' (2002, p. 131) in which the ocean is as much a centre as London, a book is as viable a route to the infinite as a global journey, and a Black female slave is as capable of commandeering a ship as a white slave-master. Its sense of infinite transformative possibility is one element that makes Wharton's novel seem to reflect a sensibility more of our age than the other three, as does its sense of a disorienting world that seems simultaneously (and paradoxically) both larger and smaller, more known and more unknown, than ever.

At one point, Amphitrite tells the others sailing on the *Bee* that 'the one great law of the ocean' is '*Sooner or later you're going to run into someone you know*' (2002, p. 230). As she takes a familiar idea from urban life and transplants it to an environment where such inevitability seems much less obvious, she establishes herself as a new kind of citizen for a new kind of eighteenth century. However sad at times her story and unfulfilled her quest, however dangerous and disorienting the 'limitless world' she is plunged into often proves to be, it is a world whose newness Amphitrite, like the Europeans on the *Bee*, accepts and functions in comfortably. These Europeans' quests, unlike Aminata's, are not for home, a notion in which none of them is terribly invested. As free-floating citizens of a globe whose strange and disorienting temporalities, geographies, and spatialities they are learning to navigate, these characters seem at home everywhere and nowhere. The oceanic modernity into which Aminata is dragged kicking and screaming is one to which they, however eccentrically, seem to belong.

One could see Wharton's choice here as deracinating Amphitrite and affiliating her with the 'cartography of celebratory journeys' that Joan Dayan critiques Gilroy's Black Atlantic for perpetrating (1996, p. 7). As she almost effortlessly trades a typically Black seafaring identity (as slave) for a normally white one (as ship captain), Amphitrite joins the *Bee* as a kind of honorary European, with reminders of her Blackness coming only occasionally – as when in London she disguises herself as a servant to avoid standing out. But as Katherine McKittrick writes in *Demonic Grounds: Black Women and the Cartographies of Struggle*, it is important to see the ship as more than a space of confinement and disempowerment for Blacks:

> Technologies of transportation [such as] the ship, while materially and ideologically enclosing Black subjects, ... also contribute to the formation of an oppositional geography: the ship as a location of Black subjectivity and human terror, Black resistance, and in some cases, Black possession. (2006, pp. x-xi)

And Amphitrite has to keep struggling; the captain she usurped chases her tirelessly round the globe in another ship and finally zeroes in on her and apparently kills her, at the end of the novel, on the Thames. But she goes down fighting, defending her ship in swashbuckling fashion because, she rhetorically asks, 'Don't you know how stories like mine have to end?' (2002, p. 362).

That she does this in London at the beginning of another ocean voyage, just as her shipmate Nicholas Flood has finally printed the infinite book he has been struggling to make, is a measure of the complex ways in which Wharton's speculative text positions the capital.

London, like the ship, is also the site of what McKittrick calls 'an oppositional geography' – a space of struggle, resistance, and incipient, tentative, insecure possession. As such, the eighteenth-century London of these four novels resembles that of the many dozens of postcolonial fictions of contemporary London, to which we might see the eighteenth-century ones, loosely speaking, as prequels.[11] In the variety of experiences, of subject positions, and of reasons for the precarious purchase – the tentative traction – of their ex-slave characters, these novels both echo and anticipate the oceanic London still haunted by the legacy of slavery and racism that subsequent generations of Black Londoners – from George Lamming and Sam Selvon to Buchi Emecheta and Joan Riley – have documented in fictions of the twentieth-century metropolis. As they speculatively and variously deploy images of the infinite city, the infinite ocean, and the infinite text, these novels, like palimpsests, add foundational, supplementary layers that overlay (or underlie) the uses of those images in dozens of other London novels written before them but set later.[12]

The four contemporary novels of eighteenth-century post-slavery examined in this essay experiment with varied fictional forms but with the shared effect, among others, of teasing out the multiple infinities implied by Black subject's move from slavery to freedom, and from sea to city. As a group, moreover, these fictions respond to the paradox at the heart of the concept of infinity, the number that cannot be quantified, by showing how readily and paradoxically slaves and ex-slaves – and the maritime, urban, and textual worlds in which they find themselves – can oscillate between the infinite and the finite. Collectively, they suggest that the binary itself needs unshackling, because if the infinite can represent the hope of possibility to the ex-slave, to the newly enslaved it can prompt the dissolution of the self; and if the finite signifies on the one hand the shackled, immobilized self of slavery's commodification and 'social death' (Smallwood, 2007, p. 59), it also, on the other, points to the rooted, grounded self that was first lost to slavery, whose recovery is sought thereafter over the sea, in the city, through the book that tells one's story.

NOTES

1. Phillips published *Cambridge* in 1991 and D'Aguiar published *Feeding the Ghosts* in 1997. The novels by Martin (1996) and Dabydeen (1999) are discussed at length in this essay, as are those of Wharton (2001) and Hill (2007).
2. A fuller contextualizing of this term, as used by Ian Baucom, is found in the discussion of his book *Specters of the Atlantic*, below. The term 'space of flows' originates with Manuel Castells; see Castells, 1989.
3. See, for instance, Bailyn, 2005, and Benjamin, 2009, among other notable works by these historians. Elizabeth Mancke, another leading Atlantic historian, notes that the Seven Years' War (1756-63) and the territorial acquisitions it brought about, 'forced Britain to reassess the kind of empire it governed. For a century and a half, the government had pursued a policy of oceanic empire, emphasizing commercial regulation and the growth of a navy to defend shipping,' but it now had to 'shift from a blue-water empire to a territorial empire' (Mancke, 2002, p. 235).
4. In 1596 Elizabeth complained in a letter to civic authorities that 'there are of late divers blackamoores brought into this realme, of which kinde of people there are already here to manie' (quoted in Fryer, 1984, p. 10).
5. Stephanie Smallwood writes that, 'in the early modern world any sailing vessel was an enclosed space, where it was impossible to create physical distance.... But the crowded conditions on slaving vessels made for a level of human density unmatched on other types of oceangoing vessels' (2007, pp. 135-36).
6. As 'African captives confronted the problem of the European merchant ship, it presented them with challenges both physical and metaphysical. With regard to physical challenges, its cavernous form signaled an eerie emptiness demanding to be filled, a powerful and dangerous capacity to consume. As for the metaphysical aspect, the very habitat of the ship – the open sea – challenged African cosmographies, for the landless realm of the deep ocean did not figure in precolonial West African societies as a domain of human (as opposed to divine) activity.... In its guiding principle – the proposition that life can be lived at sea – the ship presented an oxymoron' (Smallwood, 2007, p. 124).
7. See Yorke, 2010, for a discussion of Hill's use and subversion of features associated with the slave narrative genre.

8. Mungo's first impressions of London are described on pp. 159-60, and include hints of the city's seemingly infinite space in a passage such as the following: 'But they continue to walk all morning, going down endless lanes and crossing countless squares, as if Betty [his minder] has no intention of arriving' (Dabydeen, 1999, p. 160).
9. Lady Montague is intriguingly reminiscent of Lady Caroline in Kamala Markandaya's novel *Possession* (1963), set in 1950s London. Both ladies acquire dark-skinned tropical boys as human pets, and both Mungo and Markandaya's Valmiki are exotically but inauthentically dressed up in turbans for metropolitan display. Both are associated directly with pet monkeys. Dabydeen's Lady Montague also may be modelled after Lady Mary Wortley Montagu, the eighteenth-century writer who, in a famous portrait that appears on the cover of a 1997 Penguin Classics edition of her *Selected Letters*, appears with a Black boy servant in the background. Isobel Grundy's biography of Montagu summarizes several theories as to why this writer, known mostly for her depictions of Turkish life and not elsewhere represented as having Black servants, would be so portrayed (Grundy, 1999, pp. 301-03); in her notes, Grundy references David Dabydeen's *Hogarth's Blacks: Images of Blacks in Eighteenth Century English Art*, and specifically a section in which Dabydeen examines the eighteenth-century fashion for paintings of aristocratic white ladies posing with small Black boys who look admiringly up at them (Dabydeen, 1985, pp. 30-32), as in the portrait of Montagu.
10. The castle's own labyrinth is one whose inhabitants often appeared as if from nowhere and then 'vanished with a ripple as concealed doors silently opened and closed like the valves of some giant undersea creature' (2002, p. 31).
11. For comprehensive examinations of representations of post-war London in postcolonial fiction, see Ball, 2004 and McLeod, 2004.
12. Albert argues that contemporary writers' 'transatlantic retrospections [back to the eighteenth century] can be understood on one level as trans-historical, cross-cultural dialogues enabling the authors to better understand and represent their distinct colonial histories and current encounters with neocolonialism and racism. At the same time they reflect the fact that, like those who produced the works they confront, contemporary writers are experimenting with different modes of representation to articulate and portray their experiences in a world that continues to be traumatized by political conflict and violence' (2008, p. 5).

REFERENCES

Ackroyd, Peter. (2000). *London: The Biography*. London, Chatto.
Albert, Pamela. (2008). *Transatlantic Engagements with the British Eighteenth Century.* London: Routledge.
Bailyn, Bernard. (2005). *Atlantic History: Concepts and Contours*. Cambridge, Harvard University Press.
— (2002). Preface. *The British Atlantic World, 1500-1800*. Ed. David Armitage and Michael J. Braddick. Houndmills, Palgrave Macmillan. pp. xiv-xx.
Ball, John Clement. (2004). *Imagining London: Postcolonial Fiction and the Transnational Metropolis*. Toronto, University of Toronto Press.
Barrow, John D. (2005). *The Infinite Book: A Short Guide to the Boundless, Timeless and Endless*. London, Vintage.
Baucom, Ian. (2005). *Specters of the Atlantic: Finance Capital, Slavery, and the Philosophy of History*. Durham, Duke University Press.
Benjamin, Thomas. (2009). *The Atlantic World: Europeans, Africans, Indians and Their Shared History, 1400-1900*. Cambridge, Cambridge University Press.
Brown, Laura. (2003). 'Oceans and Floods: Fables of Global Perspective'. *The Global Eighteenth Century*. Ed. Felicity A. Nussbaum. Baltimore, Johns Hopkins University Press. pp. 107-20.
Castells, Manuel. (1989). *The Informational City: Information Technology, Economic Restructuring, and the Urban-Regional Process*. Oxford, Blackwell.
Dabydeen, David. (1999). *A Harlot's Progress*. London, Jonathan Cape.
— (1985). *Hogarth's Blacks: Images of Blacks in Eighteenth Century English Art*. Mundelstrup, Dangaroo.
D'Aguiar, Fred. (1997). *Feeding the Ghosts*. Hopewell, Ecco.
Dayan, Joan. (1996). 'Paul Gilroy's Slaves, Ships, and Routes: The Middle Passage as Metaphor'. *Research in African Literatures* 27.4: pp. 7-14.
Fryer, Peter. (1984). *Staying Power: The History of Black People in Britain.* London, Pluto.

Gerzina, Gretchen Holbrook. (1995). *Black London: Life Before Emancipation*. New Brunswick, Rutgers University Press.

Gilroy, Paul. (1993). *The Black Atlantic: Modernity and Double Consciousness*. Cambridge, Harvard University Press.

Grundy, Isobel. (1999). *Lady Mary Wortley Montagu: Comet of the Enlightenment*. Cambridge, Harvard University Press.

Hill, Lawrence. (2007). *The Book of Negroes*. Toronto, HarperCollins.

Kamali, Leila. (2005). '"Circular talk": The Social City and Atlantic Slave Routes in S. I. Martin's *Incomparable World*'. *New Formations: A Journal of Culture/Theory/Politics* 55: pp. 142-58.

Linebaugh, Peter, and Marcus Rediker. (2000). *The Many-Headed Hydra: Sailors, Slaves, Commoners, and the Hidden History of the Revolutionary Atlantic*. Boston, Beacon.

Mancke, Elizabeth. (2002). 'Negotiating an Empire: Britain and its Overseas Peripheries, c. 1550-1780'. *Negotiated Empires: Centers and Peripheries in the Americas, 1500-1820*. Ed. Christine Daniels and Michael V. Kennedy. New York, Routledge. pp. 235-65.

Martin, S. I. (1997) [1996]. *Incomparable World*. London, Quartet.

McKittrick, Katherine. (2006). *Demonic Grounds: Black Women and the Cartographies of Struggle*. Minneapolis, University of Minnesota Press.

McLeod, John. (2004). *Postcolonial London: Rewriting the Metropolis*. London, Routledge.

Nussbaum, Felicity A., ed. (2003). *The Global Eighteenth Century*. Baltimore, Johns Hopkins University Press.

Sandhu, Sukhdev. (2003) *London Calling: How Black and Asian Writers Imagined a City*. London, HarperCollins.

Smallwood, Stephanie. (2007). *Saltwater Slavery: A Middle Passage from Africa to American Diaspora*. Cambridge, Harvard University Press.

Wallace, Elizabeth Kowaleski. (2000). 'Telling Untold Stories: Philippa Gregory's *A Respectable Trade* and David Dabydeen's *A Harlot's Progress*'. *Novel* 33.2: pp. 235-52.

Wharton, Thomas. (2002) [2001]. *Salamander*. Toronto, McClelland & Stewart.

Williams, Raymond. (1993) [1973]. *The Country and the City*. London, Hogarth.

Wyile, Herb. (2002). *Speculative Fictions: Contemporary Canadian Novelists and the Writing of History*. Montreal, McGill-Queen's University Press.

Yorke, Stephanie. (2010). 'The Slave Narrative Tradition in Lawrence Hill's *The Book of Negroes*'. *Studies in Canadian Literature* 35.2: pp. 129-44.

PART II

Interviews with David Dabydeen

CHAPTER NINE

Interview between Alison Ward (AW) and David Dabydeen (DD) conducted at Warwick University in August 2013

AW: *I'd like to begin by talking about your* [then] *new novel,* **Johnson's Dictionary***; I am really pleased that you have written about slavery again! There are a lot of familiar faces in this novel, or characters that we have met in your previous works, so there's Manu, of course, but also Hogarth, Gladstone (who is now Dr. Gladstone), and Miriam. Why did you decide to create this dialogue between works?*

DD: I think I planned this novel to be my farewell to arms, my last postcolonial venture. I mean, I say farewell to arms because, as you know, postcolonial literature has been identified as writing back to the Empire, and knifing back the Empire. Well this is my seventh novel and it is the last novel I will write on the colonial or postcolonial condition. I've finished that now; no more Jews, no more Blacks, no more Indians, no more masters. I have done it, I have had enough now at this stage, because I am now in China and I want to start writing about China. I am not quite sure how I will write about China but I have been making copious notes about Chinese poetry and translation; Li Bai, Du Fu and other poets, and reading some of the Chinese classic novels. I really want to spend about two years writing something about China, because this year I have been there three years, and I think I have absorbed enough to at least attempt a novel/documentary non-fiction on China which would be completely different from everything else.

AW: *Do you think that it is likely to be historical work, or are you interested in contemporary China?*

DD: It will be historical. You have to be careful about the contemporary because I don't want to get my government into trouble, as I have a diplomatic position there. I do not do contemporary, since it takes a long time – years and years and years – before you feel comfortable enough to say anything even slightly meaningful about the livingness of the time, of the contemporary period. I am interested really in certain parts of Chinese history.

There was an empress who was strangled because of a complicated set of military strategies that went wrong, and I then read about a woman who was strangled by her enemy in a dungeon somewhere in Beijing. These are interesting things about Chinese history and the darkness that emanates from political ambitions, which are different from the Caribbean experience, except that there are parallels as well. Parallels, for example, in the slave rebellions being betrayed from within; a lot of slave rebellions were betrayed from within because the leadership had different ambitions. So, whilst you are writing about China you can still have the Caribbean at the back of your mind, but the obvious subject will not be the Caribbean.

AW: *If we can return for a moment to* **Johnson's Dictionary**. *Francis is alarmed at his unconscious acquisition of words when he calls Miriam "unblemished". He says that the word appeared in his mind "like a spirit", and it seems to me that this idea of words as haunting has a particular currency in Caribbean literature. I wonder, in the absence of direct memory of slavery or pasts like Indian indenture, if literature is the most appropriate, or indeed, the only way we have to trying to remember this past, and if some of us are, perhaps more than others, haunted by these pasts or by word jumbies?*

DD: I think that, in a practical way, to try to reimagine India, ancestral India, through the English language creates a great challenge. India becomes a kind of absence, which also has kind of a hazy presence. The absence is probably stronger than the presence, but you have to write the absence if you are to write a novel about indentureship. So I suppose that's where the ghostliness comes about; the fact that India is absent because you do not have the language, and therefore the idioms, and the metaphors, and the images, to convey an ancestral India. But at the same time obviously it has a presence, which is hazy. I suppose the tension between the absence and the presence is the ghostliness. I think that probably helps to explain something about slavery and indentureship as well; why it is that today in Guyana we all believe in jumbies. Obviously the belief in jumbies has to do with an animist outlook on life, in that my grandfather, say, would be hanging all sorts of strange things on his trees; old boots, old tin cans, bottles, sometimes painted sometimes not, so as to make the earth fertile and the tree fruit-bearing. Well, there is in that obviously an animist outlook, but I think also that it must have to do with the fact that India is ghostly. It is ghostly in the sense that it is there, but we don't really know it; it is strange, it is frightening, that's why it had to be left behind. So maybe these ideas of jumbies might not only have to do with animist practices, but also to do with the sense of an absence of history.

With regard to what you said about the English language, the submarine or the unconscious motive of writing this novel *Johnson's Dictionary* was because there was really a whole generation of West Indians in the post-war period who grew up without shoes, especially the village children, who went to schools where there were no proper teachers, certainly no books. If you were lucky you had a slate and a slate pencil. There was very little food to eat, no doubt. There were children who went to these village schools, probably run by churches as charitable schools, in the 1940s, 50s and 60s who nevertheless ended up at Oxbridge or in prestigious universities, mostly in Britain, through scholarships. So how did they get there? I mean, my own uncle started off from a little village called Brighton Village; the only reason it was called British Village is because it was on the seaside [*laughs*]! He went to a barefooted, slate-wielding school [*laughs*], and then he got a scholarship to Berbice High School, closer to the city, and then from there he got a scholarship to the University of the West Indies where he read history (he was a friend of Walter

Rodney, our great historian), then he went to Oxford. And where did he go? To Pembroke College, which is Dr. Johnson's college! So I suppose when I was writing this novel I was not thinking of it consciously, but I am sure that it is a kind of tribute to people like my uncle who moved from a situation of real, serious deprivation and semi-literacy in the English language – that's what his parents were, obviously, semi-literate in the English language – and who ended up in Johnson's college, probably staying in Johnson's room, usurping the great man's possessions and presence, right? So how did they do that? Through the dictionary, through the English language; it was the only way you could do that progression, through the mastery or mystery of language. Of course, those boys and girls would have literally studied the dictionary and they probably would have picked out and learned their choice words, and that explains why over a time we ended up being Nobel Prize winners. A long trajectory of mastering the English language to such an extent that you end up Nobel Prize winners! So, of course the other thing is, in Guyana certainly, and all over the Caribbean, it is quite wonderful to go to a church on a Sunday. I went to church three weeks ago in Guyana just to listen to the sermon, which is dramatic, extravagant, flamboyant, poignant. Through the use of words, the preacher man just sweeps you away, and seizes and creates moods, and seizes your imagination, and seizes your emotions to such an extent that you want to say: "Yes, Lord, I believe! Amen!" [*laughs*], and that's through the use of words. So I suppose in the Caribbean we are just word people.

AW: *That partly answers my next question, because I wanted to ask about the way in which you create characters that are fascinated by language, puns, and word play, which I have assumed is part of your own fascination with language. But the characters you are creating – people like Miriam, Mungo or Francis – their acquisition of the English language, their punning, their subversion of the language, is a particularly radical act given their slave status.*

DD: Of course, when they use the language they don't think of a theoretical framework within which they are speaking. Really, if I have learnt anything – many things – but if I have learnt one thing from Guyana and just listening to people, it's how rich the creole is in terms of the choreography, the potential choreography on the page, and how you can skip and dance, and how you can pun, how you can just have a delight in expression. There are many Guyanese I have listened to who actually have a sheer delight in speaking; they don't really care what they are speaking about or the truthfulness of it, they would just put their few words into any conversation going, just to enliven it. Sometimes they do it provocatively – it is almost like throwing pepper, or pepper spray, in the air – they use the words like a pepper spray to get the excitement going, to get the trauma going, get the predicament going and emotions going. I have learnt that from just listening to people in Guyana interacting through words and doing it in a salacious way, in a mischievous way, in a lewd way, you know? In a provocative way. So you try to replicate that on the page as best as you can.

AW: *The images in* **Johnson's Dictionary**, *I assume that you chose those particular images…*

DD: Yeah.

AW: *…I am interested in the interplay between the images and the text, and I wondered if you could say a bit more about why you included them?*

DD: Yes. The original idea of the novel, since it was a farewell novel, was to collect a few characters, Black characters, from different European paintings, or engravings, and weave a narrative in which they had some space and some biography and some interactions, even though they were characters from different periods and different artists. That was the idea [*laughs*], and I wrote the novel with that in mind. So the illustrations really correspond to various characters in the novel, or various events in the novel, but unfortunately they have to be studied. I suppose that was sort of a sop to academia [*laughs*], but for me it wasn't academic at all, because these are images that I've spent years and years and years and years thinking about, remembering or dreaming about. So the Hogarth Blacks are like my neighbours, or members of my family; they have been with me for 20, 30 years now. They are older than some of my brothers and sisters. So you live with them, they are not academic for me: you know them, you kind of intuit what they are. So when you come to write about them, it is not a research-driven task. It is like a family history, and maybe the writer in my case was a kind of patriarch. So you just bring the family together and let them get on with it and let them talk and just write about it. I really mean that. So before I even wrote the novel I had the illustrations in mind, the figures in mind.

AW: *So did you go back and do more research for this novel? You have, of course, written before about the eighteenth century.*

DD: No, no, no, I had to do no research because I have done the research already in terms of my teaching career. And also, you know, I always find myself hiding behind Keat's idea of negative capability, which simply put I think means you do not need to know too much. If you know too much then the novel is too knowing – it's too knowing.

AW: *I have a couple more questions about this book before I'd like to move on to talking about your works a bit more generally. I think, in a way, you have already been talking about this topic, with your next project on China, and some of these incredible histories and stories you have heard, but your narrator wonders: "Who will remember, much less record nigger-me?" It seems that it is a preoccupation of characters in your works to be remembered. Do you feel compelled to try and imagine the histories of characters who, in the main, have been forgotten?*

DD: Yes, but again not for ideological reasons, but simply because I meet these characters in the streets and the bars and villages in

Guyana. Obviously they are twentieth- and twenty-first-century characters, but how they speak and how they behave and how they curse is what I imagine the eighteenth century in England to have been, if they were actually in England in the eighteenth century. So when I write and say: "who will remember nigger-me?" I am not really talking about the slaves in the eighteenth century in an ideological way: I am really talking about these people I meet who introduce me to language and gestures and modes of being. But they don't write about it, so I write about it, see? It is not ideological in terms of an academic agenda, though there are aspects of that in there. But it is really just writing about people you actually encounter… and their lives have a kind of richness to it, obviously a tremendous deprivation as well, but it is there to be written. They happen to occupy the margins of society, but when they speak and when they joke and when they socialize and when they are *just being*, concepts like centre and margin don't really operate, they're just there.

AW: *There are lots of writers who write imaginatively about the past of slavery, and there has been a good deal written about their postmodern approaches to the historical archive; the gaps in the archive; the inaccuracies, and whose version of the past we can trust. But the way in which you return to history is striking. It is often quite antagonistic, perhaps; it is certainly exciting. Take, for example, the character of Gladstone, whom you have written about in* **The Counting House** *– in that novel, you did something different with "the facts" about Gladstone, altering the character and making him your own. In* **Johnson's Dictionary** *he's now Dr. Gladstone; I wondered what your approach to history was?*

DD: Well obviously there is a whole academic debate about what is history, whether it is Carr's book or *Tropics of Discourse*, which was…who wrote *Tropics of Discourse*?

AW: *Hayden White*.

DD: Hayden White. And there is a whole lot of debate about what is history? I think, really, it is very simple in my case, very simply, it is just two factors. One is Wilson Harris, who has been a kind of permanent presence in my imagination, let's put it like that: a permanent, almost daily, occurrence in my mind, who spoke about the unfinished genesis of the imagination, which I take to mean that the sources and outcomes are fluid at all stages. He would say that they are quantum, which means that they are inexplicable, they're immeasurable, they're impossible to define. So if you go with Harris's concept of the imagination then you can have fluidity, a flexibility, an eccentricity about history and historical events and characters. Then if you add to that my own upbringing, which was a kind of quasi-Hindu upbringing, where the belief in reincarnation was strong, then, you know, it means that Gladstone could be reincarnated as Hogarth, could be reincarnated as Dabydeen, could be reincarnated as a cockroach [*laughs*].

So, basically, at a deeper level, what it means is that the characteristics that Hogarth has, or you have, or I have, are also what Gladstone has. So we call him Gladstone and he has the historical baggage around him. You call him Hogarth and he has historical baggage, and so have I. But actually, deep down there is what D.H. Lawrence used to call the carbon element, the carbon element which connects all of us, which makes all of us anonymous, because we belong to a set of values, a set of moods and emotions which you can just call human. So I suppose the Hindu notion of reincarnation, plus the Harris, helps me to be imaginative on the page. At the same time I am still an eighteenth-century person, and I always remember Dr. Johnson saying this is all nonsense even before it was created by Harris. He said: "when you kick a stone and you stub your toe on the stone, you'll know what pain is!" So I know what reality is as well, and at the same time, reality keeps coming to you. I remember when I first arrived in China, bewildered obviously, and a bit lost, looking over the balcony in the embassy and seeing a cat playing with a bird; it was not killing the bird right away, but torturing the bird in its own cat way. And then a whole lot of birds in the trees were screaming (this must be a species of bird that look out for each other), and they were just screaming and screaming, and this cat was killing this bird slowly. But then you are suddenly braced up with reality and you think, what should I do [*laughs*]? What can you do really? Later on (well, actually what I did was, I took a plastic water bottle and pelted it all at the cat, and I don't think it really helped…), but you think about it for years later, and I also remember Herskovits the anthropologist saying you should have got off your balcony and moved among the real, and maybe you would have understood what was going on, right? And then you ask questions like; why did this happen? And then you remember what you learnt when you were young, Wittgenstein saying you are asking the wrong questions – to get an answer you have to ask the right questions. So maybe I was asking the wrong questions: why is this happening, what is the truth of it? And that is the wrong question. You know it is the wrong question, because there is no answer. So you kind of brood about these things. Harris's idea of "non-being". Harris argues that non-being is not absence, non-being is…not a state – it is a *realm* as it were, or a thing of its own. At the same time you think about the cat and the bird and other cruel things that happen, so reality braces you against the wall.

AW: *You have written about the UK, India, Guyana, Africa, and you currently live in Beijing. This is a question about labels: do you consider yourself a transnational writer, or are you still a British writer? Are these kinds of labels ever helpful?*

DD: Oh, I'd prefer it if you said I was a trans-dresser or something…a transvestite writer [*laughs*], as the other two descriptions are a little bit heavy! No, labels have been very useful in my writing career, in that you get invited to different conferences depending on which hat you are wearing. So you see the whole world as a British writer, or a Caribbean writer, or a postcolonial writer, and I suppose it has been helpful to librarians and booksellers and the trade, you know, in a practical way, in a practical economic way. In other ways I don't think it's really relevant, the label, because I remember Salman Rushdie saying that his ancestor was necessarily an Indian (well, obviously Indian), but also Lawrence Sterne, so he's an eighteenth-century Sternian, if that is the right adjective. So the labels are practical for booksellers and distributors, and maybe buyers of books, but otherwise they are not, especially now the internet has abolished time, more or less, and space.

When you get older what really, honestly, matters is the writing, not even the readership. I mean, you *hope* there is a readership, but it doesn't really matter. It's just getting the writing going, because you know time is running out and the only thing that will keep you happy for a little while, before the winged chariot hurrying near catches your arse, is the writing. And actually, therefore, after a while, you do lose ego; what matters is to get the language as lavish as you can. I go the other way, I don't go the spare way. I can see the beauty of writing in a sparse and spare way, but I would rather keep that for the poetry, and for the prose you just want to be lavish and for the language to carry the meaning by itself, so that the meaning of the work is in the language. It's in the language, yes.

It's the same way that I look at a painting. The two painters I have huge admiration for are, obviously, Aubrey Williams, and also Paul Klee. I was looking at some of Williams's Shostakovich paintings. I don't know whether you have seen that series? They are haunting, they are colourist, expressionist; expression through colour, meaning through colour, and I found the same when I once had the great privilege of going to Switzerland, and I was taken to the Paul Klee Museum. I remember thinking if I could write like these painters, Aubrey Williams and Paul Klee: layers and layers and layers of meaning without pictorial representation, but the meaning layered through colour – it's a miracle! So I thought, if I could write like these geniuses, the way they paint, then at least it's worth the venture. So I just want words to be like colours and what they convey – the message, the metaphysics as it were – what they convey should come through the colour of the words. It is hard to explain what I mean, but when I do the writing that's what I want to do.

Now, I can put it another way. I can write anywhere once there is noise and people around; in other words, once there's colour around. I found a café in Cochin [Kochi] where I could sit out, light my cigarette, have some coffee, and look out onto the road and have a table with a fan – a normal café – and I can write. You look out at the road and the most wonderful things happen. I remember the last time I was there a whole lot of tuk-tuks, auto-rickshaws, with green flags representing some party, and having a rally, hooting and waving the green flags, right? Then, after about eight minutes that was finished, they went to some other part of Cochin to propagate their political message, about seven nuns walked past. You don't normally see nuns walking, and they were eating ice cream cones, and the ice creams were green! They were eating ice cream cones, happily – Indian nuns, because Cochin is a very Catholic space (Vasco Da Gama was once buried there) – and then they walked past, and then, guess what? Two goats came walking in the middle of the road and they squatted, right in my view, and they did their goat droppings, which were again bright green, right? So what connects these three green things? Now, in the meantime, you're in the middle of a sentence, so when, by the time you see all of this magic and return to the sentence, you must make the sentence strange and the whole of that paragraph has got to be strange [*laughs*]. So really it is about using words in a way that estrange the words themselves from a recognizable reality. A lot of writers have said that. I learnt this from D.H. Lawrence as a young boy, when Lawrence said the writer should slit the umbrella of convention, and many other writers have said that it's all about estrangement; magic and estrangement. The great crime, the great killer, is obviously mister cliché, you know? So you've got to kill the cliché to get to the magic.

AW: *Do you find that most of your writing happens in these kinds of spaces: cafés, spaces like that?*

DD: Oh God, I would die if I had to get a scholarship or have to go to some Scottish castle in a room all by myself! I definitely wouldn't be able to write. I like the noise and I like the people. Coming back to this café, it is a wonderful café in Cochin because there are a lot of tourists there. So you get the hippies, of different ages. Some of them '60s hippies, '70s hippies…men have their beads and long hair, and you know, marijuana is available, and you can go to the art galleries. And then you get the young girls with their flowing robes and sandals, and they are all beautiful, you know? And you sit there and you are writing and you are having coffee, and you sit there and you look up and say hello or not hello and just…it interrupts the normalcy of writing, so that when you look back down at the page you can find some sort of inspiration to make the sentence strange.

AW: *Did you always want to be a writer?*

DD: Yes, yes. I used to write when I was about eight, nine…certainly ten, eleven. By the age of fifteen I was writing all the adolescent nobody-loves-me poetry, and by the age of sixteen I was writing my Nobel Prize speech (at the age of sixteen you are certain that this is Nobel prize quality – thank God it is all lost now!). It must have been really immature, teenage, no girls, no sex, no fun, no money kind of stuff, nobody loves me stuff. Then at the age of seventeen, I think, pompously borrowing a typewriter and doing a first novel in verse…well, you run out after two pages and then you find something else to do that is more meaningful. I never really wanted to be anything else but a writer, but of course to be a writer you have to support yourself, so then you have to be an academic, a teacher.

AW: *So, as this young aspiring writer, you went to Cambridge University and studied English. How did you end up doing a PhD on Hogarth?*

DD: Well, the syllabus in Cambridge allows you to see the interaction between literature, music and art. So I just discovered Hogarth almost by complete accident through reading. I think it was through an essay on Fielding, which talked about the influence of Hogarth on Fielding, if I remember rightly. But before then I had a wonderful boyhood friend called Philip Bradley; he and I went to school together in South London and he was very, very intelligent and cultured, and he would say; "Let's go to the Tate Gallery!" I always remember looking at Turner's steam engine painting and thinking, where is the train [*laughs*]? What is this? What nonsense is this? So I suppose through my friend Philip I got interested in art, and being at the University of Cambridge, which allowed you to look at correlations between literature and art, and in fact architecture, that helped me to move in a certain direction. I remember reading a magnificent book on medieval literature (I have forgotten the scholar's name now) where he compared Chaucer's *Trolius and Cressida* to the building of a church and a steeple, and he was able to look at the brick images and the building images in that poem and argue that, when Trolius died, that was the movement of the steeple. So basically he was able to look at the architecture embedded in the poem. And then he was also able to look at cathedral structures, floor plans, to show how certain medieval poems were also based on architectural floor plans of cathedrals. That's magnificent, isn't it? It is a magnificent way of looking at literature [*laughs*].

AW: *It is interesting, because it takes us back to your comments on Williams a moment ago: I think that, in your words, you do paint. You obviously have this engagement with artists like Turner or Hogarth, but your works are also very visual, and, although you may disagree, something that I think we can see is the fascination with the beautiful and the ugly. You've talked in the past about the use of creole in your poems in* **Slave Song** *as being useful in capturing the disturbing nature of that time of slavery and indenture; in* **Turner***, we have a wonderful, and unsettling, critique of Turner's painting, and possibly the nature of art created on slavery, but it is also a very beautiful poem. This combination of ugliness and beauty seems to be in all of your works, and I wonder if this stems from your fascination with art and your role as an art historian?*

DD: Well, it is a difficult question, but the answer is yes, because Hogarth's characters are ugly. They are ugly, he makes them ugly because he is a satirist, but then beneath the ugliness – the syphilitic sore, the grimace, the brutal forehead – there is a compassion and humanity, and I think a desire to intuit the beauty that emerges from the predicament of that particular character. So naturally that is something learned from art, but then it's being Guyanese as well, where there is ugliness all around you in terms of people being poor, people being distressed, people dying before their time, wife beating, cheating, competitiveness and stealing and all of that, which you get…well, I suppose you get in Coventry as well…you certainly get it in a deprived society, and yet you have your mother looking very beautiful, and your sisters and your aunties, and your teachers are gentle and learned and kind. So it's from, I suppose, from living itself. I may have learnt it aesthetically from looking at paintings, but it's from the actual processes of living. Yes, at the end of the day, you have to believe in the divine comedy as it were, that beauty (gosh, this is such a cliché!), but beauty is truth and truth, beauty.

AW: *You have also talked about your interest in Hogarth's work and his representation of Black subjects as being connected to a quest to belong in twentieth-century Britain.*

DD: Yes, First let me say that I have a very personal relationship with William Hogarth. Whenever I am in England I visit him and we have a few little words between us; he doesn't normally speak back and I don't actually speak, it's kind of a silent dialogue. And I normally thank him for giving me a chance to work on his art. I can't remember what he says, but he's always been a glum little bugger anyway, so I shouldn't think he should say anything generous! But after having worked with him, especially the Black characters, it made me realise obviously that we have been living in Britain, in a visible way, for hundreds of years, and once I realised that through my initial research on Hogarth, you felt more at home, you know? And then you did other research in Black British history, which was very nascent in the 1980s, and then the more you read, the more you realise, that yes – we have been part of the making of this society, and therefore I have a claim to belongingness. So studying Hogarth's Black figures certainly brought me to that level of comfort in terms of a sense of belonging to space, which I can say my ancestors or my friends' ancestors occupied and contributed to. But I would not say it's all one-sided; I would say I helped Hogarth a lot, he owes me as well, in that I brought out his Black people which nobody before had done. So if you go to Hogarth's house now there is a whole panel on Black people in Hogarth; I helped to bring out my friend's hidden agenda, so it has been a two-way act. And then, because of *Hogarth's Blacks*, friends of mine, Steven Martin (S.I. Martin, who wrote that lovely book *Incomparable World*) and Lawrence Scott, have acknowledged the influence of *Hogarth's Blacks* on their work. So then we are taking Hogarth from being a dead, white, eighteenth-century man and, first of all, we are revealing hidden layers of his work, and then we have West Indian and Black British people writing about him. So we have also rescued him from being dead. And he, in return, has given my imagination characters who become live on the page; it's a mutuality.

AW: *It's been almost 30 years since* **Hogarth's Blacks** *was published, in which your traced the relationship between art and slavery, and you returned to this area again in* **Turner**, *also in* **A Harlot's Progress** *and once more in* **Johnson's Dictionary**. *I wondered if you thought, in this 30-year period, that Britain has become more aware of its role in the past of slavery, or slavery's embeddedness not just in its past but in the present?*

DD: Yes, I think 30 years on there's been a tremendous evolution in the awareness of Black British history; of the need to acknowledge the role that, say, the Caribbean played in the construction of modern Britain, and therefore the need for academies and schools to try to incorporate into the syllabi literatures that deal with our histories and cultures and our experience of encountering Britain. There is no doubt that has happened over the last 30 years. It has also happened because

Black people have been in Britain creating, constructing, achieving, and rioting as well, when occasion merits it, according to certain opinion. London now is more multicultural, more visually multicultural, multiethnic, certainly than 30 years ago. So there is movement in Britain over 30 years. Of course there are drawbacks, and two steps forward, one step back. I think I am optimistic about the recognition of Britain as a multiethnic space, a multiethnic place, and that makes it more comfortable to live in Britain now than, say, 30 years ago, or certainly 40 years ago. Forty years ago it was still skinhead time, and the nakedness of racism was there. You would see it scrawled on the pavements, on the walls, on the train stations, "niggers go home" or "NF". That is now unacceptable. I have not seen racist graffiti for a long time in England. So things have moved ahead to such an extent that Princess Diana may have married a Muslim. So one has to be optimistic about the human capacity to understand, and to rationalise and to recognize each other.

AW: *Could we continue this talk about how Britain has changed, about the presence of Black people in the UK, by thinking about your work* **Disappearance***? This is such an important book, in placing a Black migrant from Guyana in rural Britain. So often, as you know, there is a link between urban centres and Blackness, and your work challenges that assumption. I know that its speaks to Naipaul's novel* **The Enigma of Arrival***, but I wondered what else drew you to write about the English countryside in this work?*

DD: Honestly, the sheer horror of finding myself in an English village or an English village pub, where you squirm with embarrassment because visually you are an oddity. I mean, this came across quite strongly in Naipaul's *Enigma* as well, where he is walking down this Salisbury countryside and looking at and absorbing the landscape, and he turns a corner and there is a white person there and suddenly he falls back on his ethnicity, or his sense of colour, or his sense of alienness. I found myself in an English village on many occasions because I had an indigenous English girlfriend outside of Hastings, a place called Fairlight – even the name of the village, "Fairlight", suggests how genteel it was, or how white it was. So I used to go and visit her in the evenings so as not to disturb the social equilibrium of the place, and then gradually in the daytime, and then I got to learn about the village. I borrowed her dog, so I would go walking with the dog, and you'd meet white people who were also walking their dogs, and we would have conversations; the dogs broke the ice, basically. The novel is actually dedicated to the dog. So it's the sense of isolation. It's just the sense that Black people and the English countryside are oxymoronic, but now it is different...a little bit different, though I shouldn't imagine too different, because we find security and employment in cities sooner than we would find them in the villages. I would imagine that in England the villages are still alien territory to Caribbean, African or Asian people – still ye olde England, ye olde England would welcome neighbours, but probably not too many.

AW: *You also talked about seeing the English countryside through a lens or a frame of Constable or Wordsworth, but the countryside has changed a lot since their work. What does the British countryside represent to you today?*

DD: Well, I could never, ever, ever connect with the English countryside, because I always felt estranged there, always completely lonely and completely...you had a complete sense of not belonging to the country, never mind the countryside, the only way you appreciated the countryside, was through art and literature, certainly Wordsworth, D.H. Lawrence, Ted Hughes, Dylan Thomas, Thomas Hardy. So the countryside was always mythic; iconic and mythic. I mean, I can't see myself walking, going on a walk in the English countryside. It just feels alien, it'll take some time before we grow into the countryside. I think I said that in *Disappearance*, it might take centuries for us to grow into the countryside. I think it is the last bastion of Englishness, and if we get in there creatively (and when I say "we" and "get in" I mean colloquially) – creatively, imaginatively – I think that is when we can have, or I can have, a sense of true belonging.

AW: *Your writing is always very playful and very ironic. You include references to figures like Naipaul or other people that you have known – other writers and friends – and I get the impression, rightly or wrongly, that you are sometimes having a chuckle at the critics or at the academy. Of course, I am thinking in part of your wonderful poem* 'Coolie Odyssey' *and its lines that have been quoted over and over again (I am going to quote them once more now!): "See the applause fluttering from their white hands/Like so many messy table napkins."*

DD: Well, I have changed that line: I have changed "white", which is a nasty word in that context, to "fair", which is more ironic and more ambiguous. Fair meaning white, but fair also meaning maybe there is something there to the applause, right? There is some justice to it, right? The academy had fed me, and sustained me, and inspired me, but I have never really been an academic, or never wanted to be an academic, or be a scholar and write books, scholarly books. You had to do one or two to show your credentials, to get your tenure as it were, but once that was done, you kind of kept a low profile and did your poetry and your fiction, and hoped that nobody bothered you. So therefore you can chuckle, not maliciously, about your academic past and at a type of pretentiousness; getting up to read Foucault, Derrida and Lacan, and trying to impress your students with your knowledge of theory, when deep down you really did not care a damn, but you had to do it to inspire them to study and write their essays [*laughs*]. And therefore you are chuckling at yourself and at your fraudulence. That's a heavy work, but I suppose I was a bit of a fraud as an academic, or a pretend academic. And therefore you have to have a sense that you have survived by the skin of your teeth. And again, the laughter has to with Anancy; you survive on your wits. You duck and dive, and you keep a low profile, and you do your work and try to persuade the opposition that actually you are on their side, and then basically you work up to your pension! So yes, taking you back to the word "fraudulence", I would say I was certainly an Anancy character. When we were children in Guyana we grew up on Anancy stories; we never knew Anancy was West African, we used to call them Nancy stories. So we all told each other at bedtime Nancy stories and these are obviously stories about surviving and trickery, the trickster figure, you know? Obviously, as children we didn't know we were doing trickster figures, but that is what we were doing. So yes, some of the characters, many of the characters of the fiction I write, are trickster figures.

AW: *Until very recently you've been in the position of being both author and critic...*

DD: Yes.

AW: *...You have provided notes to **Slave Song**, for example, as a nod to T.S. Eliot, and you have produced numerous excellent critical works alongside the creative ones: ae you ever conscious of Dabydeen the critic as you write, or is that a part of yourself that you have to put aside in order to write creatively?*

DD: No, I don't think you have to put it aside. I mean, you try to separate yourself from theory, if I can put it like this, but not necessarily criticism. I grew up with literary criticism, which was largely non-theoretical, which as basically F.R. Leavis saying: just look at the text, look at it closely. When I was studying literature, that was the approach; always an appeal to the text and textuality of the text, by which I mean the rhythm, or the image, or the colour. So the textuality of the text was always privileged over the philosophy of the text, so I don't want to ever separate myself from that. But to write, one tries to keep a complete distance from theory. Unfortunately it does creep in, but then if it creeps in too much, obviously you've failed.

AW: *Lots of writers say that they never read reviews of their novels or poetry collections, but I get the sense that you are quite interested in the reception of your work. Am I correct in saying that?*

DD: Yes, when I was younger, because of the boost to your ego and the encouragement to keep writing, and when you are older because you don't want to be forgotten or neglected [*laughs*]. Not in the process of writing – in the process of writing you don't think about anything other than the writing, I tell you that honestly. I remember having not written anything for four months and going to the university library, and taking up my pen and my notepad and writing, and actually looking at my hand moving, not so much attending to the words – obviously the words come out intelligently – but actually marveling at my hand moving, thinking: my God something is happening! So in the process of writing, that is what you think about, the magic of your hand moving. As Walcott would say: "from the left hand margin to the right hand margin". That's all you think about, the left hand margin and the right hand margin, and then you know how many lines there are in a page, which is 33 lines, and then you have to think: left hand margin, right hand margin, top of the page, middle of the page, end of the page. So that's all you are concerned about really, and not reviews or what will happen tomorrow. In the making of the thing it is just the sheer pleasure in the making of the thing. When you have made it and people curse you for it, I have had a little bit of revenge. In my first novel I had a really bad review, and being young I took it very badly and I did say to my agent: "Could we sue?" And she said: "No, you cannot sue!" So what I did was, in the second novel I created a character who was slightly pornographic, and lazy, and lascivious, and I named it after this critic, but kept enough space in the names for the critic not to be recognised, but also to be recognised. So you do get your revenge on the page [*laughs*]. I have to be honest with you, if someone really upsets you it helps you to write a bit, encourages you to carry on, so that you can get your revenge [*laughs*]!

AW: *I shall be careful what I say...* [*laughs*]!

DD: I can say very briefly that the new novel has characters in it who were rooted in the University of Warwick's break up of the Centre for Translation and Comparative Studies. The novel got to the point of tedium for me, or stasis, and suddenly a big fight happened at Warwick, not just at Warwick but many other universities, a big departmental fight happened. I was on study leave so I was involved with it, but not very involved with it. But it really gave the novel a spurt because suddenly I was able to create these characters who were partly inspired by what was going on, but obviously not ultimately. But that breakdown, you try to salvage something from it.

AW: *In the past you have talked about the influence of Caribbean writers on your works; in particular, the first time you read Naipaul's novel* **Miguel Street** *you felt that it was about you, and quite a few Caribbean writers have spoken of a similar sense of joy of recognising themselves in literature. But unlike that first generation of Indian-Caribbean writers like Naipaul and Selvon, in* **The Counting House** *and your poetry collections you chose to explore the past of Indian indenture. What made you want to write about this past in the first place?*

DD: Well, it's the context in which you live, isn't it? I grew up as an Indian, or an Indo-Guyanese and, coming to England, moved more easily within an Asian community, so it is in your makeup, and at some stage you will write about it. In my case, I had no desire to write about it except when a Black Rastafarian woman pulled me up at London University in 1985 when I was giving a talk on the iconography of Black people in English art, and said to me: "Why are you writing about *our* people? Why don't you write about your own people?" So that pushed me back to that sense of ethnicity, and so therefore I thought, fine, I will take your advice, and I wrote *Coolie Odyssey*. Why do you write? You write because it is there to be written, it is largely unwritten. It is a new subject, it is a new layer to Caribbean historiography and Caribbean literature. It is a challenge, and you don't have to be Indian to write about Indians. I quarrelled strongly with Brathwaite, who said he doesn't know what the Indo-Caribbean character is because it does not emerge as prolifically in literature as, say, the Afro-Caribbean history and culture. And I wanted to say to Brathwaite, well you go and write about it, go and imagine it! The writer's imagination is sovereign, as Harris would say, the imagination is sovereign, and I feel I can have a go at writing about Chinese characters. I might not write it as richly as somebody else might, but that's probably because of the poverty of my imagination, but I can write about it. So here is a whole new area, relatively new area, of Caribbean history that can be explored by writers of any ethnicity, and that goes for the Chinese and certainly for the Portuguese in the Caribbean. So, yes, it was exciting – I really enjoyed it. It was a serious pleasure writing *The Counting House*, but this is how it works, though: I did not know how to end it. I really didn't know how to end it, until I invited Pauline Melville to Warwick, my Guyanese friend, and she read from *The Ventriloquist's Tale*; a whole splurge of words, and you know that novel finished within about 10 days because of Pauline. I have told her that. So you are inspired by another writer and not by your ethnicity. And that novel would have been stuck if Pauline by the grace of God did not come to do her reading! So yes, it is exciting, it is an exciting frontier and I hope a lot of writers take it up; I know a lot of scholars are, an increasing number of scholars – scholars like yourself and Miriam Pirbhai, and so on.

AW: *In some Indian-Trinidadian novels, like Ramabai Espinet's* **The Swinging Bridge** *or Peggy Mohan's* **Jahajin**, *it seems for older generations that the past of Indian indenture was something that was best forgotten; they were in some ways too close to that past to want to remember it. Instead, it has been the younger generation that have wanted to learn more about their indentured ancestors, and I wanted to know how India and the past of indenture was remembered when you were growing up as a child in Guyana?*

DD: Simply, it was not. The only India we knew was through Bollywood and through the *Ramayana* where India was a mystical space, and there was Rama and Sita, and there were fables around them, and India was a magical narrative. Or else India was

Bollywood, which is another magical narrative, and my friend Prof. Clem Seecharan has written brilliantly about this – India and the Caribbean imagination. So Clem has argued (and I would agree with him) that there are two reasons why the older generation do not remember India and did not pass that memory down to their children: A, they were too busy working and saving and getting on, and B, they probably came from carnage and dark pasts. Maybe they were fleeing moneylenders? I did say when I launched my edition of *The Richmond Diary* that it may well be, and actually I hope, that my great-great grandmother was a prostitute fleeing from India, or a widow; that would give her something special – at least I can speak about her in a special way. So many of us were running away from prostitution, the badge of widowhood, poverty, famine, imperialism and the Indian mutiny, and I don't think those people wanted to remember that. And they started again wonderfully by renaming themselves; many of them gave themselves Brahmin names – they upgraded and travelled imaginatively First Class! Yes, they didn't want to be known as *chamars* or whatever, low castes, and what is wonderful today about Guyana (I do not know so much about Trinidad), but no Indian knows their caste. A few people will tell you they are Brahmins, and you just snigger at them. It is meaningless to be Brahmin in Guyana: they don't know the language, they can't read the Sanskrit, so what is the point in being a Brahmin? So it has been a great equalizer, the middle passage, and it is for that reason that it differs from the middle passage for Africans…Well, it was an equalizer for Africans, too – people of different tribes were all on the same boat and fed the same food – the same with the Indians, except that the Indians in the early boats had special Muslim chefs, and so on. So there are very fruitful and creative comparisons between the two middle passages which I hope scholars are now working on.

AW: *You said that your literary imagination is very much Guyanese, and you are of course the Guyanese Ambassador to China. I wondered if you still consider Guyana to be your home, and if not, what Guyana means to you?*

DD: Well, I am Guyana's Ambassador to China, Japan, Malaysia, South Korea, Thailand and Singapore, so now I feel an incipient Asianness descending on me, which is why I want to write about China at least. Home? That's a very difficult one, but certainly it is not Guyana – just imaginatively. I have only lived there just a few years of my life. England…I am still not comfortable living in England. Maybe in the metropolis, where the multiculturalism is an event, and daily, and lived. China, not really. I was thinking of going to live in India, but maybe India is a little bit too crazy and uncertain, and then ultimately I do not have the language. So I have really seriously been thinking in the three years since I left England where to move to. The latest thinking in Barbados, which is called "Little England". You are still in England, but far away from it, so, yes, there is no home as such. Well, put it this way – that sounds too poignant or self-pitying – there are many homes, or many potential homes, and it is just a matter of deciding where to settle down, but whatever I do, I would always be writing about Guyana in some shape or form; even through it might be writing about China or India, it would be echoes of Guyana. In the same way, when I write about slavery I am also echoing indentureship and vice versa. Manu was African, but Manu is also the writer of the Hindu laws of India.

AW: *Can I ask you about your ambassadorial role: is there such a thing as a typical day?*

DD: I think, yes; one has got accustomed to saying; "one has got accustomed!" I have got accustomed to wearing a suit on a regular basis and biting my tongue. For example, in China, since you are representing your country, you cannot talk about censorship or human rights, because you are only a small country. So what you do instead, when you do official talks in front of officials about the Caribbean, you always mention the Nobel Prize. I also mention that we came from a relatively deprived – well, not relatively – a deprived background. A background of deprivation and dispossession and colonization, and we rose up and read and ate the dictionary, and got two Nobel Prize winners, Naipaul and

Walcott. That is a way of talking about human rights and about freedom of expression without insulting the Chinese or preaching to the Chinese. The "N" word in China is like the "F" word in England, because their Nobel Prize winner, Lui Xiaobo is in prison for quite a while. China does not like criticism from outsiders. China gets upset from criticisms from outsiders, many of which are misguided. The West is so envious of China that they only report what is bad about China, and China has removed 300 million people from abject poverty, which is the greatest act of human rights the world has ever seen. People are eating now, and going to school, and being able to travel, and having a mobile phone – that's human rights, access to material rights. So I do not criticize China for human rights in a way that is westernised or automatic. I recognize what China has achieved, where China is going or promises to go, and then you still have to talk about writing as a necessity for writers to be free. So I do that through the Nobel Prize. I do that through Naipaul and Walcott. I'm sure they don't realise they have those roles in China, but I have given them those roles! Basically, you are engaged in those kinds of intellectual discussions, but actually most of the work is applied physics rather than theoretical physics. It is about accessing foreign aid as well as concessional loans for your government, to do certain infrastructural and economic projects. So basically you are dealing in millions of dollars; as an academic, if you are lucky someone might get the office a scanner, but in China you deal with hundreds of millions of dollars, none of which is yours. So, basically I see the job as promoting the interests of Guyana through accessing loans from the Chinese; loans and aid. Now and again you can do something cultural. I have asked the Chinese for the last two years for some money to build an arts centre, a performing arts centre, an art gallery, a museum, a cinema, a film-editing studio, a children's library, and so on, in Guyana and they have more or less agreed. They are sending a physical feasibility team in August/September to see exactly what it is that we want. So now and again you can push the arts and the culture. The Chinese government has also agreed to set up a Confucius Institute at the University of Guyana, which is a huge boost for our University and makes a linguistic bridge between China and Guyana. So there's occasion to do that kind of work and, above all, the Chinese people are unbelievably courteous. There's something about the Chinese character – I don't want to generalise – but there is a certain type of courtesy and courteousness there. As a foreigner, if you stop a Chinese person to ask where something is, they will walk you there if necessary. There is just something about the Chinese character – I can't generalise – but the Chinese people I meet; there is just a certain kind of decency.

AW: *Thank you so much for your time.*

DD: Thank you.

CHAPTER TEN

Interview between Diane Barlee (DB) and David Dabydeen (DD) conducted at Warwick University on 18 May 2016

DB: *So what got you interested in poetry?*

DD: I think a sound colonial education. In that the curriculum that I had as a boy in school was basically – the English curriculum, that involved having to read – not having to *read*, but exposure to Shakespeare and Wordsworth and the great English poets. I think this is just not in Guyana, but all over the Caribbean now. So a sound colonial education. That coupled with our own native literatures. Whether it's the religious literature of the Hindus or the Holy *Quran* of the Muslims, because those are books that are sung. They're sung. They're recited. They're not just read silently. So certainly that would have been an influence in terms of ones awareness of how words have rhythm and music. Certainly from the *Gita*, and the *Ramayana*, the Hindus and the Muslim and the *Quran*. And then I grew up in England obviously and followed the curriculum.

DB: *Did you have books in your house at home?*

DD: Well, in, in, in – not really. Not really. Not really, and the schools didn't provide books. It was a largely – unless you lived in the city and you were part of a literate, literary middle class, aspiring to the condition of Afro-Saxondom. In other words you wanted to have a shirt and tie, wear gloves, and have tea, and all that stuff, right? And there was a class of people who were part of that colonial set up. They knew, really promoted literature and the arts. So we had very early on a literary magazine. We had theatres and so on, but that was for the city folks. They would have books. In the country side? No. You'd get religious texts. Yah, religious texts. I tell you this because in my first novel I went back to my village in the countryside and I left one of my novels there. It was a novel based in that village. And when I came back a few days later to go and visit there was a man there called – he said, "My name is Gura," and I thought maybe he was somebody had interfered with his grandmother, some Scottish man, because Guaire [sp?] is a Scottish name. So, as I was pondering all of this colonialist history he said, "It's short for gorilla." Because everybody calls him Gorilla. Everybody in Guyana has a nickname: Big Foot, Big Eye. [Laughter]

He said to me, "Why?" and he was very serious. He was a drunkard, but he was sober when he spoke to me. He said, "Why did you use the word 'F'' in your novel?" (I'd used the 'F'' word.) He said, "Did you get permission?" I said, "Well, you don't really need permission, you know." He said – and he really confronted me on this, but in a lovely way, but in a serious manner, right? And he said, "Why didn't you use the word, if you had permission, why didn't you use the word 'sex' instead?" I apologized. Later on I found out that his only acquaintance with books were the holy books – the religious books. Especially the *Ramayana* and so a book for him was something that—

DB: *It was holy.*

DD: It also had nothing to do with his own life, because his life was to look after cows and sheep. He's swearing all day, he's cussing, he's pissing, he's drinking, so a book was something sacred. Everything that he was not is what that book was, right? A book is cleanliness. He is not clean. He drinks rum, he spits, he has a girlfriend here and there, maybe shags his wife. But the Rayamana is clean so it must not have the word 'F' in it. I think the Jamaican and the Barbadians didn't have the same ethnic mix and the same multi-religious mix. So their influences are probably different from our influences.

DB: *And how old were you when you moved over here?*

DD: Thirteen. So basically the exposure to books – colonial, but also native. And poetry, I always had an interest in writing. You don't know where it comes from.

DB: *How old were you when you first started writing poetry?*

DD: Certainly, certainly, certainly at the age of ten. Certainly. And I remember writing these poems; they were probably all this trashy stuff, but I was boarding and the teacher, the boarder next door was a Spanish teacher in my school and he used to read the poems and say, "Oh god, there is something here!" In fact, he spoke to my father and said, "The boy has got some real talent here." Then when I went to school I had a wonderful teacher in Georgetown who was a literary man. He's now Professor of Literature and Linguistics at Stanford University, John Rickford, who was brilliant at promoting literature among us. Promoting reading. At the back of classroom for example he set up a library, with an exercise book and he encouraged us to take a book out, to read it and make a note. He was really inspirational.

DB: *That was actually the next question that I was going to ask you is whether or not you had any mentors. So that would be somebody*

DD: Oh certainly. And, in an odd way, my uncle. My grandfather couldn't read or write English. He just grew watermelons and he had a few cows and sheep and he lived in a village. His son went to Oxford. His son got a scholarship from the village to the city. From the city to University of the West Indies. From the University of the West Indies to Pembroke College, Oxford. Pembroke College, Oxford is where, in 1755, Dr Samuel Johnson was a graduate. He wrote the English dictionary in 1755.

So, here was the son of an illiterate peasant farmer going to Oxford. Now I grew up with that memory. My grandmother would say (she couldn't pronounce the word 'Oxford', she would say: *Acksfard*) "He went to *Acksfard*...[?] study hard in in *Acksfard*." [Laughter] So I grew up with that. In fact, my last novel is a kind of – it's called *Johnson's Dictionary* and it really is a look at how the importance of Johnson's dictionary had in the Caribbean, in terms of our understanding of English words.

DB: *Well, just as an aside, I was reading the other day that the term 'buttonhole' you know when you buttonhole somebody? That is actually came from Johnson because he used to buttonhole people when he was talking to him.*

DD: Oh really? I didn't know that.

DB: *I don't know if it's apocryphal.* [Note: unable to verify. Interviewer later remembers that a friend in Canada told her the anecdote].

DD: So, the colonial education, the dictionary, certainly the bible because that's where a lot of African Guyanese poetry is inspired by the myths and the stories of Babylon and Exodus and so on. And our Hindu texts and our Muslim texts.

DB: *You went to Selwyn when you went to Cambridge didn't you?*

DD: Yah, I went there in '74.

DB: *So how did you – I'm going to get back to Cambridge in couple of questions, but how did your first poetry publication Slave Song come about?*

DD: Well, I was at Cambridge and they started a prize called the…the…after a famous professor there. So they named this prize after him, a Victorian professor – I've forgotten what the name of the prize is. You had to write a piece of creative writing, so I submitted some of the poems in *Slave Song* and it won the prize. It was the first time the prize was awarded and it won the English prize…God you know, I can't remember his name! Anyway, he was a Victorian professor; I think the first professor in Cambridge. Anyway, Google will tell you.

So that was ok. I was just lucky to get into Cambridge, because the two people who interviewed me – you know at Cambridge, you don't get in. So I grew up in care at the time so I suppose they felt a bit sorry for me. And also, you should be applying to five universities; I only applied to Cambridge. Bluff. Bluff. So when the man said to me – when he said to me, "Well, if you don't get in, what will you do?" I said, "I'll apply again." [Laughter] And the two blokes who were interviewing me, one was an Irish man who was a war – he objected to the Second World War. He was a pacifist and they sent him to work in a croft all the way in Scotland. So he was a pacifist, left wing, socialist type who believed in comprehensive schools, which was the school I went to. And the other guy was the son of a very famous Shakespeare scholar, but he didn't like the elitism of Cambridge and after two years he left to work in adult education. I was so lucky to be interviewed! Not by two rich buggers [Laughter] but by two people who were sympathetic. Otherwise how would I get in?

DB: *Right. That's interesting. So, let's talk a little bit more about Cambridge. So, were you in the poetry scene at Cambridge?*

DD: No. I more or less withdrew from Cambridge because it was much too elitist for me. So I went to – I think the first two years – I dropped out after two years there.

DB: *Oh, that's interesting.*

DD: Yah, I dropped out. It was too elitist. It was too – what can I say? Elitist. It was rich, it was elitist, it was posh and so I left and went back to Guyana, but my mother sent me back. So Cambridge took me back.

DB: *How long did you go back to Guyana for?*

DD: For about a good four months, which was wonderful. Which was the very first time I'd gone home having left when I was a boy in England. So I was immersed again in all that Creole and all that fighting and all of that. And so when I came back to Cambridge in my last year I was able to write *Slave Song*. Because I got the language back. So I was able to write *Slave Song*. So then by the third year in Cambridge I felt much more confident. Much more confident. Much more confident because I'd spent some time at home drinking rum and chasing girls, whatever you do, you know? You know you're at home right? I came back full of confidence. In fact, I have to say that I was a little bit popular. [Laughter] I used to have a little court of four or five people come and see me to chat and chat about literature, whatever. Because you came back with an enormous amount of confidence.

DB: *It's so interesting.*

DD: When you grow up in England as an immigrant it does, it does – it can sap your confidence and your self-es – I'm not moaning, there's lots of compensations. It's only when you connect with something of value and something that you're rooted in some emotional and cultural way that you can then come back with confidence.

DB: *Did your life change at all after your first poetry publication?*

DD: Um, well my life changed as a result of Cambridge definitely.

DB: *How so?*

DD: Well, it was easier. They say that – and you know it's true – that if you're a graduate of Oxbridge people take you seriously. So even if you're drunk in the gutter the police will probably not slap you around the face or whatever, right? [Laughter] You know what I mean, once you're a graduate of Oxford or Cambridge. So I was able to get a grant [?] to do my PhD and I wanted to be an academic. But then I met a West Indian writer. A very venerable kind and brilliant West Indian novelist who lived in London for most of his life, called Sir Wilson Harris. He was knighted recently. He became my friend, I met him and he said to me, "David, oh you've finished your PhD…" I said, "Yah, I've also written this book of poems." He said, "Oh don't worry about that PhD, just do the poetry." In other words: *be a writer rather than a critic, David*. So I stopped doing criticism more or less. I got a job at Warwick. They didn't ask me here to – you had to churn out a few little, you had turn out a few [?], you had to churn out a few academic books. But the University of Warwick were very kind, they said: you do your creative writing.

DB: *And then did they award you a PhD?*

DD: No, at London University, then I came to Warwick in '82. [DD corrects himself] London University then '84 Warwick.

DB: *So when you were at London University, did you hang out with a poetry crowd there?*

DD: No, no, no.

DB: *No. Just the—*

DD: It's very solitary doing your PhD. Very solitary.

DB: *That's for sure.*

DD: Did I meet – I met a Jewish guy. He said he was Jewish and we met and we talked and we…he told me – I invited him to my house and we had a curry and he was telling me how people used to spit at him and say how he killed Christ. He couldn't figure it out. [Laughter] It was interesting, but he was the only person I met. I lost touch with him.

DB: *What did you do – what was the title of your PhD?*

DD: It was on William Hogarth. Hogarth – I argued, probably completely wrongly, that Hogarth was an early kind of socialist. He was – he's normally depicted as a good, solid, middleclass Englishman and I was saying, no, no, he's a bit more radical than that. He's more radical than that. Well, although he died before the French Revolution he painted people, he painted the ordinary people. Prostitutes and tax collectors – the people of Jesus moved him up [?]. Prostitutes and tax collectors. And when he painted them he made them into religious icons. He elevated their status. So when he paints the prostitute meeting the pimp, he paints it as Elizabeth meeting Mary. Anyway, I'm convinced – I, you know, I developed a really good relationship with Hogarth. I used to go and visit him in his grave obviously. Chat to him silently.

DB: *Where was he buried?*

DD: He was at Chiswick. I went to his house and we did a television programme filmed in his house. And then I discovered that a lot of Black people – he painted a lot of Black people in all of his major paintings. So I did a book on Hogarth's Blacks. The Black figure, which has been – for some reason it's been completely overlooked, but now if you go to Hogarth's house, there's a whole panel of all the Blacks. He had a mulberry tree in his garden and it was dying, so I took my handkerchief and squeezed some juice out of it, so I got the DNA of it. [Laughter] So you kind of build up a relationship with these old folk. [Laughter]

DB: *I had a mulberry tree in my yard as a child. I love mulberry trees and they get huge, they can be enormous.*

DD: Of course on Hogarth's grave, Johnson had written the epitaph.

DB: *What was the epitaph?*

DD: It was four lines, simple stuff: here lies a great artist or whatever—

DB: *Isn't that interesting.*

DD: Yah. I haven't seen him for a while. The last time I went to see him his grave looked a bit overrun.

DB: *A little shabby?*

DD: Yah, it did look a bit shabby. [Laughter]

DB: *So, now when I was looking on WorldCat I saw that you haven't published any books of poetry since 1994, why?*

DD: Because I got diverted into prose. Partly because of the challenge of it and then for the money as well. But not the money really – the challenge of it. And it suggested itself, so I wrote prose. I'm still writing poetry, but it's bubbling away. I want to end up writing a long poem, which I've planned. I've got to do research on it, so it's there. I've written a few lines and I think about it but [?]. I'm doing a novel at the moment so that's going to take some priority. When that is finished that's me finished.

DB: *I'm curious – this doesn't really have anything to do with my thesis, but when you're writing prose as opposed to writing poetry, which is easier for you to write?*

DD: Um…I would probably say, I would probably say prose. Because once you start writing you have a story; it follows your characters. You've got buildings – it's like Lego as it were. You build, you build. But with a poem what do you do? It either comes or you can sit and write a line and if the coffee is not good, or cigarette, or whatever, the second line doesn't come. And then the second line comes and it's too bloody long and then are you going to rhyme the first and the second line? It's just difficult. It's not difficult, it's joyous, but it's hard. It's harder than prose. It's harder than prose.

DB: *OK. So, you work as a director, a professor—*

DD: No, I'm no longer – I'm a professor in the Centre for Caribbean studies. But not at – I've just come back from China. I was ambassador there for five years.

DB: *Oh, I did read that.*

DD: From 2010 until 2015. The university gave me leave, but I'm coming back in October to resume my chair – professorship.

DB: *So, with all of those things, when you do resume your professorship, how [will] you carve out the time to write creatively?*

DD: Well, the three things are: work, obviously academic work. Family, I have a wife and two little kids, and then socializing. You know – easier to socialize than to write. With my mates, go drinking, chatting and whatever. So that is the issue. Certainly in China I could hardly write anything. So, I've got a third of a novel set in China that I'm vaguely excited by and so I just have to sit and write the bloody thing. And I like to write in spaces like this. I don't like quiet.

DB: *That's interesting.*

DD: Yah, I like noise. I like – you look around, when you're bored you look around. I found a lovely café in India. I went about three times with my family. They went swimming and I sat in a café. The café looked out, it was called [?], it looked out on the main road. Fantastic!

DB: *You see life go by.*

DD: You see tuk-tuk, tuk-tuk, tuk-tuk. And then there were political tuk-tuks with flags waving. Four or five nuns, this was a Catholic space [?] had been there, eating ice cream. How often do you see four of five nuns in their full habit, followed by a goat that pooed in the middle of – I mean it's brilliant, right? You have your coffee and your fags and you do your writing. I need to find a space like that. [Laughter]

DB: *That's funny. That's great. So, and this is a question that I ask most of the poets that I interview—*

DD: What time is it now, sorry? I just have to get my hair cut.

DB: *Twenty-five to. When do you have to go?*

DD: Two forty-five.

DB: *Oh no, we'll be done.*

DD: I've got some time.

DB: *That's plenty. Um, so you write poetry, you write fiction –*

DD: Can I say something, Diane?

DB: *Yes, of course.*

DD: I mean I was being a bit jocular about me and Hogarth, but I have built a relationship with this old guy. I'm nearly as old as him now. Over – since 1978 when I first wrote about him at Cambridge, right? I wrote my undergraduate dissertation on him. And I've had a peculiar kind of relationship with him mentally. Sometimes I dream that I discovered a missing painting. I go to see him, I chat with him. Now, he is a white English guy who didn't like foreigners. He disliked the French and the Italians, oh God. I don't know what he would have thought of Africans – no, I think he was more sympathetic to Africans, through his paintings right? And there I am in the 20th century, the 21st century, a completely different people. Completely and yet I have a sense of kinship. So, almost everything I've written creatively has been about Hogarth. My last novel has a painter in it who's a drunk; whom I sent to Guyana. I call Masta Hogarth. The previous novel was called *A Harlot's Progress* – vaguely based on one of his paintings, right.

DB: *So, it's a touchstone?*

DD: Well, yes. Because he introduced me to the 18th century. And the 18th century is full of gutters and people emptying their piss pots and, you know, diseases and rudeness and drunkenness and all of that, right? It's got a smell to it. You can smell the 18th century land. The stews and the gutters and the piss pots. The dead cats in the gutter. So, Hogarth introduced me to an aspect of life, 18th century life, which I still live in my mind. I love the 18th century. That period anyway, after he died in 1757 I'm not quite sure what happens after that in England. I've not been really interested. 1698 to 1757, when he died in '57 I've never checked the other 50 years, which is the important one. That's when the French Revolution happened, but I can't be bothered. [Laughter]

DB: *So, when you're—*

DD: So one thing, poetry can be inspired even though we are – we seem to come from the margins of empire. And maybe here we live in the margins of mainstream society being minorities. You soon can have these profoundly – literary ancestors or even you can make them your literary ancestors in the way that Walcott, Derek Walcott—

DD's phone rings. Takes call from his wife.

DD: Walcott as well talks about the importance to him – Homer onwards, you know. So, it may be that the other part doesn't work as well. In other words maybe the English poets are not as inspired by our stuff. Maybe they don't know it as well as we know their stuff. I always remember Walcott saying, I remember Walcott saying that when he started writing at the age of 16 or whatever, he could not put the word 'mango' in one of his poems, because mango was not an iconic, poetic fruit. A cherry was. A peach was. An apple was. A mango? Apart from the difficultly of finding a rhyme for mango: mango pango, wango, jango—

DB: *Never mind orange.*

DD: So he felt a little bit timid, but then his greatness was that he named the landscape. He named the landscape. So it may be that – I don't know how influenced contemporary English poets are by what we write or whether they feel estranged from it because some of it is in Creole, some of it is very local. I don't know whether we integrate at that level, whether we integrate at the level of poetry. I don't know whether it's important. I don't know whether it's important anyway.

DB: *Is it important to you?*

DD: Um, no. A good poem is a good poem, you know. It's of no importance to me. I mean, politically it's important in terms of – actually no, literature should be exempt from all that nonsense by integration. Because people write what they want to write.

DB: *So, speaking of writing, because you've written as a poet, you've written as a—*

DD: May I say something?

DB: *Yes, of course you may.*

DD: I judged a national – talking about integration – I judged a National Poetry Competition, which is the big poetry competition in England, about twelve years ago.

DB: *Did you judge with anybody else?*

DD: Yes, I judged with two writers. Fine poets. Three of us judged and we all came to the conclusion: *this one poem is the winner*. It was anonymous obviously, but there was a number. It was a beautiful poem written in Creole about a horse being taken to water and a shark attacking it. Beautifully done. Beautifully, beautifully written, right? And we all agreed. And we were not Black or West Indian. I was the West Indian, the other two thought it was a West Indian poet, a Jamaican poet and so then we excitedly looked up her name and it was a woman from Devon.

So, I said to my friends, "Oh bloody hell, we'll look like real wallies if she turns out to be a middle-aged woman," right? But you know what? She was. She turned up at the poetry award, she turned up – first of all *The Guardian* reported that we had said well we would look like really wallies. *The Guardian* did that: *Dabydeen said that we'd look like real wallies*, right? [Laughter] She turned up, I can't remember her name now, we communicated. She turned up and I wrote back to *The Guardian* to say look, if it excited the imagination, it excited the imagination. All we've got to do is look at the poem and form [?] the language. Well, she did turn up. The other two judges, God bless them, exempted themselves – you cowards, right? (DD speaks closely to recording device) And when she turned up I was so, I was so – not embarrassed. It was a strange moment. She turned up late from Devon because the train was late. She had a Devon accent – a kind of English accent. Obviously a woman of substance and class and whatever. But she'd lived in Jamaica for a few years and it had inspired her. But I remember one of my fellow poets – I won't mention his name, but one of my fellow West Indian buddy poets, said to me, "David, you did the judging did you?" I said, "No, it's the other two!" [Laughter]

But it showed that it doesn't matter: race, class and gender. Race, class and gender.

DB: *It was her poem.*

DD: And she was inspired by it. And I'll tell you, her Creole is better than a whole lot of Caribbean Creole. Without a doubt, I would say, I would put it as one of the top ten, right. [Laughter]

DB: *That's so interesting. Ok, this leads me to a question I was going to ask you later on, but I'm going to ask you now: how important are prizes and awards to you as a writer?*

DD: I think, well, first of all I think, if you hang in there you're going to get a prize, because there's so many of them. [Laughter] Unless you're very good or unlucky, right? [Laughter] ...Quiller-Couch is the professor! He did the Oxford book of Victorian poetry. That's another irony I want to [?]. And then I bought a book on Hogarth with the prize money. It was twenty quid. So I bought a collection of Hogarth's engravings. Anyway, what were we talking about?

DB: *Prizes and awards.*

DD: I'll tell you why they're important, not just to me but to other people, because nobody reads your stuff. I mean, you can't make a living – a few people can make a living writing. Most of us sell – these days if you sell 500 books of poems, you're really lucky, you know?

DB: *Yep.*

DD: And therefore if somebody gives you a prize it gives you confidence doesn't it? You feel, well, somebody has read the bloody thing and thinks highly of it, right? Prose not so much. Prose is much more commercial obviously. And you get dropped if you don't sell. And actually these days it doesn't matter how famous you are. If you don't sell publishers will drop you. Or they'll contemplate dropping you. So, poetry especially, it's nice for prizes to be given to poets: A) because it's such a minority activity and people don't get money out of it and they have to make a living. So, I should imagine a prize, certainly the Commonwealth Prize certainly made me feel emboldened that I could write. They were saying: *You can write. It's not just an error on your part.* Well, it probably is, but at least nobody's spotted it yet, so carry on. [Laughter] Yah, of course they are important.

DB: *So, do you self-define as a poet, a novelist, an academic? All of those things? Or a writer?*

DD: That's what I do.

DB: *So, a writer then?*

DD: Yah, a writer and an academic.

DB: *OK.*

DD: A writer and an academic.

DB: *Would it be writer first?*

DD: Mm-mm. [Yes]

DB: *That's interesting.*

DD: The academic was to pay the bills really. And also the complete joy of being with the best writers young brains.

DB: *Well, that leads to another question that I was going to ask you. So, do you think that people can be taught to write poetry?*

DD: Um. I don't think so. I think people can be taught to *read* poetry. And the more they read obviously the more they may pick up some ideas from other poets. They can be taught – they can be taught more how to write prose.

DB: *That's interesting.*

DD: Because, because poetry is such an individual and instinctual work, which then is cleaned up and edited. Prose has got more easier rules I think, you know. If two people start talking [?] just drop them. Or if you drop them then you can add something else. I think you can teach prose. There are certain tricks in prose that my editor taught me – Robin Robertson. He said, "Look you put the donkey on page 18 and then the donkey didn't reappear until page 110. Why don't you flag up the donkey a bit more?" So, that's a little trick you can learn. You can't do that in poetry, can you?

DB: *No you can't.*

DD: So, he was saying flag it up more and then, "Well, you ended – that character was just terminated. Why did you terminate that character? You just killed the bugger off." I said, "Well, I was fucking bored. I didn't know what to do with this character. It was easier to kill him wasn't it?" He said, "No, no, no. Your character has to go on for another two pages" so you can learn prose more.

DB: *Huh. That's interesting. So, when you were writing poetry, and I know you said, you're still writing a little bit now, but would you get anybody – because clearly Robin Robertson was helping with editing your prose, but would you get anybody to help edit your poetry?*

DD: Well, not edit, but certainly suggest. I had a friend who was completely poetic and that friend would actually now and again suggest a better line. In conversation, you know. That's it. I normally send things to my friends to read because they're trusted friends and I say to them, "Just kick the balls, just kick the balls of it in." I mean kick it in, right? I mean I regret it now and again. The last novel I sent to my dear, dear, friend, the godmother of my daughter. She's been my friend for years; I taught her here. I said, "Just kick it in, this novel." She got back saying, "Actually, after page 60 I couldn't give a damn what happened to the characters…" [Laughter] She said, "I lost interest."

DB: *Oh boy. That is a kick.*

DD: Then you have to look at it again and revise it, so criticism is fantastic, right?

DB: *Isn't that interesting.*

DD: And I try to give criticism – when I say criticism, I try to copyedit and edit poets who are friends of mine by just saying, "If you put a comma there I think it might work." I love to fiddle about with peoples' poetry.

DB: *Did you ever belong to any workshops or anything like that?*

DD: No. I did give a couple of workshops with the Avon – the *Arvon*. Not Avon, Avon is a skin cream. The Arvon Foundation. Two I think, but no workshops. Basically, because you've immersed yourself into literature and you're teaching the stuff – maybe I could have benefited from workshops. [Laughter] But I never – I didn't feel a need to do that. By the way, John Burnside have you talked to him?

DB: *No, but I'm going up to Edinburgh this summer for a month.*

DD: He's a genius.

DB: *I know – he's a genius. He's a genius.*

DD: He's brilliant. He and I had a nice – he and I were published together by Robin, so we spent a little bit of time going to readings everywhere and drinking some red wine and what have you. He met my Mum and I met his people, and then I lost contact with him, but he's a really lovely bloke and super talented, super talented.

DB: *He's very bright isn't he?*

DD: He's informal, he's not precious. Give him my regards.

DB: *Well, if he agrees to it* [an interview]. *We'll have to see.*

DD: Tell him I told him, because I did a reference for him once. Tell him I told him, I told you—

DB: *I will do that.*

DD: Say Dabydeen said do it! Say Dabydeen said, "John Burnside is brilliant and you ought to do it."

DB: *Thank you. I will! So, you published with Dangeroo, Hansib and Cape. How did you find them, or did they find you?*

DD: I found Dangeroo by accident, because I met the editor by accident in the Africa Centre in London. So that was an accident and then when I sent her the poems, she was very keen to do them, but then I put it to the back because I just finished my PhD. Then I met Mr Harris, Wilson Harris, and he said, "Do the poetry." So it was an accident, it was an accident. The second one was, I knew a small publisher and so he published that. And then my first novel was by Cape – no by Secker and Warburg and then the editor Robin moved over to Cape and then I did another novel with him. And then they were doing poetry and so I did a poem and then another two novels with him, but then I put the poetry aside to bubble away. Then I sent him the fifth novel, which he didn't like. Probably quite rightly. [Laughter] Who knows? So, I published that with a friend of mine who had set up a small press. Arrow – oh yes! Then it was published by the largest independent Caribbean publisher in Britain called the Peepal Tree Press.

DB: *Oh yes, I've heard of them.*

DD: And the good thing about Peepal Tree Press, although they're not mainstream, everybody in that area reads them. So, if you're interested in Caribbean literature that's where you go. So my fifth novel was published by – I don't think I bothered to send it to Robin. Because I got an offer from MacMillan Caribbean and I went with them and then I haven't gone back to – I've stayed with Peepal Tree as a loyalty. And then this novel, I don't know what's going to happen. But I think I wasn't selling enough for Cape. Definitely not.

DB: *OK, so you did touch upon having a loyalty with publishers. So, you do have a loyalty if somebody's—*

DD: Well, I mean I suppose you have a loyalty, but at the end of the day the loyalty is to the bloody writing, isn't it? You want it to be out there, you want it to be out there. And Cape obviously – I mean it was wonderful with Cape because they took you all over Britain. Very nice wine and there was lovely food and nice hotels. People turn up to listen to little old you. And you're getting a couple dosh, a couple quid here and there. Whereas the smaller presses they can't really. The pay your train fare and that. [Laughter] Oh dear.

DB: *OK, so some of the poets I've been speaking with, they'll harken back to other British poets like Auden, Heaney, MacDiarmid, Hughes: do you think that there's an equivalent poet at the helm right now in British poetry?*

DD: Well, first of all I definitely – if I had to fit myself in the tradition of English poetry it would be *Sir Gawain and the Green Knight*. The nature poetry, Thomas Hardy, D.H. Lawrence and Ted Hughes. And maybe Dylan Thomas. That non-cerebral, non-intellectual, non T.S. Eliot tradition, right? I think that's where I feel – I feel more comfortable there. And again *Gawain* was an obsession for quite a while. In fact *Gawain* was the one who gave me the courage to write in Creole, because *Gawain* was written in English Creole and Northumberland, Northeast England Creole. And Chaucer, who was out in the south actually, took the piss out of the northern poets.

DB: *I didn't know that.*

DD: In *Canterbury Tales* he said, "They go yar, yar, yar". Something like that he said – I can't remember what it was. Because he was a court poet. Now with regard to contemporary English writing, is that what you're asking me?

DB: *Yes.*

DD: Do you know I've been out of it for so long – five years I've been in China and only now am I coming back. Only now am I coming back. I'm reading some Guyanese poetry at the moment, a very fine collection of Guyanese poetry published by Peterloo Press, by one of our finest poets in Guyana. And then I have to get a hold of John Burnside again, because I've not read his – the last book of his I read, I'm sorry to say, is ten years ago. *The Myth of the Twain* I think? Wonderful. Amazing stuff.

DB: *Yah, his autobiographies are supposed to be incredible too.*

DD: I've not read it. No, see I've been out of it. So, I have to go back. I remember reading with Don Paterson being astonished at the distillation of ideas and the – well the accomplishment of it! It's just accomplished. So I've got to read a bit more. Certainly when I come to do this book of poems, I was going to read poetry all day, right? For inspiration. You know the last thing I can say to you, in 1995 I think I published a novel called *The Counting House* set in Guyana and India. Cape published it. Robin published it. And I couldn't end it. I knew I had about six pages to go and I had no idea how to end it. No idea – couldn't end the bloody thing. And I invited a fantastic writer from Britain called Pauline Melville. Do you know Pauline Melville?

DB: *I've heard of Pauline Melville, yah.*

DD: She's written poetry, but mostly prose. She won the Guardian Fiction Prize. The Commonwealth Writer's Prize—

DB: *Does she write short stories?*

DD: Short stories—

DB: *I think I know her.*

DD: I tell you what, she's a really terrific writer and a decent human being. She's in London if ever you want to meet her I can give you her contacts. I don't know whether she likes interviews, but never mind. She came to Warwick and she read from her novel called *A Ventriloquist's Tale*.

DB: *Yes, I have heard of her because I worked in a bookstore for a long time.*

DD: Oh you did? Now the first six pages – she only read six pages – were inspirational because they were written in a fantastic, vivid English. And I told her the other day, I met her the other day (I've told her before and I've met her before as well) and I said to her, "I was able to go back to my desk and finish off this novel because of you." Because you know how people inspire you.

DB: *That's amazing. What a compliment for her too.*

DD: I said, "I'm not giving you any royalties though". I told her I didn't get much anyway. [Laughter] But no, people inspire you. You got to a reading – obviously in Beijing there's nothing – but the odd reading you go to, you go "Oh gee!" I mean sometimes you look at some lines – I just read a beautiful poem, some poetry, by a girl called Harris. Maggie Harris who lives in England from Wales; was born in Guyana. And I was just blown away by them! It was really – you know when you come across a good poem—

DB: *I know.*

DD: It makes you feel a bit happy.

DB: *It takes your breath away.*

DD: And no jealousy.

DB: *That's impressive. That's impressive.*

DD: You actually think, "Hey Maggie! How did you do that?" You're genuinely moved and impressed by it. Prose is probably a little bit more competitive. I'm not sure. This writer gets paid more than this writer, this writer. I don't know how that – I'm not sure—

DB: *Because the undercurrent, I mean because poetry there isn't—*

DD: There's no money in it. We're all mendicants. [Laughter]

DB: *OK, I've only got three more questions. This one is really broad; it's a two-parter. One is how would describe the poetry community in the United Kingdom and what changes have you noticed in the poetry community, I know you've been away as you said, within the last say thirty years.*

DD: Thirty years. Well, I suppose the same names keep cropping up, which is not a bad thing because there are substantial writers rooted in the composition of poetry. That might mean that other writers are crowded out, you know. But this has always been so. Being an 18th century person, those guys used to stab each other. If you read Alexander Pope, he hated Colley Cibber; he called him a dunce . Cibber was a poet laureate – he was a dunce. And you know the battle of the books: "Swift, you bastard, you're getting all of this money for *Gulliver's Travels*! Give us a couple of dollars!" right? Highly competitive. And each poet had his own patron. If you were my patron I would write a lovely encomium for you and you would give me a couple of dollars; I'll write something nasty about your enemy, who is the patron of another poet. So, it's a dog-eat-dog. But now today I suppose maybe *The Guardian* is a patron of two or three particular writers and maybe the *Independent* – well it's gone now – has it's own favourites you know. Who knows?

I'm not going to sit down – I'm too old now to cuss people. When I was younger I used to get a bit more angry about these things, but now…I used to talk about minority writing and people not being published because they're Black and all that blah, blah,

blah and arguing for more diversity in publications and so on, which I think is quite right in the '80s and the '90s to do that. Now when you hit your age, my age, you just want to do the right thing. And even if a dog passes by and vomits over it at least it's been attended to – at least it's been attended to, do you know what I mean? [Laughter] And also, I'll tell you, if you finish the book and your friends, who kicked it in, say "It's ok now," you're happy. You're happy. It's done. Then you feel, *well, that's eight novels done, is that enough? Yes, that's enough. Bollocks. No more*, right? *Let's go back to poetry*. And then I think I will probably make a serious attempt to go see John Burnside wherever the hell he is.

DB: *I think he's living close to Edinburgh, maybe half an hour [away] maybe.*

DD: Is he?

DB: *I can't remember where exactly. He's not in England anymore.*

DD: Oh, he's not? I did ask – who did I ask? That fine English poet who won the poetry – oh, Jo Schapcott. I saw her about seven years ago. She had a reading that she did. Fantastic! I said to her, "How did you write that!" Again, I was amazed. I said "Jo, you've done something that nobody has done yet, as far as I know." And she said, "Well, you know…". [Laughter]

[Further discussion of the whereabouts of Burnside]

DD: John is just our best, I think. From what I can see and what I've read of him. As I say, *The Myth of the Twain* and some other things, just John right?

DB: *Yah, I've read excerpts of his and he's a terrific writer, he really is.*

DD: Yah, he is. I look forward to meeting him again. Yah, I'd like to go and see him again.

DB: *OK, last question.*

DD: Right.

DB: *What impacts do you think that modern technology, specifically the internet have had on the field of poetry?*

DD: I honestly can't answer that question except that I suspect it might be a neg – I sound like an old man by saying that it might be a negative impact in that it's easier to clean. Maybe too easy to clean. I don't type. I type with one finger. I write. I write by hand.

DB: *Oh, you write longhand.*

DD: I write by hand and then I speak it, I do it all, I speak into a microphone, tape recorder and I pay some person to type it out.

DB: *Oh, that's really interesting.*

DD: It means that when you tape, you think that doesn't sound right, it doesn't sound right. So you can edit –

DB: *Yah, because you're saying it out loud.*

DD: But the best thing of all is when it comes back from your desk and the typist has made some beautiful errors, typing errors, which sometimes improves—

DB: *It works! Like it's wordplay, right?*

DD: It improves. And I remember Auden himself – was it Auden who said, he'd written a line, I'm not sure if this was the line but: *every port, every sea has it's port*. I think that was the original line and the typist made an error and said, "Every sea has its poet". Much richer. Much richer. That little error that that typist made changed – I'm sure it's [?] that the quotation was richer than that. That each sea has it's poet. Wonderful.

DB: *Incredible wordplay. That's good.*

DD: Yah, you get puns.

DB: *They say apparently, I read an article recently, that when you're writing longhand it utilizes a different part of your brain than typing, which is interesting.*

DD: I don't know. I really hadn't – I can't type. I just can't type. That's why my letters to you have just one line. Where's the H? Oh, there's the H. [Laughter]

DB: *Well, that's it. Thanks so much!*

CHAPTER ELEVEN

Interview between Ruzbeh Babaee (RB) and David Dabydeen (DD) conducted online in spring 2016

RB: *You are both a writer and a university professor of comparative literature. Do you know yourself first as a writer or a university professor?*

DD: First as a writer. When I was a boy that is basically all I wanted to be. As a teenager I wrote the usual self-pitying stuff and, at 16 or 17, I attempted a novel in verse, inspired by some story in the Bible, I [have] forgotten which; but gave up after a couple of pages. Why [did I] want to be a writer? I don't know. In my youth in Guyana I never encountered a writer. I think it must have been youthful aspiration to emulate the writers of Nancy Drew and Hardy Boys novels, which were standard childhood fare in Guyana. Also, since I come from a large family, it must have been the regular escape to the New Amsterdam public library to be alone, and whilst there (the place was usually empty), discovering books in the Ladybird series on great scientists, great politicians etc. I distinctly remember reading about Benjamin Franklin, Madame Curie, Alexander the Great, and others, at the age of nine or ten. There were also the odd books on Greek myths, lavishly illustrated for children. The story of Andromeda chained and naked and threatened by a monster, before being saved by Perseus, awakened unfamiliar boyish erotic feelings... perhaps not 'unfamiliar' (I was 8 or 9), but certainly the first time a **book** had aroused such feelings. When I was about 11 or 12 I came across V.S. Naipaul's *Miguel Street* and was awed by how it made our lives in Guyana so familiar. It was set in Trinidad, but the characters lived down my street. A great contrast to the Andromeda story which was exotic and erotic as opposed to the familiar lives of ordinary folk described by Naipaul.

Being an academic has also been important to my writing. Firstly, you get a lot of time to read and discuss books with very bright students. Teaching in seminar groups has been amazingly exciting at times, and that intellectual excitement, sensuous in intensity, inspires the act of writing. I used to teach MA courses on Black British Literature and on Literature and Slavery. Certainly, Olaudah Equiano's autobiography in 1789, which I read multiple times for teaching purposes, left an impact on my writing which is dotted with 'Equiano' figures (people who moved from deprivation to the craft of writing, through cunning and an inclination for mischief mostly). Secondly, as an academic, you are exposed to theory, which can fertilize your writing and give it a 'metaphysical' content. Overexposure leads to didacticism, which I am sure my writing suffers from. As Derek Walcott says, you shouldn't "put Descartes before the horse". Most importantly, being an academic pays the bills, so whilst hunger has provoked a lot of writers, I preferred to have a house rather than a hovel. Growing up in Guyana was to exist in relative lack of material things. Many years ago I met Maya Angelou, she had kindly invited me to her house, and she cooked a lovely Southern meal. She said: "I drive a Cadillac. I don't do bicycles, which were my youth. And I eat meat, because all I had as a child was garden vegetables." I appreciated her extravagance, though deep down she was a kindly person, and generous.

RB: *You are also a politician. In 2010 you were appointed as Guyana's Ambassador in China. How have you proved yourself as a politician?*

DD: I don't belong to any political party in Guyana, but I enjoyed a close friendship with Cheddi and Janet Jagan. Cheddi had been cheated out of office as a result of the CIA and the British Government, in the 1960s, because he was a committed man of the left. In 1984, when I was appointed to Warwick University, I invited Cheddi to lecture there. He had no money, so the University and a travel agent friend, Vino Patel, were persuaded to provide his economy ticket and accommodation whilst at Warwick. We treated him as the true President of Guyana. All the national elections had been fiddled, and he was kept out of office for decades. Warwick offered him a platform, when other places thought of him as a 'has been'. He visited about five times, then in 1992, the Berlin Wall having fallen and the Cold War ended, the Americans allowed us to have free and fair elections, supervised by President Carter and Cheddi Jagan won and became President of Guyana.

I was his regular houseguest from 1992 until 1997 when he died. He taught me more about how colonialism behaved than any textbook. He had lived through the colonial period and was jailed by the British in 1953. All his life was dedicated to the betterment of the poor: he was fiercely concerned with reducing and eliminating poverty. In return for his great hospitality, all I could do was edit and publish some of his political speeches. He also asked me to be his Ambassador at Large and to sit on the UNESCO Executive Board representing Guyana. He had no money, since he inherited a bankrupt country in 1992, so it was an amazing honour to serve him pro bono. One day I will write something more extensive about him…one of the stories he told me was about Fidel Castro. The two of them were friends and political comrades in the late 50s and early 60s. It was Cuba who supplied us with food in the early 1960s when the CIA fomented strikes and shortages in Guyana. Castro, however, needed allies in the region, against American embargo, so when Cheddi was manoeuvred out of Office, Castro started to court the friendship of our new autocratic Prime Minister, Forbes Burnham, and more or less dropped his relationship with Cheddi. I learn from this that politics trumps decency; that politicians by and large are opportunists. Learning this first hand from a great and ethical politician like Cheddi Jagan was more powerful than learning this from textbooks.

As to Janet Jagan, his wife, who, when he died, was elected President in our national elections, with an enhanced vote, she was an astonishingly generous host. My role was to edit and publish her short stories for children. She was a bit lonely in Guyana, in terms of only a few people to share her passion for the arts, so whenever I showed up, a bottle of wine was uncorked, or better still, a bottle of Bailey's Irish Cream (we had a local equivalent). She too had been jailed by the British in 1953, so, again, I learnt from her intimate details of Guyana's struggle for independence, and the callousness of politicians (Forbes Burnham had attempted to murder her in 1964, but his bomb went off in the wrong place in the Party's Headquarters, killing a young activist instead, Michel Forde. Janet suffered from minor injuries).

As to Walter Rodney, Guyana's internationally renowned historian, assassinated by Forbes Burnham and the State apparatus in 1980 [the International Commission of Enquiry into his death was issued to Guyana's Parliament last month], it was an enlightened decision on the part of the University of Warwick to set up an annual Memorial Lecture. The Walter Rodney lecture has been given, since 1985, by some of our leading Caribbean scholars, like Hilary Beckles, Carolyn Cooper, Harold Goulbourne, Michael Gilkes, Clem Seecharan, Ken Ramchand, Verene Shepherd and others. I don't think I have proved myself as a politician in any concrete way. My only possible 'political' act was, in 2012-2013 lobbying the Government of Guyana vigorously and regularly to set up an International Commission of Enquiry into the death of Walter Rodney. I took full advantage of my friendship with the then President, Donald Ramotar, who was readily sympathetic to Pat Rodney's written request for such an Enquiry [Walter's widow]. As a member of the Walter Rodney Foundation's Advisory Group, I liaised with Pat Rodney and in 2013 the Government of Guyana agreed to set up the Commission. I don't think this was a 'political' act on my part, merely the obligation I felt to Walter Rodney, a fellow academic whose books were monumental.

RB: *How do you define politics?*

DD: In a small underdeveloped or developing country, politics normally is about the acquisition of power over state resources for the benefit of family and friends. Idealism goes out of the window as soon as the politician assumes Office; the struggle then is for survival and continuation of Office, so very little good gets done, political energy being spent on maintaining and expanding the arena of privilege. Exceptions are rare, people like Cheddi Jagan, Nelson Mandela...Cheddi was famous for his frugal lifestyle. He died intestate, owning no property. He never stole from the national treasury, rare for a politician from the developing world. Had Rodney lived, he would have been a leader of exemplary ethics. I should add my admiration for a previous, undemocratically elected President of Guyana, Desmond Hoyte, who, long before the Rio Summit and long before 'Climate Change' was topical, bequeathed a million acres of Guyana's rainforest to the Commonwealth, for the study of sustainable development (the Iwokrama Project). This was in 1989. It was an act of rare vision by a Caribbean politician. So, politicians like Hoyte might have been elected by crookery, but can prove to be significant and visionary leaders. I enjoyed cordial relations with him, when he was President [1985-1992], as well as when he was Leader of the Opposition, again based on books. We talked a lot about Egbert Martin, the first Guyanese poet and short story writer [19th century], and about the Guyana Prize for Literature which he had instituted in 1987, in the hope of bolstering the literary and intellectual life of Guyana and its Diaspora. He had a wonderful library, and he cared deeply for literary achievement. We talked little about party politics, except about the sharing of political power and the Mandela Rainbow ideal. Towards the end of his life he was all for power sharing, though he had enough integrity to worry about where oppositional ideas would come from if we were all in alliance.

RB: *Do your political affairs affect your creative writing?*

DD: There is no direct link, though I have written about the dereliction of Guyana under the autocratic rule of Forbes Burnham. My new novel-in-progress, set partly in China, is provoked by the unimaginable cruelty imposed on the people by the Emperors and their warlords. So, politics breeds in me a despair which can stimulate writing. One of the great disappointments, living in Britain, was Tony Blair's loss of idealism (he seemed abundantly idealistic, which is why people voted him into Office in 1992), and the lies he told about Iraq's military capacity to justify a hideous and bloody invasion of Iraq. On the other hand, in Britain, there were politicians like Jo Cox, who was visionary and full of promise (she was murdered recently), and who made all of us feel hopeful and glad to be alive. If only we had a handful of such politicians in Guyana! I am privileged to enjoy a long-standing friendship with Clare Short, the former Labour politician whose heart is as big as Mount Kilimanjaro.

RB: *You have often depicted Guyanese characters and settings in your fiction such as* **Disappearance** *(1993),* **The Counting House** *(1996), and* **Our Lady of Demerara** *(2004). Does it mean that you still live in your past and that you know yourself devoted to your homeland?*

DD: I do live in the past, in that my childhood in Guyana left indelible memories of family and friends and village landscape. Especially the creole language we spoke at home, and the creative tension with the 'proper' English we spoke at school. The slippages between the two are fascinating, with potential for comedy and pathos. The vigour of creole is always with me.

Leaving Guyana as a boy was exciting (the prospect of adventure), but then proved to be lonely and hurtful, since I was never settled in England. On the one hand, England was a world of books, but at the same time a world of grunting and guttural 'skinheads' daubing racist slogans on walls and threatening to assault immigrants. London has changed profoundly since the 60s and 70s, it is now a diverse space, enriched by waves of immigrants from the Commonwealth and from Europe. There is still a strong undercurrent of racial hostility, but more in the north of England, hence the recent vote to leave the European Community. Many in the north of England have not got accustomed to the loss of Empire and the new order of the free movement of goods and people. This hostility is at the ideological level, and contradictory, because on a day to day level, people are, by and large, decent to each other, irrespective of ethnicity. London is different; it is run by people of immigrant backgrounds: nurses, doctors, builders, hotel and retail staff, care workers. I am astonished at how much has changed, and I am excited to be living in London. The creative energy of the city is palpable, and the diversity of people is inspiring. I no longer feel culturally or physically threatened, as in the 1960s and 1970s. In other words, I feel London is home, but so is Guyana. I return to Guyana at least once a year, to renew my sense of the past, to be refreshed by creole language and creole ways, and to be awed and terrified by the rainforest. I also keep writing about Guyana partly out of a sense of obligation to the place. We only have a handful of writers, so I feel it is important to write about the place. Guyana came into modern being, in a sense, through literature: I am thinking specifically of Walter Raleigh's *Discoverie of Guiana* (1596), the first text about us.

RB: *Why do you often depict historical tensions and challenge traditional cultural representations of the slave in your novels?*

DD: Guyanese history, in relation to contact with Europe, is stark: the decimation of indigenous people, the enslavement of Africans, the system on Indian indentureship. It is stark in terms of the immensity of suffering, and the sheer injustices of colonial rule. Yet, we became acquainted with Samuel Johnson's *Dictionary* and the magical properties of the English language; with the lyricism and storytelling of the Bible, of Shakespeare, of Victorian poetry. These new texts supplemented the ones we brought from Africa and India (the *Koran*, the *Ramayana*). Ancient and living Carib, Arawak and other Amerindian stories fertilized the situation. We rewrote and reimagined our inheritance, hence Walcott, Naipaul, Jean Rhys, Pauline Melville, Grace Nichols, John Agard, and a host of others. I write about the injustice (historical, but also self-inflicted in our postcolonial condition), but more about the urge to creativity and expression that emerged from being on the margins; the fierce resolve to become educated, literate, creative, venturing beyond boundaries. Our postcolonial politicians may have failed us repeatedly, but I am forever astonished at how resilient Guyanese are. When I visit parts of India, parts of China, the nature of poverty there is brutal and overwhelming. We don't have that level of deprivation, because we have created the means of survival and the prospect of abundance, whether on the plate or on the page.

RB: *Do you believe that there is any nation on earth that enjoys true freedom and independence?*

DD: I don't know what true freedom or independence mean, we are all constrained and liberated and catapulted into creativity by being with each other. However, I recall what Walcott said about slavery: that the enslaved African being herded to the cane fields would have seen something sensationally beautiful along the way, given how lush Caribbean landscapes are. A hummingbird or kiskadee or blue-saki or brightly coloured viper…Walcott said that such encounters with beauty were moments of freedom which could only be partially understood, partially described, because they also contained the seeds of tragedy and terror. If you venture into Guyana's rainforest, you will experience the sublime which contains elemental terror and a tragic sense of how life is constantly being destroyed and remade and destroyed by tooth and claw.

ABOUT THE CONTRIBUTORS

John Clement Ball is professor and chair of English at the University of New Brunswick. He is author of two books, *Imagining London: Postcolonial Fiction and the Transnational Metropolis* (University of Toronto Press 2004) and *Satire and the Postcolonial Novel: V. S. Naipaul, Chinua Achebe, Salman Rushdie* (Routledge 2003), and editor of the *World Fiction* volume of *The Encyclopedia of Twentieth-Century Fiction* (Wiley-Blackwell 2011). He was editor or co-editor of *Studies in Canadian Literature* from 1996 to 2013, and in addition to his work on Dabydeen in this volume, he has published articles or book chapters on oceanic resonances in Jamaica Kincaid's *Mr. Potter*, Yann Martel's *Life of Pi*, and Tim Winton's *Breath*.

Marta Fratczak-Dabrowska is an assistant professor at Faculty of English, Adam Mickiewicz University, Poland. She gained her PhD in postcolonial studies with a thesis on the contemporary Anglo Guyanese novel (Poznañ, 2015), and is currently continuing her research in the field of Anglo Caribbean fiction, postcolonial literature and postcolonial economics.

Najnin Islam is Assistant Professor of English at Colorado College where she teaches classes on Postcolonial Literature, Caribbean Literature and Culture, and Global Anglophone Literatures with a focus on histories of race, labour, and capital. Her scholarship examines nineteenth century and contemporary cultural productions about Indian indentured servitude in the Caribbean and the Indian Ocean world. She is currently working on her first book manuscript provisionally titled, "Recasting the Coolie: Racialization, Caste, and Indian Indentureship". Research from this project appears in *Interventions: International Journal of Postcolonial Studies*.

Renée Landell is a PhD candidate in the School of Humanities at Royal Holloway, University of London, and a fully funded AHRC Techne scholar. Her research combines postcolonial and ecocritical approaches to Caribbean literature, with a specific focus on a literary resistance to popular and pervasive anti-Black stereotypes.

Lynne Macedo has a PhD in Caribbean Studies and is an Honorary Research Fellow of the Yesu Persaud Centre for Caribbean Studies at the University of Warwick. She has previously taught at the Universities of Warwick, Aston and London Metropolitan, and has worked as General Editor for the Caribbean Press. Her publications include *The Hook of Desire* (Hansib Publications, 2023), *Talking Words* (UWI Press, 2011), *Pak's Britannica* (UWI Press, 2011), *No Land, No Mother* (Peepal Tree Press, 2007), and *Fiction & Film* (Dido Press, 2003). She is currently compiling a Bibliography of Indentureship for the Ameena Gafoor Institute.

Sten Pultz Moslund is Associate Professor in Comparative Literature at the University of Southern Denmark. His research focuses on postcolonial literature and theory. He has published a range of books and articles on literature and issues of migration, hybridity, place and geocriticism, including *Migration Literature and Hybridity. The Different Speeds of Transcultural Change* (Palgrave-Macmillan 2010), *Literature's Sensuous Geographies. Postcolonial Matters of Place* (Palgrave-Macmillan 2015), and the co-authored *Reframing Migration, Diversity and the Arts: The Postmigrant Condition* (Routledge 2019).

Sofia Muñoz-Valdivieso is Associate Professor in the English Department at the University of Malaga. She has published on adaptations of English classics and appropriations of Shakespeare on screen and literature. She has worked on the interaction between historical and fictional texts and her current research focuses on the rewriting of history in Black British fiction, in particular texts that engage with issues of slavery in Britain and the British Empire. She has published articles in such journals as *Afroeuropa*, *Ariel*, *Cahiers Charles V*, *Changing English*, *Interactions*, *Journal of European Studies*, *Journal of Postcolonial Writing*, *Obsidian III: Literature in the African Diaspora*, and *SEDERI*.

Mark Tumbridge read English at Brunel University, Uxbridge, graduating in 2005 with a first class honours degree. He spent two years teaching in London and Poland, before returning to Brunel to complete his MA in Contemporary Literature and Culture. In July 2008, he won the David Nicholls Memorial Trust Scholarship, and by July 2012 he had successfully defended his PhD thesis in Comparative Cultural Studies at the Yesu Persaud Centre for Caribbean Studies, University of Warwick. His research interests include Caribbean literature and culture, world literature, literary representations of indentureship and slavery, critical theory, and the presence of tropical products such as opium and sugar in literature. He is currently lecturing at the University of Guyana.

INTERVIEWERS

Ruybeh Babaee holds a PhD in English literature. He has been a visiting fellow at the University of Southampton, and has published mainly on utopia/dystopian literature.

Diane Barlee is a cultural sociologist interested in finding new theoretical insights into the study of arts and popular culture. Currently, she is working on a series of articles and a manuscript which explores and analyses the field of contemporary print-based British poetry. She holds a PhD from the University of Cambridge.

Abigail Ward has taught at the UK universities of Leeds, Nottingham Trent and Nottingham. A Leverhulme Research

Fellowship examining representations of human trafficking brought her to the University of Calgary, and she now lives in rural northern BC, Canada, where she is the Director of McBride and District Public Library and also teaches at the University of Northern British Columbia. She has written many journal articles and chapters on postcolonial literature, with a particular focus on slavery and Indian indenture, and is the author of *Caryl Phillips, David Dabydeen and Fred D'Aguiar: Representations of Slavery* (Manchester UP 2011) and editor of *Postcolonial Traumas* (Palgrave Macmillan 2015).